James Fenimore Cooper

STUDIES IN LITERATURE 12

James Fenimore Cooper

New Historical and Literary Contexts

Edited by
W.M. Verhoeven

Amsterdam - Atlanta, GA
1993

CIP-gegevens Koninklijke Bibliotheek, Den Haag

Cooper

James Fenimore Cooper: New Historical and Literary Contexts / ed. by W.M. Verhoeven. Amsterdam - Atlanta, GA 1993 : Rodopi. - Ill. - (DQR Studies in Literature, ISSN 0921-2507 ; 12)
ISBN 90-5183-333-4 bound
Trefw. : Cooper, James Fenimore / Amerikaanse letterkunde ; geschiedenis ; 19e eeuw

Cover design: Hendrik van Delft

Printed in The Netherlands

CONTENTS

INTRODUCTION: RECONSIDERING COOPER

W.M. VERHOEVEN

In February 1852 a memorial meeting was held New York's Metropolitan Hall to commemorate the death of James Fenimore Cooper, five months earlier. Among the celebrities whose letters of tribute were read during the meeting were such people as Emerson, Hawthorne, Longfellow, Prescott and Parkman. But perhaps the most laudatory assessment of Cooper's contribution to American literature came from Herman Melville, who wrote about Cooper: "He was a great, robust-souled man, all whose merits are not seen, yet fully appreciated. But a grateful posterity will take the best care of Fenimore Cooper."[1] At first sight it seems remarkable that a "serious" writer like Melville, who had just finished his complex and artistically ambitious novel *Pierre* in which he lashes out with extreme vehemence at the popular writers of the day, should speak so highly of Cooper, who was after all, in Edgar Allan Poe's words, "at the head of the more popular division" of American literature.[2] Yet despite his lengthy and bitter struggle to stem the tide of popular culture in general, Melville apparently felt he had to acknowledge the central position Cooper occupied in the development of American fiction; in fact, Melville was one of the first to draw a distinction between the popular rhetoric of Cooper's novels and their intrinsic meaning, between the romance and the myth. Leaving aside whether Melville's assessment of Cooper's contemporary literary fame was an accurate one, the question that remains to be answered today is, of course, Was posterity as appreciative of Cooper's status and talents as Melville had predicted? Clearly not.

---

1. *The Letters of Herman Melville*, eds Merrell R. Davies and William H. Gilman (New Haven: Yale University Press, 1960), 145.

2. *Selected Writings of Edgar Allan Poe: Poems, Tales, Essays and Reviews*, ed. David Galloway (Harmondsworth: Penguin Books, 1967), 422.

During the second half of the nineteenth century Cooper's name gradually disappeared from the forefront of American letters (despite — or as a result of? — continuing popular support). Symptomatic of Cooper's fate among academic critics and highbrow readers was the treatment he received at the hands of Mark Twain; for many years Twain's hilarious criticism of *The Deerslayer* in his essay "Fenimore Cooper's Literary Offenses" summed up the knowledge and appreciation the average literate American had of Cooper's novels.[3] By way of compensation, so to speak, his tales of the sea and forest gained him a questionable reputation as a writer romantic children's books, while the rest of his novels were left unread on the shelves of libraries.[4] Not surprisingly, one the first critics to take Cooper's novels seriously, James Grossman, was a professional lawyer rather than a professional academic.[5] Barring Cooper pioneers like Robert E. Spiller, it was only in the fifties that Cooper first became the object of widespread scholarly interest — even though in Lewis's assessment of Cooper in his seminal study *The American Adam* phrases like "marginal," "astonishing lack of co-ordination" and "unbearably sentimental" still abound.[6] For despite the efforts of such critics as R.W.B. Lewis, James Franklin Beard, Marius Bewley, George Dekker, James Grossman, Donald A. Ringe and Henry Nash Smith to rehabilitate Cooper,[7] the New Critical climate of the forties and fifties

3. "Fenimore Cooper's Literary Offenses," in *The Complete Humorous Sketches and Tales of Mark Twain*, ed. Charles Neider (New York: Doubleday, 1961), 631-42.

4. Writing in 1968, Leslie A. Fiedler observed: "Cooper's status is at the moment shaky in the extreme: a writer demoted by adults to the children's departments of libraries, and there unread by children who would, if they could, doubtless ship him back to the adult shelves again" (*The Return of the Vanishing America* [1968; rpt. London: Paladin, 1972], 122).

5. See James Grossman, *James Fenimore Cooper* (New York: Sloan, 1949).

6. R.W.B. Lewis, *The American Adam: Innocence, Tragedy, and Tradition in the Nineteenth Century* (Chicago: University of Chicago Press, 1955), 101.

7. See R.W.B. Lewis, *The American Adam*; *The Letters and Journals of James Fenimore Cooper*, ed. James Franklin Beard, 6 vols (Cambridge, MA: Harvard University Press, 1960-68) — hereafter *Letters and Journals*; Marius Bewley, *The Eccentric Design: Form in the Classic American Novel* (New York: Columbia University Press, 1959); George Dekker, *James Fenimore Cooper: The American*

was generally hostile to a technically limited writer like Cooper. As a result, Cooper was — at best — only a marginal presence in the major anthologies and he was never included in the canon of "serious" or "great" American literature.[8]

It was only in the course of the sixties, when less formalistic winds began to prevail in the field of American literary criticism and when an author's success with the popular audience was no longer seen as a sure sign of artistic inferiority, that Cooper's star began to rise. Soon Cooper had earned a secure place in the American literary history as one of America's earliest mythographers, one of the architects of the American national consciousness, "the most mythopoetically gifted of all American writers" — in the words of Leslie A. Fiedler.[9] Fiedler was of course taking his cue from D.H. Lawrence, who was one of the first to offer a reading of Cooper's tales in terms of transcendent national myth. Writing back in 1923, Lawrence — undoubtedly still one of Cooper's most perceptive commentators, despite the idiosyncratic, impressionistic nature of his criticism — had already defined the Leatherstocking tales as "the true myth of America" and Natty Bumppo as "the very intrinsic-most American."[10] And although some revisionist literary historians have in recent years been trying to stigmatize Cooper as a sexist, a racist and, generally, a distorter of historical facts,[11] the majority of critics would now, I believe, agree

---

Scott (London: Routledge & Kegan Paul, 1967); James Grossman, *James Fenimore Cooper*; Donald A. Ringe, *James Fenimore Cooper* (New York: Twayne, 1962); Henry Nash Smith, *Virgin Land: The American West as Symbol and Myth* (Cambridge, MA: Harvard University Press, 1970).

8. See, for instance, Fiedler's remarks that "Only the sort of snobbism prompted by Henry James, confirmed by T.S. Eliot and academicized by F.R. Leavis, learned to regard the historical romance in general as *infra dig* and its Western form in particular as beneath contempt" (*The Return of the Vanishing America*, 123).

9. Fiedler, *The Return of the Vanishing America*, 122.

10. D.H. Lawrence, *Studies in Classic American Literature* (1923; rpt. Harmondsworth: Penguin, 1971), 60, 69.

11. See, for instance, Philip Fisher, *Hard Facts: Setting and Form in the American Novel* (New York: Oxford University Press, 1985), 22-86; Gordon Brotherstone, "*The Prairie* and Cooper's Invention of the West," in *James Fenimore Cooper: New Critical Essays*, ed. Robert Clark (London: Vision Press, 1985), 162-86; Jane

with what Beard wrote in his edition of Cooper's letters, that "[n]o other imaginative writer had so successfully interpreted distinctly American experience for America and the world" and that "[n]o other major American writer had so consistently identified himself, in love and in anger, with the multitudinous problems besetting the young Republic."[12]

Cooper would have been greatly pleased with the modern assessment of his career. Reading the letters Cooper wrote to his first publisher, Goodrich, one cannot fail to notice how very self-conscious and ambitious he was as a budding author; Warren Motley aptly refers in this context to Cooper's "precocious confidence in his literary power."[13] It is a well-known fact that with his first very novel, *Precaution*, Cooper did not merely want to be a successful writer: he consciously set out to rival the popular British writers of the day in recognition and fame (even though he admitted that it was a hastily and carelessly written book): "I am much more sanguine," he admitted to Goodrich, "of its success in England than in this Country and much more in Boston and Philadelphia than in New York."[14] The financial predicament he was in at the time is certainly one of the reasons why he wanted to become a popular and commercial success; but it is evident that from the beginning of his career onward, Cooper was particularly sensitive to the powerful role the popular author could play in deciding the nation's ideological debates.[15] Thus he declared in *Precaution*: "Books are, in a great measure, the instruments of controlling the opinions of a nation like ours. They are an engine alike powerful to save or to destroy."[16] In contrast to *Precaution*, his second novel, *The*

Tompkins, *Sensational Designs: The Cultural Work of American Fiction, 1790-1860* (New York: Oxford University Press, 1985), 94-121

12. *Letters and Journals*, I, xviii.

13. Warren Motley, *The American Abraham: James Fenimore Cooper and the Frontier Patriarch* (Cambridge: Cambridge University Press, 1987), 60.

14. *Letters and Journals*, I, 64.

15. For a discussion of Cooper's ambitions as a budding novelist, see James D. Wallace, *Early Cooper and His Audience* (New York: Columbia University Press, 1986).

16. Cited in *Letters and Journals*, I, xxi.

Spy, was launched as "an American novel professedly";[17] dealing with a crucial phase in America's genesis, it was specifically designed to discover whether the American audience was ready for American subjects, in particular for subjects that touched upon the nation's cultural identity and ideological status quo. "The task of making American Manners and American scenes interesting to an American reader," Cooper wrote to Goodrich in connection with *The Spy*, "is an arduous one — I am unable to say whether I shall succeed or not."[18] Judging from the success of *The Spy* — the book rapidly went through three editions, was translated and adapted for the stage — , Cooper had struck gold. And after his third novel, *The Pioneers*, had confirmed his talent for gathering large audiences (the first edition of 3,500 copies was sold on the morning of publication), Cooper was soon acknowledged, both at home and abroad, as the voice of the American people.[19] If Cooper's literary example, Sir Walter Scott, had become "the Wizard of the North," then Cooper could with justice be styled "the Wizard of the West."

The fact that the modern assessment of Cooper — i.e. as an artist who has successfully translated the essence of the American experience into sustained myth — has come to coincide with Cooper's favorite pose as the nation's bard, ironically enough threatens to undermine his authoritative position in American literary history. Cooper's status now generally being considered to be that of mythmonger, there is a tendency — among some critics at least — to "read" the artist Cooper the way Cooper "read" American culture: as unified, centripetal myth, attempting to construct a sense of order out of what is basically an elusive conglomerate of ambiguous meanings. In other words: whereas it took nearly a century before critics began to distill Cooper-the-mythmonger out of the opaque stuff of his novels, we have now come to a point where the novels are in danger of being overwhelmed by the looming presence of their mythical creator. Again, it was D.H.

---

17. Letter to Andrew Thompson Goodrich, in *Letters and Journals*, I, 49.

18. Letter to Goodrich, in *Letters and Journals*, I, 44.

19. Thus, Prescott asserted in his 1852 tribute to Cooper that Cooper's writings "are instinct with the spirit of nationality," and that there "is no one … in [the] country, from the north to the south, who does not look on the fame of Cooper as the property of the nation." Longfellow declared in his tribute that he had been "in no country of Europe where the name of Cooper was not familiarly known" (cited in *Letters and Journals*, I, xvii).

Lawrence who foresaw this problem long before Cooper had been mythologized — at his instigation — by modern critics. Perhaps it was Lawrence's own lifelong concern with the duality of human nature that made him see so lucidly that Cooper's "yearning myth" only barely covers a fundamental psychological rift, both in artist himself and in the society he had mythologized. Instead of there being just one Cooper, the man, Lawrence maintained, was seriously divided against himself, never being able to make up his mind whether he preferred the wigwam to his Paris hotel, Chingachgook to his wife, or Natty Bumppo to his "humble self."[20] Ultimately, Cooper wanted to realize both options, but that was as likely to happen as Natty Bumppo, that "saint with a gun," actually slaying deer on the shores of Lake Otsego.

It would of course be untrue to say that modern Cooper criticism is not sensitive to the numerous discrepancies that dominate Cooper's life, art and thoughts. On the contrary: his uneasy patriotism (what Beard called Cooper's "uneasy love affair with his country");[21] his ambivalent political stance (somewhere half-way between Federalists and Anti-Federalists); the awkward double life he tried to live, of the gentleman and the pioneer, the entrepreneur and the writer; the attempt to combine cultural elitism with cultural egalitarianism — all of these have been amply documented by recent criticism. A critic like Warren Motley, for instance, emphasizes the choices of allegiance that Cooper had to make throughout his life. In his recent study *The American Abraham* Motley argues that the attempt to come to terms with the legacy of the Revolutionary fathers is one of the basic modes in Cooper's work. More specifically, he sees Cooper's search for paternal authority as a major rationale in his novels: "To Cooper, Abraham's story offered a mythic typology of generational conflict and historical change," and he goes on to say that Abraham's story "takes on archetypal significance in Cooper's work."[22] However, when he subsequently asserts that Cooper's eagerness to become a literary success was essentially the flip side of a crippling inferiority complex that he suffered from as a second generation child of the Revolution — the urge to become popular author as an attempt to boost his deflated ego — Motley is turning the man Cooper into the archetype Cooper."

---

20. Lawrence, 54.

21. *Letters and Journals*, I, xviii.

22. Motley, 7, 8.

That is, he is trying to sublimate the ambivalent biographical facts of Cooper's life into a sustained myth of the post-Revolutionary writer.[23]

I would like to illustrate this point by juxtaposing Motley's thesis — that Cooper's career as a writer was a conscious attempt to compensate for a frustrating lack of self-respect and a sense of social isolation — with what Emory Elliott has elsewhere said about the status of the author in the post-Revolutionary era, notably in his book *Revolutionary Writers: Literature and Authority in the New Republic*. Elliott has found that literature in the post-Revolutionary period was in a serious crisis; after initial optimism about the role of literature in the new republic (that of spreading knowledge and the light of reason among free citizens), writers of fiction from the mid-1780s onward found that the people did not recognize their spiritual and cultural authority any more. As a result, Elliott says, there was a marked tendency toward isolation of the artist, a tendency which was reinforced by "a crude notion of American manliness," which flourished in the years after the Revolution.[24] According to Elliott, an attitude began to emerge between 1780 and 1815 "that literary and religious activity belonged to the domestic world of women" and "the stereotype of the minister or poet as a weak, effeminate, and impractical person became ... firmly established during these years."[25] Writers like Joel Barlow and Charles Brockden Brown, Elliott continues, discovered that their republican readers were "inclined to resent anyone, whether preacher, politician, or poet, who presented himself as an authority figure."

Given the status of the writer of fiction during the late eighteenth and early nineteenth century, it is hard to imagine how Cooper could have — in Motley's words — "conceived of writing explicitly as a route to authority" or as a conscious attempt to emulate the patriarchal authority of William Cooper, the epitomy of the staunch and successful frontiersman.[26] Of course, Cooper *did* become a literary authority soon after he moved to New York in 1822 — the living image of a

23. Cf.: "Writing had solved the crisis in his sense of self-worth .... As his progeny, literature will connect him to the society and to the future. For Cooper, that avenue to authority was essential to a credible identity" (Motley, 60-61).

24. Emory Elliott, *Revolutionary Writers: Literature and Authority in the New Republic, 1725-1810* (New York: Oxford University Press, 1982), 46.

25. Elliott, 47.

26. Motley, 56.

transcendent national leader — but the letters he wrote at the *outset* of his career reveal that he was at the time as much concerned with the pecuniary success of his first two novels as with their literary reputation. Indeed, despite his novice's arrogance in the letters to his publisher, Cooper kept a very low profile as an author while he was writing *Precaution* and *The Spy*.[27] These first two novels in fact reveal that Cooper was very much aware of the precarious position the author held among his audience. Thus both novels were clearly written from a position of (seeming) detachment and distance, the author taking great care all the time to avoid provocation of any kind, and to instruct his audience without alienating them.[28] Especially *Precaution*, which was modeled on the English novel of domestic manners, is the product of a self-effacing, almost obsequious author who knew exactly what his (predominantly) female audience expected of him: a discreet theme, an elevated tone, an edifying moral, and, above all, a narrative voice that had no recognizable, authoritative identity.[29] The myth of Cooper as a

---

27. Looking back on the start of his career in the 1849 "Introduction" to the revised edition of *The Spy*, Cooper makes the following observations concerning the authority of literature and of the artist in the first quarter of the nineteenth century:

> Five-and-twenty years have been as ages with most things connected with America. Among other advances, that of her literature has not been the least. So little was expected from the publication of an original work of this description, at the time it was written, that the first volume of "The Spy" was actually printed several months, before the author felt a sufficient inducement to write a line of the second .... (*The Spy; A Tale of the Neutral Ground* [1821; rpt. London: Routledge, n.d.], ix).

28. See Elliott, 47-48.

29. In *Precaution* Cooper repeatedly professes to be a champion of woman as the superior sex. Thus: "the writer of these pages is a man — one who has seen much of the other sex, and he is happy to have an opportunity of paying a tribute to female purity and female truth. That there are hearts so disinterested as to lose the considerations of self, in advancing the happiness of those they love; that there are minds so pure, as to recoil with disgust from the admission of deception, indelicacy, or management, he knows, for he has seen it from long and close examination. He regrets that the very artlessness of those who are most pure in the one sex subjects them to the suspicions of the grosser materials which compose the other. He believes that innocency, singleness of heart, ardency of feeling, and unalloyed, shrinking delicacy, sometimes exist in the female bosom, to an extent that but few men are happy enough to discover and that most men believe

second-generation American who *consciously* set out to seek a sense of self through the authority of his writing is, therefore, truly a myth.

Cooper, it appears, owed his success as an author much less to a sort of existential drive to gain a credible identity than to an *intuitive* understanding of the contending cultural and ideological forces that existed in the American experiment and to the degree in which he succeeded — somewhat to his own surprise — in amalgamating those diverse forces into powerful and vitalizing myth.[30] In the final analysis it was the unexpected popular success of his romances of the Revolution — *The Spy* and *Lionel Lincoln* — and of the frontier — *The Last of the Mohicans* and *The Prairie* — that gave rise to Cooper's self-image of "a man of letters, a gentleman whose pen was in his nation's service,"[31] rather than the other way around; and it was this overwhelming success with the popular audience that accounts for the remarkable transformation of that pedantic, zealous young author — a kind of male Jane Austen — that scribbled away at the manuscript of *Precaution* into the transcendent national authority that apparently could afford to opine in his *Notions of the Americans* (published only eight years after his début as an author): "I have never seen a nation so much alike in my life, as the people of the United States, and what is more, they are not only like each other, but they are remarkably like that which common sense tells them they ought to resemble."[32]

Since poststructuralism has opened our eyes to the insidious mechanisms of historiography — selection, suppression, appropriation and marginalization — such attempts to project "ideal significations and indefinite teleologies" (to borrow Foucault's phrase) on to the chaotic interplay of events we call the past, can no longer fool us. Deconstruction and New Historicism have recast Cooper's mythical America as at best an embryonic nation of questionable antecedents and

---

incompatible with the frailties of human nature" (*Precaution*, vol. XIII of *The Novels and Tales of J. Fenimore Cooper*, [1820; rpt. London: Routledge, n.d.], 95).

30. A similar point is made — *passim* — by Leslie A. Fiedler in *Love and Death in the American Novel*, rev. edn (1960; rpt. Harmondsworth: Penguin, 1984), 187.

31. John P. McWilliams, *Political Justice in a Republic: James Fenimore Cooper's America* (Berkeley: University of California Press, 1972), 1.

32. *Notions of the Americans: Picked up by a Travelling Bachelor* (1828; rpt. Philadelphia: Carey, Lea & Blanchard, 1836), II, 108-109.

an uncertain future. Although in Cooper's time America had gone some way toward a recognizable, national identity (marked by such formative rites as the War of Independence, the debate over the Constitution, and the process of rapid territorial expansion), a great many crucial dilemmas still had to be resolved before anything of a unique, transcendent ideology could emerge: there was still serious political maneuvering going on following the "great national discussion" of 1787-88, when the Federalists and Anti-Federalists fought a fierce battle over the Constitution, the echoes of which had still not subsided;[33] there was also the unresolved race question, involving mainly blacks and Indians; there were the social frictions that arose between the urban rich, emigrant laborers, and rural gentry (a conflict that figures prominently in the Littlepage Trilogy); and there was the woman question.

Most of the essays in the present volume are either directly or indirectly informed by the need to confront Cooper's tales with the indeterminate historical context from which they arose; those that are not, start from the premise that our understanding of Cooper's work can benefit significantly from displacing it from its traditional position in American literary history and by realigning it in a new literary context; what unites all essays is a commitment to see Cooper's works as historical documents that both give us access to and reflect the complex, equivocal mind that created them.

Among the essays that attempt to recontextualize Cooper's work by explicitly setting up a dialogical opposition between one or more of his fictional texts and a selected corpus of historical, or other non-literary sources are the contributions by Robert Lawson-Peebles (on the role of landscaping, property, marriage, and women in Cooper's early fictions), John P. McWilliams (on *Lionel Lincoln* and the Battles of Lexington, Concord and Bunker Hill), Susan Scheckel (on land rights and the legitimation of American national identity in *The Pioneers*), and Charles H. Adams (on Cooper's employment of contemporary theories of natural history in *The Crater*). By focusing on Cooper's literary modes of expression, the essays by Donald A. Ringe (on the Gothic discourse in *The Last of the Mohicans*), Richard D. Rust (on the choice of names, the multivaried and intricate relations of characters, elements of plot and the use of poetic language in *The Pathfinder*), and Theo D'haen (on the central role of naming in the rhetorical construction of

33. James Madison, Alexander Hamilton, and John Jay, *The Federalist Papers*, ed. Isaac Kramnick (1788; rpt. Harmondsworth: Penguin, 1987), 88.

Satanstoe) want to challenge the inordinate amount of negative criticism Cooper's stylistic excesses have traditionally come in for, and present a strong case for a radical revaluation of Cooper's use of language and style. The essays by John G. Cawelti (on Cooper's myth of the American wilderness and the anti-myth which it contains within itself), A. Robert Lee (on the mythologization of the American Revolution in *The Spy*), and W.M. Verhoeven (on the authority of myth, and the myth of authority, also in *The Spy*), analyze various aspects of the intriguing but ambiguous relationship in Cooper's work between history and fiction, between fiction and myth, between myth and history. Finally, the essays by George Dekker (on how the critical reception of Cooper's work has always gone hand in hand with the contemporary critical stance toward the genre of the American romance) and Jan Bakker (on the thematic and ideological correspondences between Cooper's Leatherstocking Tales and Pynchon's postmodern parable *Gravity's Rainbow*) try to reposition Cooper's work in terms of the development of American literary history in general.

While the essays in this volume all aim at some degree of historical or literary-historical (re)contextualization of Cooper's work, this is not to say that they share a common methodological approach; indeed, the essays were commissioned and selected with the specific idea in mind to apply contending approaches in contemporary literary discourse to the canonical Cooper. While the array of critical approaches represented in the book is by no means exhaustive, interpretive strategies vary from textual, formalistic New Critical readings, to "old" historical, contextual readings, and from "new" historical, revisionist readings, to deconstructive readings. It is hoped that through their critical diversity these essays will cast a new light on Cooper's work in relation to its historical context, and on the relevance of Cooper's work to both nineteenth-century and modern literary, historical, and ideological debates.

This book originates in a conference which was held at the University of Groningen, The Netherlands, in October 1989, in commemoration of the two-hundredth anniversary of James Fenimore Cooper's birth. I would like to thank the co-organizer of the conference, Jan Bakker, and the editors of the *Dutch Quarterly Review* for permission to reprint material that originally appeared, in somewhat different form, in the pages of their journal. The illustration on page 49 ("Elizabeth Conversing with Mohegan") is reproduced by permission of the Huntington Library, San Marino, California, whose co-operation is hereby gratefully acknowledged. I am indebted to the Faculty of Arts of the University of Groningen for a research grant which enabled me to do most of the editorial work in the congenial environment of the Huntington Library, and to the library staff, for their kindness and assistance.

JAMES FENIMORE COOPER AND THE AMERICAN ROMANCE TRADITION

GEORGE DEKKER

The argument I wish to pursue here is that the critical fortunes of the novelistic subgenre to which Cooper's fictions are usually supposed to belong deeply affected both the ways he wrote them and the ways they have been received over the years. Conversely, the rise or fall of Cooper's reputation for other, sometimes extraliterary, reasons has no doubt greatly affected the reputation of the romance novel or, as it is more simply, more often, and more misleadingly called, the "romance." He was, after all, one of its earliest and best known practitioners, and what he was perceived to have accomplished or failed to accomplish as a novelist inevitably influenced critical perception of generic limits and possibilities. But my focus here will be on Cooper as the victim or beneficiary of changing attitudes to the romance, and it is as much with those attitudes as with Cooper himself that this article will be concerned. I will begin, *in medias res* as it were, with the book by Richard Chase that taught us to think of "romance" whenever we begin thinking about the American novel tradition.

You will recall that in *The American Novel and Its Tradition* (1957) Chase argues that the greatest American fictionalists were rarely much interested in the manners and morals, the social reality and role, which preoccupied their British and European counterparts.[1] Hence American fiction's great tradition, that of the romance novel, has been characterized by melodramatic extremes and Manichean division; by the complex ambiguities of the symbolic mode; by an emphasis on action rather character and on individuals in isolation rather than in social relation with each other; and by a "penchant for the marvelous, the sensational, the legendary, and in general the heightened effect" (21). Chase contends that, with the partial exception of Henry James,

1. Richard Chase, *The American Novel and Its Tradition* (Garden City, NY: Doubleday, 1957).

American fictionalists whose work resembles that of the great British novelists of morals and manners have been writers of the second or third rank (158).

One measure of the widespread influence of the romance thesis is the sales record of Chase's book. Academic books that sell as many as a thousand copies are doing very well, and ones that sell two thousand are likely to have an impact on the way other scholars study and discuss the same topic. *The American Novel and Its Tradition* has sold over 100,000 copies since 1957.[2] This is only a crude quantitive measure, to be sure, but it points out the direction the wind is blowing and suggests something about its force. To gauge the impact of the romance thesis more accurately, we should have to look closely at the many articles and books that have been published over the past thirty years seeking to refine Chase's arguments or, on the contrary, to refute them as fundamentally unsound and misleading. This would be no small task, since by my count there have been over twenty articles and at least seven booklength studies (including one of my own), all published since Chase's book and all containing respectful references to it, whose titles declare their author's conviction that "romance" is a useful critical term and concept and that in one shape or another this kind of fiction has flourished in America.[3]

---

2. I owe this datum, and much else besides, to John P. McWilliams, Jr., "The Rationale for 'The American Romance,'" *Boundary 2* 17.1 (Spring 1990), 71-82.

3. The articles are too numerous to list, but the books in question are the following: Joel Porte, *The Romance in America: Studies in Cooper, Poe, Hawthorne, Melville, and James* (Middletown, CT: Wesleyan University Press, 1969); Michael Bell, *The Development of American Romance: The Sacrifice of Relation* (Chicago: University of Chicago Press, 1980); Evan Carton, *The Rhetoric of American Romance: Dialectic and Identity in Emerson, Dickinson, Poe, and Hawthorne* (Baltimore: Johns Hopkins University Press, 1985); George Dekker, *The American Historical Romance* (Cambridge/New York: Cambridge University Press, 1987); Edgar Dryden, *The Form of American Romance* (Baltimore: Johns Hopkins University Press, 1988); Emily Miller Budick, *Fictional and Historical Consciousness: The American Romance Tradition* (New Haven: Yale University Press, 1989); Robert S. Levine, *Conspiracy and Romance: Studies in Brockden Brown, Cooper, Hawthorne, and Melville* (Cambridge/New York: Cambridge University Press, 1989). Many other books about American fiction devote some or many pages to the same generic questions, but their titles do not highlight "romance" as the issue with which they are centrally concerned. I have doubtless overlooked some discussions of the topic worth knowing about.

Dissenters from the romance thesis have included some eminent Americanists, including two who are important in the history of Cooper scholarship, Robert E. Spiller and John P. McWilliams.[4] McWilliams's case against the romance thesis is especially pertinent here because it is recent enough to take account of refinements on Chase and also to gain the historical perspective necessary to see his work as a characteristic cultural product of the 1950s.

His most telling criticism concerns the effect of the romance thesis on the American literary canon: which books and authors does it foreground or center, which does it push to the margins or out of sight? "*The Blithedale Romance* but not *Uncle Tom's Cabin,*" answers McWilliams, "Henry James, but not Edith Wharton ... Scott Fitzgerald, but not Willa Cather; William Faulkner, but not Richard Wright." In sum, the thesis favors white highbrow males and marginalizes the kind of writers who are more likely to write novels of manners or social protest. Expanding on McWilliams just a little, I might add that, in the case of Cooper, Chase judges the historical novel of manners *Satanstoe* clearly inferior to *The Prairie* with its solitary hero in retreat from society, its brooding symbolic landscapes, and its commitment to the myth of a doomed American pastoral. Of course it is possible for a reader to prefer *The Prairie* to *Satanstoe* with or without ever having heard of the romance thesis; but a reader who finds *Satanstoe* the richer, more moving, and more artistically satisfying book is likely to suspect that Chase's thesis dictated his preference for *The Prairie* rather than the other way around. McWilliams also points out that one of the problematic consequences of Chase's book has been to entrench Hawthorne as the indispensable central figure in the tradition. Subsequent wideranging studies of the American novel that favor the romance thesis omit or include any other fictionalist as best suits their convenience or focus, but Hawthorne is always there. After all, if we did not have his prefaces and his novelistic fictions prominently labeled as "romances," how much immediate authority or plausibility would the thesis have?

Although I have some reservations about aspects of McWilliams's critique of the romance thesis, I believe that he does not exaggerate its

---

4. Spiller's biographical, bibliographical, and editorial work laid the foundation for modern Cooper studies. His most important publication on Cooper is *Fenimore Cooper: Critic of His Times* (New York: Minton, Balch, & Co., 1931). McWilliams's major Cooper study is *Political Justice in a Republic: James Fenimore Cooper's America* (Berkeley: University of California Press, 1972).

Procrustean tendencies. To say so is not to deny that a strikingly high percentage of the greatest American novels are packed with features common in ancient forms of the romance and uncommon in novels of manners and morals; this is a phenomenon that deserves the scholarly attention it has received. But — to move from the general to some particular instances — it is or should be a scandal that Chase finds Edith Wharton a writer "of second or third rank" (158) and employs the romance thesis to explain why this should be so. And it is a worse scandal that he does not so much as mention Willa Cather, whose novels give the lie once and for all to the Eurocentric notion that (as Chase restates it) "the novelist who undertakes to reflect our social scene, or some segment of it, in literal detail ... finds that not all his wit and perspicuity can save his novel from reflecting too strongly the comparative social dullness of America" (160). McWilliams is also brilliantly right about the way the romance thesis privileges Hawthorne. This last point is important for the present discussion; for if Hawthorne is the foundational figure for the American novel tradition and epitomizes what is best in it, what are we to think of Cooper, who is like Hawthorne in some respects but is radically unlike him in many others? Spare, allusive, allegorical, formally elegant, introspective, ironically equivocal — obviously I am not talking about Cooper. If these are the things chiefly to be valued in fiction, then Cooper is a decidedly minor writer.

However, the argument I want to make is not that the romance thesis of recent times has done nothing to promote a just appreciation of Cooper — I will return to this complicated issue later — but rather that ideas about the nature and value of the romance influenced the way Cooper wrote his fictions and have *always* had the effect of limiting or enlarging what readers find in them, with direct consequences for his reputation as a serious literary figure. In the remainder of my discussion I will trace this pattern of limitation and enlargement from Cooper's time to ours.

To find out what Cooper and his contemporaries thought about the romance form, a good place to start is Michael Davitt Bell's *The Development of American Romance*. Bell argues that in public parlance "romance" was less often opposed to "novel" or "realism" than to "truth" or non-fiction. The latter opposition, which links romance with the unreal and morally dangerous vagaries of the imagination, made romancers themselves appear suspect, socially deviant figures. Some writers — whom Bell calls "conservative romancers," followers of Sir Walter Scott like Cooper and Simms — were able to bridge the gap between imagination and reality, and thus make themselves and their works acceptable, or even patriotically respectable, by working with "certain native materials [which supposedly] were already imbued with 'storied and poetical association' or could be so imbued."[5] Other writers — notably Brown, Hawthorne, Poe, and Melville, whom Bell calls "experimental romancers" — accepted the subversive role of cultural outsider and explored the discrepancies between the ideal and reality of American institutions, pretension and practice in American manners.

Bell's account is informed and helpful, but it needs some amplification. The writers Bell calls experimental romancers belong to a tradition that has gothic antecedents and includes the British writers William Godwin, Ann Radcliffe, Mary Shelley, James Hogg, and Emily Brontë. Cooper was affected by this strain of romance, particularly in his portraits of demonic Indian leaders in *The Prairie* and *The Last of the Mohicans*, but it was Scott's historical romance that provided the crucial model.

Cooper inherited not only Scott's fictional form but also his ambivalent feelings about it. Althought their romances dealt, at least in part, with the heroic "matter" of epic and were historical in a far from superficial way, Scott and Cooper tended to share the view of most educated readers that any kind of novel was primarily an ephemeral income-producing form of family entertainment which wanted the dignity of both epic poetry and "real" history. Lacking reverence for their form and faith in its durability, they wrote too much too rapidly; they skirted important subjects that were supposedly not fit for the family circle; and as they got older and more financially pressed, their prose and their plots tended to become increasingly loose and repetitive. This was not always the case; some of Cooper's strongest novels, notably *Satanstoe*, belong to his later years; but they are outnumbered by weak performances.

However, critics who conclude that Scott and Cooper chose the romance form merely because of its money-spinning possibilities do not know much about human nature — or at any rate about the nature of these two writers. Among other advantages, it offered them a well-established vehicle for expending their seemingly inexhaustible funds of imaginative energy and playfulness. Further, enlarged and historically grounded as Scott was able to make it in *Waverley*, the romance also

5. Bell, 21.

became wonderfully accommodated to writers whose intellectual interests had an Enlightenment range and variety and whose political commitments were strong and carefully pondered. Although contemporary reviews sometimes objected to the potentially confusing mixture of fiction and history, it appears that Scott's innovation was generally successful in spiking the guns of critics who equated fiction with falsehood or frivolous nonfactuality. To Cooper, then, Scott bequeathed a form of romance that not only suited many of his needs and powers but that also had more respectability than romance had previously known. Scott also bequeathed an immense readership for historical romances.

That Cooper was soon being called "the American Scott" indicates how well he made use of his opportunities, but it was a sobriquet he understandably resented — partly because it implicitly denied his own originality and partly because he disliked Scott's British aristocratic political values. Cooper was an American nationalist and democrat, and much of his fiction implicitly or explicitly argues for a union of interests not only between the states but between the social classes of the new nation. For instance, in his first and best-known historical romance of the American Revolution, *The Spy* (1821), Cooper cheerfully provided the suspenseful physical adventure and courtship interest demanded by younger or at least more ingenuous readers; but, at the same time, his action featured a unified front of New York and Virginian military forces against the common British enemy and a cordial meeting of hearts and minds between the aristocratic American commander George Washington and the plebeian secret patriot Harvey Birch. Cooper's efforts on behalf of national union were not overlooked by reviewers, who urged him to continue in the same vein and commented on how the historical romance could help overcome regional misunderstandings and jealousies.[6]

I cite *The Spy* here not because I think it is one of Cooper's masterpieces but because it well illustrates how, at the outset of his career, he was as successful as Scott in overcoming objections to romance by making the entertainment he provided upliftingly instructive and civic-minded. To forstall any inference of cynicism, I should emphasize that the impulses to be instructive and civic-minded belonged

6. See W.H. Gardiner's review of *The Spy*, *North American Review* (July 1822); rpt. in *Fenimore Cooper: The Critical Heritage*, eds George Dekker and John P. McWilliams (London: Routledge & Kegan Paul, 1973), 55-66.

to the man rather than to a deliberate strategy of placating moralistic critics of romance. Or, rather, both propositions are true. For Cooper was himself a moralistic critic of literature and society, and he was able to justify the writing of romances only by investing them with a pedagogical design calculated to make his readers more thoughtful and informed citizens. This is true even of a work like *The Last of the Mohicans* which on the surface is an escapist adventure story with a sentimentally agreeable sad ending. Look at it a little more carefully and one sees that his characters, regarded as representatives of different races, regions, and social classes, are engaged in an action that tests the possibility of racial and regional harmony in America and arrives at pessimistic conclusions. Take another look at *The Spy* and one is struck by the amount of sordid villainy, anarchic violence, and anxious uncertainty concerning motives and identities that Cooper slips into a novel which, on the surface, seems to project an uncritically sunny view of the Revolution and American national destiny. In these and other early romances, then, he was able to please all parties, and I am aware of no evidence that Cooper or anybody else sensed that this success depended on a balancing act and on compromises that he might not be able to sustain.

In retrospect, it seems clear that early popular romances like *The Spy* and *The Last of the Mohicans* created expectations which Cooper could continue to satisfy only by keeping his pedagogical design and pessimistic conclusions submerged, by developing historical contexts as sparsely as possible, by subordinating character and motive to action, and by keeping that action going at a feverish pace. Sometimes he was able to deviate from this recipe for popular success. Just as Scott managed to please readers even while developing his historical contexts in loving, sometimes antiquarian, particularity, so did Cooper enjoy one of his greatest popular triumphs in the *The Pioneers* (1823), a novel that draws on his earliest recollections of Cooperstown and that abounds in what his English-speaking contemporaries called "Dutch" detail. But *The Pioneers* is special in more ways than one; it is suffused with a genial charm and affectionate humor more characteristic of Scott than of Cooper, who by temperament was more prone to dwell on the dark aspects of human nature and history and more inclined to take a forthright stand in favor of unpopular views.

When he turned to stark, unrelieved tragedy in *The Wept of Wish-ton-Wish* (1829) and *The Bravo* (1831) and doubly damned these romances by making the first richly but unflatteringly historical and the second passionately political, his departures from recipe were met with bemused silence or open hostility. Although these books contain many of the ingredients that won him fame unprecedented for an American writer, fat royalties, and a readership that cut across social classes and national boundaries, the winning balance is lost. For these novels are addressed primarily to an adult audience; the playfulness has a sardonically ironic edge; and altogether there is more moral urgency and a deeper imaginative engagement with the tragic realities of racial prejudice and colonial conquest than are to be found in the Leatherstocking tales. This was not what his contemporaries expected from romance or wanted to know about America, and so Cooper was widely supposed to have violated a kind of generic compact with his readers and also to have suffered an imaginative decline.

For twentieth-century readers who know *The Wept of Wish-ton-Wish* and *The Bravo* and also know something about the history of literary taste and canon formation in the United States, the parallel with Melville is irresistible if somewhat misleading. It is misleading inasmuch as later nineteenth-century American readers were scarcely aware of the existence of Melville's masterwork, whereas they went on reading the five Leatherstocking romances, which together do undoubtedly constitute not only Cooper's greatest achievement but also a cultural monument that deserves all, or nearly all, it has received in the way of ridicule, execration, love, rapt readership, and interpretive overload. The parallel with Melville is just inasmuch as the readers who remembered Melville only for his early narratives of exotic adventure also knew Cooper only by romances that had survived chiefly as classics of children's adventure literature — books whose virtues, if any, were not those of the "grown-up" realist novel. This meant that Cooper was an easy target for Mark Twain, who had a sharp eye for the absurdity in other men's writings and who in all likelihood had not read works like *The Wept of Wish-ton-Wish* or *Satanstoe*. And so it was with other and subtler exponents of novelistic realism. To Howells and James the romance novels that had enthralled earlier generations appeared obsolete and juvenile, although James's sympathies were sufficiently catholic that he placed Scott with Balzac and Zola in the select company of writers with "the largest responding imagination before the human scene," writers whose "current remains therefore extraordinarily rich and mixed, washing us successively with the warm wave of the near and familiar and the tonic shock ... of the far and strange."[7] Although much the same could have been said of Cooper, James only remembered *him*, fondly but condescendingly, as an author who had charmed the idle hours of early boyhood with stories about Indians, canoes, lakes, and forests.[8] Had he known the unknown Cooper, the author rejected and effectively buried by romance-loving readers of the earlier nineteenth century, James might have seen that "adult" American fiction did not begin with Hawthorne.

During our own century the process of rescuing Cooper's romances for an educated adult readership has gone through several phases. Each of these phases has involved a new perspective on the romance novel, and each of these perspectives has been made possible or even necessary by fundamental shifts in the academic study of American literature and, not unrelatedly, in the American political climate. I will conclude by venturing a brief and perhaps overbold sketch of the main phases of this process.

The recovery of the unknown Cooper came fairly late in the astonishing period of canon reformation that began shortly after World War I with the recognition of Melville, Dickinson, and Whitman as major — possibly *the* major — American writers of the previous century. That several of the figures discovered or rediscovered were New Yorkers rather than New Englanders probably owed not a little to two closely connected developments in American intellectual and institutional life at this time: the displacement of the great New England universities from the uncontested center of academic prestige and influence, and the emergence of the new discipline of American Studies with its self-consciously national perspective. Surely it is no accident that the most searching critical reassessment of Cooper's fiction came not from Yale or Harvard but from Yvor Winters in California and that the groundbreaking study of Cooper's achievements as a social critic came from Robert Spiller in Pennsylvania.[9] These seminal studies were published during the Depression years when educated Americans were

---

7. Henry James, Preface to *The American* (New York: Scribner's, 1907), xv.

8. James mentions Cooper in passing on several occasions, most interestingly perhaps in *The American Scene* (1907; rpt. Bloomington: Indiana University Press, 1968), where a chance encounter with Indians or a view of a New England lake triggers off nostalgic recollections of the Leatherstocking tales (18, 364).

9. Cf. Spiller's *Fenimore Cooper: Critic of His Times*, and Yvor Winters, "Fenimore Cooper, or The Ruins of Time," *Maule's Curse: Seven Studies in the History of American Obscurantism*, (Norfolk, CT: New Directions, 1938), 25-50.

more than usually prepared to honor the qualities of candor, ethical depth, and broad humanity that both Spiller and Winters discerned in Cooper. Although neither undertook a systematic defense of Cooper's historical romance form, between them they provided a basis for taking the entire Cooper *oeuvre* seriously and particularly for appreciating the importance of *The Bravo*, *The Wept of Wish-ton-Wish*, and *Satanstoe*.

The next major phase in the development of American literary studies came during the period of political reaction and social disengagement by liberal intellectuals that followed World War II. This was the heyday of New Criticism, Myth Criticism, and Psychoanalytic Criticism, approaches to literature based on theories that regarded the social and cultural contexts of literature as "extrinsic." Fortunately, American Studies was largely proof against the extremes of formalism, ahistoricism, and psycho-reductivism that these theories fostered, and the theories had a mainly fructifying effect on the leading Americanists of that era. Developing an approach pioneered several decades earlier by D.H. Lawrence, Henry Nash Smith, R.W.B. Lewis, Richard Chase, and Leslie Fiedler demonstrated the power and importance of the romance novel as a principal vehicle for expressing the cultural myths of America.[10] Moreover, they — and especially Chase — perceived that the romance was capable of a kind of formal elegance and intellectual depth rarely attained by novels of manners and morals; and they prized these excellences in the fiction especially of Hawthorne and James even while they mined them and other — artistically inferior — romances for cultural mythology. For Cooper, this approach to the American romance entailed both gains and losses. On the one hand, a portion of his work received much space and serious examination in several of the most influential books in the field. On the other, these

---

10. In addition to *The American Novel and Its Tradition*, the books in question are Smith's *Virgin Land: The American West as Symbol and Myth* (Cambridge, MA: Harvard University Press, 1950); Lewis's *The American Adam: Innocence, Tragedy, and Tradition in the Nineteenth Century* (Chicago: University of Chicago Press, 1955); and Fiedler's *Love and Death in the American Novel* (1960; rpt. New York: Dell, 1966). Charles Feidelson's *Symbolism in American Literature* (Chicago: University of Chicago Press, 1953) exemplifies another kind of influential book of the period, that had little direct effect on the way Cooper's romance were read and taught but that reinforced the notion that our classic writers levitated themselves and their fictions outside of society and history by means of myths, symbolism, and allegory.

books had the effect of temporarily undoing the good work of Spiller and Winters by concentrating attention on the Leatherstocking tales again and on Cooper as the dreamer of timeless, antihistorical myths. And they encouraged the notion that the mythic vein in Cooper's fiction was so rich and accessible precisely because its author was an artless, slapdash worker. This was the Cooper and the American romance of my own student days, and it was not until I started teaching that I learned to question them.

At that time, the mid 1960s, a good many American intellectuals began to question the ideological constructs, academic and otherwise, of the Cold War era. Risky though it is to generalize about the relationship between politics and scholarly methodology, I can at least testify that my own commitment to historicism was confirmed by a growing realization that Americans were fighting in Vietnam because of a failure of understanding that basically was even more historical than it was moral or military. I do not mean to suggest, by the way, that the great scholar-critics of the 1950s would have failed to see that proponents of American involvement in Vietnam were prisoners of Cold War myths which effectively precluded any deep historical understanding; on the contrary, that generation taught mine to appreciate the blinding power of such myths. But the dominant '50s approaches to literary study themselves had a systemic tendency to encourage subtle forms of historical blindness and hubris, leading professors to overestimate their own interpretive authority and to underestimate the thoughtfulness, historical awareness, social responsiveness, and deliberate artistry of the great American romancers.

Since the Vietnam War, we have been better placed to see that these romancers were not only myth-makers extraordinary but also, and at the same time, shrewd critics of the prevailing myths of their age. The most striking and welcome trend discernible in recent reworkings of the romance thesis has been their effort to rehistoricize the American romance, insisting that its major practitioners have always been profoundly concerned with what might be called the mental or ideological "manners" of American society, and that their seemingly anti-mimetic fictions both represent and criticize those manners. For the study of Cooper's romances these developments have meant great gains in the historical understanding of the Leatherstocking tales and a new appreciation of some of the romances that his own reading public had contrived, like a spellbinding wizard out of medieval romance, to submerge in oblivion for a century.

MAKING HISTORY, MAKING FICTION: COOPER'S *THE SPY*

A. ROBERT LEE

> [B]y persuasion of Mrs. Cooper I have commenced another tale to be called the "Spy" scene [set] in West-Chester County, and [at the] time of the revolutionary war .... [M]y female Mentor says it throws Precaution far in the back-ground — I confess I am more partial to this new work myself as being a Country-man and perhaps a younger child .... The task of making American manners and American scenes interesting to an American reader is an arduous one — I am unable to say whether I shall succeed or not ....[1]

> The "Spy" goes on slowly and it will not be finish'd until late in the fall — I take more pains with it — as it is to be an American novel professedly — I think it far better than "Precaution" — more interest — and better writing ....[2]

I

James Fenimore Cooper's bow into *American* literature rests upon a well enough known irony, that of having written a first novel almost assiduously given to imitation of *English* "manners and scenes." Although, for sure, a work important for its anticipation of later Cooper interests and themes, and not without its ingenuities — the near *mésalliance* of Jane Moseley with Colonel Egerton and related other "family" mistakes of apparent over actual character — *Precaution* (1820), even so, delineates a world inevitably known only second-hand,

1. *The Letters and Journals of James Fenimore Cooper*, ed. James Franklin Beard, 6 vols (Cambridge, MA: Harvard University Press, 1960-68), I, 44: Letter to Andrew Thompson Goodrich, June 28, 1820.

2. *Letters and Journals*, I, 49: Letter to Andrew Thompson Goodrich, July 12, 1820.

a society written into being from an Atlantic away and thus from the margins of the historical world it seeks to recreate.

The upshot could not be more evident, a kind of socially unparticularized, even inert, "shadow" text. Why, then, the choice at all of an English theme and setting? What implications, in turn, beyond the given shift of national locale, arise out of this transition from *Precaution* to *The Spy: A Tale of the Neutral Ground* (1821), Cooper's first truly American novel? Two key, and closely related, kinds of insecurity initially might be said to have come into play.[3]

First, as a putative American writer, how in general to break free of so determining an imaginative legacy as "England" and to help inaugurate an indigenous literary culture fully the equivalent of political Independence? Emerson's call, a few years ahead in "The American Scholar" (1837), to abandon "the courtly muses of Europe," "to write [our] own books," or Melville's, in "Hawthorne and His Mosses," (1850) to "let America ... prize and cherish her writers; yea, let her glorify them," inspirational, and even epochal, as both might have been thought, could not at the same time more have bespoken an anxiety of influence.[4] Second, and more locally, could Cooper have looked to his

3. The following criticism has been of immediate benefit in writing this essay: William Charvat, *The Profession of Authorship in America, 1800-1870* (Columbus, OH: Ohio State University Press, 1968); George Dekker, *James Fenimore Cooper: The Novelist* (London: Routledge & Kegan Paul, 1967); Donald A. Ringe, *The Pictorial Mode: Space and Time in the Art of Bryant, Irving, and Cooper* (Lexington: University of Kentucky Press, 1971); Richard Slotkin, *Regeneration Through Violence: The Mythology of The American Frontier, 1600-1860* (Middletown, CT: Wesleyan University Press, 1973); *James Fenimore Cooper: A Collection of Critical Essays*, ed. Wayne Fields (Englewood Cliffs, NJ: Prentice-Hall, 1979); James D. Wallace, "Cultivating an Audience: From *Precaution* to *The Spy*," in *James Fenimore Cooper: New Critical Essays*, ed. Robert Clark (London: Vision Press, 1985), 38-54; James D. Wallace: *Early Cooper and His Audience* (New York: Columbia University Press, 1986), Charles Hansford Adams, *"The Guardian of The Law": Authority and Identity in James Fenimore Cooper*, (University Park and London: Pennsylvania State University Press, 1990); W.M. Verhoeven, "Art as Neutral Ground: The Problem of Authority in *The Spy*," *Dutch Quarterly Review* 20.3 (1990), 224-38 (for a revised version of this article, see 71-87 below).

4. Ralph Waldo Emerson, "The American Scholar" (1837 [orig. title "An Oration Delivered before the Phi Beta Kappa Society, at Cambridge, August 31, 1837"]; rpt. in *Essays*, First Series (1841); Herman Melville, "Hawthorne and His Mosses" (1850; rpt. in *Moby-Dick*, eds Harrison Hayford and Hershel Parker [New York:

own hitherto untested powers of creation to do more than rework (and then through plot-line more than anything else) an inherited genre, the "domestic" English novel?

Cooper's replacement of the "Moseley Hall" of *Precaution* with the "Westchester" of *The Spy* anticipates in some degree the literary nationalism adumbrated by Emerson and Melville. But if so, yet another paradox arises. For however short-term, not to say ironic, this assumed mask of Englishness in so self-vaunting a patriot as Cooper, would not the footfalls of a Toryish, nostalgic anglophilia play across virtually all his eventual fiction, be it the five Natty Bumppo-Chingachgook Leatherstocking narratives, the no less than eleven sea-novels from *The Pilot* (1824) to *The Sea Lions* (1849), the Littlepage Anti-Rent and land-ownership trilogy — *Satanstoe* (1845), *The Chainbearer* (1845) and *The Redskins* (1846) — and the late, quasi-religious, Utopian writing of *The Crater* (1847), *The Oak Openings* (1848) and *The Ways of The Hour* (1850)? The same inclination, too, unlikely as it might have been thought in so "nationalist" a body of polemic, even shows through in *Notions of the Americans* (1828), *A Letter to His Countrymen* (1834), and, axially, *Home as Found* (1838) and *The American Democrat* (1838). Nor, to add to the roster, could his *The History of the Navy of The United States* (1839) be held to reflect other than a thoroughly patrician, officer's eye, viewpoint.

For despite his lifelong republicanism, Cooper never ceased to be a true-believer in a hierarchy of natural worth for which "Old England," and, relatedly, upper-class, Anglo-Dutch, "Old New York," the latter a legacy which counts Washington Irving, Herman Melville and Edith Wharton in its gallery, had long supplied the working social and cultural models. Little wonder he found himself increasingly out of sorts with the leveling sway of Jacksonianism, more and more cantankerous and litigious from the 1830s onwards, and even, eventually, a kind of Rip Van Winkle in the view of many of his countrymen. His conservativism also drew definition from his seven-year sojourn (1826-33) on an upper-crust European circuit of England, France, The Low Countries, Switzerland, Italy, and France again (where he renewed his friendship with Lafayette), and which came to an end with a last British Summer before he once more embarked in September 1833 for the United States.

W.W. Norton, 1967], 4).

"Arduous" may have been Cooper's term for writing in general, but it also signals the immediate problem he had before him. How to write himself out of *Precaution*, with its echo of Jane Austen's *Persuasion* both in its title and in its story of the well-bred English family of the Moseleys exercised as to right and wrong suitors for the two daughters, and into, as he himself said, "an American novel professedly," a "tale" born of his own first-hand observations and past? How, in other words, to bring to bear an American historical or social round, a world drawn anything but from afar, thereby making good in *The Spy* on the absence of local texture which had so debilitated *Precaution*?

And could he, even then, win over a readership still accustomed to looking across the Atlantic for its literary fiction, to a Henry Fielding or Samuel Richardson, to a Maria Edgeworth or Amelia Opie, or, supremely, to a Sir Walter Scott? Could he, too, as he saw it, make his own fiction more consequential than hitherto American-written novels like Susanna Haswell Rowson's *Charlotte Temple* (1791, 1794), a seduction narrative by appearance but in fact a key proto-feminist text, or, notably, Hugh Henry Brackenridge's four-part, compendious *Modern Chivalry* (1792-1815), Cervantean picaresque turned satirically upon the foibles and crudities of frontier democracy?

One name, however, perplexed him more than the rest, that of Charles Brockden Brown. *Wieland* (1798), he more or less saw, went beyond Gothic surface. The dramatization of messianic self-delusion and of too ready a trust in Lockean sense-data arose out of flare, an authentic, fiercely Enlightenment curiosity. Then, too, in *Notions of the Americans* (1828), whether offered out of patriotic solidarity or some buried irony, he would go on to write "This author … enjoys a high reputation among his countrymen."[5] But so much acknowledged, it is hard to resist the conclusion that Cooper felt other than a deep sense of competition toward the Philadelphia author whose *annus mirabilis* of 1798-99 had produced no less than five full-length novels — in the first place *Wieland* (1798), but also his conspiracy-novel, *Ormond* (1799), his Philadelphia *Bildungsroman* and plague-epic, *Arthur Mervyn, First Part* (1799) and *Arthur Mervyn, Second Part* (1800), and his densely worked portrait of somnambulism and psychological break-down, *Edgar Huntly* (1799).

5. *Notions of the Americans: Picked up by a Travelling Bachelor* (Philadelphia: Carey, Lea & Blanchard, 1828), I, 60.

Firstly, Gothicism in general as against "ordinary American life" evidently dismayed Cooper as he makes clear in *Home as Found* (1838).[6] There can, too, be no mistaking the slight he intends towards Brown in his Preface to *The Spy* when he dubs him "not the rival that every man would select."[7] Brown's *Edgar Huntly*, even more notoriously, brought matters to a head. A sop to "English critics," Cooper goes on to call it dismissively, an "account" not of "American manners" but of a spurious, merely crowd-pleasing, "Indian manners," especially on the basis of the famous cave scene containing "an American, a savage, a wild cat and a tomahawk, in a conjunction that never did, or ever will occur" (8).

Two related factors thus again would seem to come into the reckoning, both of which, directly or not, bear upon Cooper's emergence as an "American" writer: the conviction that he knew "Indian" America infinitely better than Brown, almost in fact as a birthright, and the likely first stirrings in his imagination of how frontierism might yield a new, inerasably American narrative. Further, too, if his coming great theme of "Virgin Land" and the clash of two civilizations, white and Native-American, lay close to hand, it did so as part of Cooper's larger call to full-time literary life.

As to the first issue, had not his father, Judge William Cooper, Federalist, settlement-founder in upstate New York, a self-made man of wealth for all his lowly Quaker heritage, acquired formidable tracts of land around Lake Otsego, the source of the Susquehanna River, where as a boy Cooper doubtless saw the few remaining tribal peoples? And would Cooper not later write an Introduction to William Cooper's *A Guide in the Wilderness; or the History of the First Settlements in the Western Countries of New York, with Useful Instructions to Future Settlements* (1810), with its references-back to the original Mohawk, Mohican, Mingo and other Iroquoian Confederacy habitations?[8] Secondly, the Leatherstocking-Chingachgook cycle indeed looks to have already taken root in his mind, certainly the "descriptive tale" soon to be published as *The Pioneers* (1823), and even, conceivably, *The Last*

---

6. *Home as Found*, Preface (1838; rpt. New York: Capricorn, 1961), xxxviii.

7. *The Spy; A Tale of the Neutral Ground*, Preface (1821; rpt. New York: Popular Library, 1972), 7. Further references to this edition will be cited parenthetically within the text.

8. Reprinted in *Jahrbuch für Amerikastudien* V (1960), 308-39.

of The Mohicans (1826) and *The Prairie* (1827). Yet "Indian" America, and Cooper's momentous transformation of it into frontier epic, still lay slightly ahead. For the moment he had in *The Spy* other American materials to make over from fact into fiction, reality into myth.

There were, too, genuine doubts, obstacles, to overcome. He may well have had within himself a social confidence born of his family's relatively new but considerable wealth. He may well have been able to look to his landed New York patrimony (heir to Judge Cooper and Cooperstown), to his studies, though brief, at Yale (1803-1805), to his year spent at his father's insistence as a common sailor aboard the *Stirling* (1810) prior to entering the Navy proper, to his squirarchical, grand-alliance marriage in 1811 to Susan DeLancey and her Dutch-patroon clan, and to his gentleman-farming and management of the two family properties at Cooperstown and Angevine Farm, Scarsdale. But as an outsetting writer, Cooper at the same time had every reason to think himself up against odds. How with matching confidence to play literary founder, the maker of a New World art for a New World history? How to alight upon credible innovations not only of subject but of voice, design, viewpoint and the rest?

The Spy understandably has long come to be recognized as indeed marking his advertion to "American Manners and American scenes," as signifying literally enough his first "American novel professedly." Among the "pros," as Cooper designates matters in his Preface, for choosing "his own country for the scene of his story," he mentions "untrodden ground," "all the charms of novelty" (9-10). What better subject, too, it might be thought, especially given the novel's closing perspective of "thirty-three years after" and "The War of 1812," than "1776," The Birth of the Nation (or at least its military prelude), itself the very inscription of "America" in terms of a politics and history? Where more appropriately to begin an American literary career than with The War of Independence, Washington's patriot soldiery cast against the army of The British Crown and its loyalist supporters? Whether by chance or not, two "beginnings" so come together — America as a political dispensation free as for the first time of the ancestral British yoke (and by force of arms no less) and Cooper as an American author equally free as for the first time of British literary pre-emption.

But so much acknowledged about the "Americanness" of *The Spy*, and that consideration has tended to hold sway in most critical discussion of the novel, Cooper himself hints of still another, actually far cannier, shaping impetus behind this first of his novels set in his own country. The indications lie in terms like "I am more partial to this new work," "goes very slowly," "I take more pains with it," "more interest," and above all, "better writing." For *The Spy* carries not only the inscription of his nation's genesis, its revolutionary and beginning history, but of nothing less than his own true writerly genesis, the first, most fully engaged, awakening and realization of his own imagination.

In *The Spy*, as had been possible only in silhouette in *Precaution*, he, too, could "make" history, that is, take upon himself to invent or fictionalize fact, an "impersonation," so to speak, which, whether obliquely or otherwise, in every way underwrites all the specific impersonations in the novel. For overall, like the Wharton home of "The Locusts," and around it, "The Neutral Ground" itself, *The Spy* positively abounds in self-inventions, masquerades, actings-out, "passes" of the kind held by Harvey and Henry, in all, a gamut of different kinds of metamorphosis and false shows of appearance. "Great numbers wore ... masks," Cooper discloses early on, on the one hand those assumed by "useful agent(s) of the leaders of the Revolution," and on the other hand those assumed by "divers flaming patriots" (12). It remains a strength of *The Spy* that it finds, and then sustains, the imaginative wherewithal to dramatize precisely these "masks," the game of impersonation itself impersonated.

The Spy cannot have more claimed for it than in truth it merits, a "first" novel with a seeming proneness to formula symmetries (Mr Wharton/Mr Harper, Henry Wharton/Peyton Dunwoodie, Sarah/Frances, etc.) and related other besetting flaws and longueurs. But at the same time it also displays a virtual relish of the art of fabulation in its own right, of "impersonation" as a process of invention and self-creation whose reflexivity — nothing if not pervasive — gives a truly individuating animus to the story as a whole. In this respect, however less so in others, Cooper's "new work" — for which in his letter of June 1820 to the publisher-bookseller Andrew Thompson Goodrich he revealingly declares himself "partial ... as being a Country-man and perhaps a younger child" — cannot even yet be said to have had its full interpretative due.

II

Consider, first, the quality of imagining behind Cooper's "history" in his opening chapter. "Chilling dampness," "increasing violence," "darkness," "the approach of a storm," might all indicate climate (11). But they speak coevally, and figurally, to both the history, the

Revolutionary War in process, and to the geography, the Neutral Ground as miasma or natural labyrinth, through which Harper as "solitary traveller" traverses en route to his rendezvous with the spy-peddler, Harvey Birch. Westchester, thus, a "midway" valley, could not be better conceived, an actual but also in Faulkner's phrase for Yoknapatawpha a "mythical kingdom," a state-of-nature but also a state-of-the-nation, which draws into a single configuration of time and place both a disguised American patriarch (George Washington) and a disguised English-Loyalist patriarch (Mr Wharton).

A kind of double-helix of matching dispensations can immediately so be seen to have been come into the imaginative reckoning: Old Order as against New, Imperium as against Colony, True as against False. Yet, as in Hawthorne's later "My Kinsman, Major Molineux," each amounts to more than a simple binary. They play against each other obliquely, disguisedly, hedged about with an ambiguity to reflect the anxiety of crossed or uncertain loyalties as America ceases to be English domain.

Within these apparent antimonies, appropriately, still more disguise proliferates: the coded interchange between Harper and Wharton about tobacco with its pointers to the troop dispositions of the two sides; the competing, love-affected political loyalties of Sarah and Frances Wharton; the "weather-beaten," red-wigged, and falsely stooping Henry Wharton who has crossed lines on a forged pass, a spurious sign of identity; the black manservant Caesar Thompson with his acting-out or "putt'n on ol' massa" routines; and the references to the double-dealing of the Skinners. Little wonder Cooper returns, at his chapter's end, to the "violence" of the storm, the perfect synecdoche for all the radical and interwoven displacements — the guises and disguises — of the Anglo-American historical order whose break-up his novel seeks to explore and inscribe.

III

"Are you what you seem?" (233). So, infinitely to the point, Captain Lawton interrogates the peddler-spy. For as title-figure, Harvey Birch follows in suit, the True Patriot masked as Falsehood and doubly suspected by both parties. To Lawton he ranks as "a spectre," an "inexplicable man," who, before "plunging into the darkness," allows himself (not a little bitterly) to be thought "a royal spy" (233). To Major Dunwoodie, having first "captured" Birch, then himself been made his prisoner, and then been freed, he ranks as a "mysterious being" (189). To Katy Hayes, housekeeper to the Birches, he likewise signifies "a mystified body," "a man that no calculation can be made on" (255). Betty Flanagan, having come upon a golden guinea at his hands and in a nice touch of two-way Irish brogue, calls him an "honest divil" (239). And relatedly, to Caesar Thompson, in African-American patois, he ranks as a "berry clebber man" (219).

On his own reckoning, he remains his own "true character," "truly alone — none knows me but my God and *Him*" (189). An isolato, thus, *par excellence*, it adds to the irony that he is thought so many different things, one of a "multitude of agents" (345). Even the words of George Washington nominating Birch as an "unrequited servant of his country" become hidden (350), an anonymous honorific quite literally enboxed until accidentally discovered by a later generation. The "veil which conceals your true character" (343), as Washington writes, thus holds from start to finish, Birch's self-masking an integral part of the novel's "plot."

Yet, and at every turn, Washington's view, as each of the others, serves as a test of, a stalking-horse for, Cooper's own powers of invention. For all these several identities ("Necessity," says the peddler, "has made me a dexterous pilot among these hills"; 299), when seen from a readerly distance, bespeak an altogether larger, self-mirroring authoriality. How to "invent" Birch as a spy whose very own business is "invention," the simulation of what he is not? On a forward note, too, can it not also be said that Birch likely represents a first shy at none other than Natty Bumppo, the Leatherstocking?

If, accordingly, the essence of upright probity, and abrim in frontier savvy to boot, Birch operates throughout as a double, a riddle, the very spirit of "the imperfect culture of the Neutral Ground" (322). Firstly he carries his pack in true allegorized and Bunyanesque fashion, the bearer not merely of goods for trade but of secrets, espionage, things seen and yet concealed. An unmasker of others, the bigamous Wellmere notably, he wears always a mask himself, most right when most wrongly accused. As, too, a rogue frontiersman, a seemingly white "Indian," he speaks almost always with his own forked tongue, first of all and symptomatically in the early Harper-Wharton scenes where with "knowing looks and portentous warnings" he plays out a linguistic charade (52), a game of double-entendre and cypher. Whatever his straightness of purpose, his is the spy's double-speak intuitively sensed and exploited by Cooper as being among the prime working staples in all "mystery" writing.

Birch's inventedness in these respects scores from the outset, a living fiction in himself obliged to self-invent and re-invent at almost every turn. Cooper's portrait of the inner man hidden inside the outer guise becomes a comment in itself on a world historically turned upside down, inside out, or, almost literally, about-face. Harvey Birch undoubtedly has his fictive betters among the ranks of nineteenth-century American "doubles." He hardly matches, say, Poe's Dirk Peters, the Herculean yet bald and dwarf-like "singular being" in *The Narrative of Arthur Gordon Pym*, or Melville's Queequeg, "a wondrous work in one volume," "a living parchment," "a riddle to unfold" in *Moby-Dick*, or the Duke and Dauphin, "low-down humbugs and frauds" yet perfect burlesques of the St Petersburg gentry of the Judge Thatchers and Miss Watsons in Twain's *Huckleberry Finn*.[9] But if lesser kin, especially of that supreme Proteus, Melville's The Cosmopolitan in *The Confidence-Man* ("QUITE AN ORIGINAL" as the text capitalizes him provocatively),[10] does he not belong at least somewhere in this American gallery?

Nor is this to pretend that Birch cannot wear or irritate at times. His Diggory Venn-like omniscience and habit of turning up just in time, his repeated "bird's eye view of the valley," and his mournful recitations of duty (especially to Washington/Harper — "Your grace" or, in the commander's absence, "Him") border on the implausible if not unintendedly comic. Likewise, his bitter self-murmurings ("Have I not been the hunted beast of these hills for three years past?"; 296) hint of oddity, the maunder of the village atheist or eccentric. Equally, he undergoes suspiciously top-heavy doses of misfortune, whether the death of his father, the twice-over loss of his possessions and savings, the burning down of his house, or his own final eclipse by history. Yet, and given his "melancholy smile" or not, he remains a virtuoso piece of imagining.

The first full bead Cooper offers of his spy runs as follows:

---

9. Edgar Allan Poe, *The Narrative of Arthur Gordon Pym of Nantucket* (1838; rpt. Harmondsworth: Penguin, 1975), 85; Melville, *Moby-Dick*, 399; Mark Twain, *The Adventures of Huckleberry Finn* (1884; rpt. Cambridge, MA: Houghton, Mifflin & Co., 1958), 106.

10. Herman Melville, *The Confidence-Man: His Masquerade* (1857; rpt. New York: Signet, 1964), 245.

> In person, the pedler was a man above the middle height, spare, but full of bone and muscle. At first sight, his strength seemed unequal to manage the unwieldly burden of his pack; yet he threw it on and off with great dexterity, and with as much apparent ease as if it had been filled with feathers. His eyes were grey, sunken, restless, and, for the flitting moments that they dwelt on the countenances of those with whom he conversed, they seemed to read the very soul. They possessed, however, two distinct expressions, which in a great measure, characterized the whole man. When engaged in traffic, the intelligence of his face appeared lively, active, and flexible, though uncommonly acute; if the conversation turned on the ordinary transactions of life, his air became abstracted and restless; but if, by chance, the revolution and the country were the topic, his whole system seemed altered — all his faculties were concentrated; he would listen for a great length of time, without speaking, and then would break silence by some light and jocular remark, that was too much at variance with his former manner, not to be affectation. But of the war, and of his father, he seldom spoke, and always from some very obvious necessity. (33-34)

Some shrewdly-turned local portraiture immediately comes into play — Birch's "heavy" pack (and the implied word-play of "pedler"), "seeing" eyes, character-as-physiology, and alternating styles of attention as pointers to the essential man. But the text, in fact, "imagines" even more. It sets up the spy both as himself a "double" speaker and as obliged to listen in others for language which plays the equivocal for the true, the feigned for the authentic.

This same self-aware inventedness clearly extends to each of Birch's reversals (his capture by the Skinners as "the pedler spy"), near-misses (his closeness to being shot or hanged), and different interventions (his exposure of Wellmere or help in the escape of the "masquerading" Wharton). In this latter respect a classic piece of self-reflexivity occurs when as indeed a "royal spy" he guides Captain Wharton, a one-time neighbor yet an officer of the opposing army, to the safety of the British navy. This marks a service to the Wharton family to whom, the text alleges earlier, "it was no new intelligence ... that Harvey Birch was distrusted and greatly harassed by the American officers" (110). To Wharton, Birch now alleges "I thought you knew me too well, to be uncertain which part I favoured" (325), his equivocation, his self-authoring, the perfect surrogate for Cooper's own. "Paying mysterious visits," "lingering," "a strange figure that had been seen gliding by in the mists of the evening," all phrasing used and echoed in characterizing Birch, again does typical double-service.

Three explicit "disguise" scenes which involve Birch give still further emphasis to the point. In the first, the spy plays ghost, a ruse to escape the Skinners. This classic "invention," clever enough in itself, gains from being modulated through Caesar — Birch's father as a "spook," "a being from another world" (117). Cooper is again not to be denied his bluff, his invented invention. Even more so does that apply when Birch eludes his captors in the guise of Betty Flanagan, an ingenious piece of cross-dressing and ventriloquism with the Irish washerwoman paid off with her guinea into the bargain. Cooper's casting of him as a Calvinist divine (with full-blown props of wig, powder, gown and bible) in the rescue of Captain Wharton yields the added bonus of a mock-religious rhetoric, a teasingly invented hellfire and damnation idiom. Dressed to suit, and with Wharton as Caesar (white become black and *vice versa*), Birch could not better ape the whole drama of impersonation in *The Spy*, one charade engagingly in service for another.

IV

A similarly "double" inventedness underwrites all the other principals and their mutual encounters in the novel. Even Harper/Washington, whom many readers find wooden, too obvious or staid, Cooper signals as a making-over of the historical commander-in-chief into an imagined creature of his own. The cue lies less in the opening episodes with the Whartons, or in his subsequent disguised appearances, than in the episode where Frances Wharton makes her way to his hut, "this singular edifice" (306), to seek his help in the reprieve of her brother.

Harper/Washington, in one sense, fulfils to perfection his role as Father of the Nation, wise, benign, solemn even to the point of formula. He also doubles as a "true" father to Frances as against her own "false" father; so much the gesture to "history." But, at the very same time, having in time of need, uncertainly, and at night, found her way to him, France sees the following in the hut:

> Against the walls and rocks were suspended, from pegs forced into the crevices, various garments, and such as were apparently fitted for all ages and conditions, and for either sex. British and American uniforms hung peaceably by the side of each other; and on the peg that supported a gown of striped calico, such as

> was the usual country wear, was also depending a well-powdered wig — in short, the attire was numerous, and as various as if a whole parish were to be equipped from this one wardrobe. (307)

The Washington of *The Spy*, it seems hard not to infer, much as he acts in required historical image, also belongs to Cooper's "wardrobe" — a repository of "various garments," "uniforms," "wigs" and "attire," in all the very "equipment" of a literary fiction. Even, thus, with his only "historical" figure in the novel, Cooper more or less acknowledges an invention, a quite knowingly costumed or "imagined" portrait.

That applies the more so to the rest of his cast. In Mr Wharton, his family coach bedecked in British armorial arms (as against Washington on his lone horse), he develops another masquerade — that of the Loyalist to the British Crown who pretends to be a "political neutral." Wharton's balancing-act, American yet given to "the manners of England" and "aristocratic notions of blood and alliances" (23), proves a nice challenge to Cooper: how to portray, in line with the name of the house, a Locust, the feigned "moderate"? As a study in weakness, vacillation, Mr Wharton deserves his due, another self-disguised "invention" at the behest of Cooper's own inventing powers.

Each of the other Whartons, in turn, "act out" parts which hide their actual selves, yet further stand-ins as it might be thought for Cooper's own invention. Captain Henry Wharton — principled, brave — becomes the literally twice-over disguised son (initially when he crosses lines to visit The Locusts and again as Caesar in Birch's rescue). His trial, particularly, seems to stand in for the novel as itself an imagined "theatre." There gather the "different actors in the approaching investigation" (259); Henry is accused of "disguise"; it is said of him that "deceit never formed part of his character" (263); one of the American military judges asks "Was he in disguise?" (262); and he is indicted and sentenced as "a spy — artful, delusive and penetrating beyond the abilities of any of his class" (266). Much as these exchanges serve the drama of Henry's capture, they could not be mistaken as other than loaded up with self-reference, markers also for Cooper's own disguise and artfulness.

Sarah and Frances Wharton are both led into mistaken perceptions of love — Sarah with the already married Wellmere and Frances over the misconstrued Isabella Singleton. Sarah will undergo transformation into an American Ophelia, a "lonely maniac," her "madness" the perfect upshot of Perfidious Albion in the form of Wellmere (244). Frances has to work through her misperception of Peyton Dunwoodie ("you know not yourself nor me" he tells her in her jealousy; 197), in fact as true a lover as he is American patriot. Even the aunt, Miss Jeanette Peyton, has her equivocations, the matching interest she has in General Montrose on the one hand and in Dr Sitgreaves on the other.

The minor presences operate no less reflexively. Katy Haynes goes through life self-deludingly the would-be wife to a supremely unuxorious Harvey Birch, a "love" nicely counterpointed in the playful Betty Flanagan-Sergeant Hollister liaison. Cooper's shy at Smollettism in Dr Sitgreaves (with his *leitmotif* of the unsurgical swordplay of the American troopers) depicts an outwardly robust medic actually full of sensitivity as his reaction to the death of Jack Lawton and his respective attitudes to the truly wounded Singleton and falsely wounded Wellmere confirms. Wellmere as bigamist, in fact, "acts" as a perfect double, the deceiver, yet at Birch's hands, eventually himself the un-deceived and disgraced. The Skinner leader, too, in one of the more graphic scenes in the novel, mistakes his own likely hanging for a ruse by the Cow-boys, one more mistaken charade of many. For his part, Caesar Thompson veers, to be sure, between stereotype and something only slightly better. But he remains one of the first white-written "African" portraits in American fiction. His jibes to the soldiery, his insistent servant role (especially in the dinner scene of "American profusion" at The Locusts), and above all, his actorly parts in the ghost and the Wharton rescue episodes, again shadow the designing hand behind them. Here, as elsewhere, Cooper's implied recognition of his own will to invention could not be more firmly indicated.

V

"At the time of which we write, we were a divided people" (132). The narrator's observation typically for *The Spy* serves several ends at once. For the "divisions" so ingeniously exploited by Cooper — America and England, Patriot and Loyalist — are matched by the different internal divisions of Birch, the Whartons, Harper, Wellmere and the rest. Thus if the novel delineates a "divided" history, it does the same for the men and women who live that history, a well-taken match of the humanly particular within the general. And as they, like the histories to which they belong, mask and unmask, they become also the very instances of Cooper's own imagining.

Each "staged" scene does likewise, notably the central battle with Washington and Howe as overall commanders, Lawton and Wellmere as the field officers, and Henry Wharton aided to flight by Caesar only to be recaptured almost immediately. The whole draws a tone of sardonicism from Sitgreaves's attitude to Wharton's hand injury ("a scientific operation ... might tempt a younger man, in the hurry of business, to overlook the particulars of the case"; 92). Similarly the different trial scenes, first of Birch, then of Wharton, and with the gallows threateningly close to hand, clearly give Cooper the opportunity to imagine the division of life and death, of sentence and execution — an action he goes on to see through to its completion in the dispatch of the Skinner chieftain.

Nor does the "division" stop there: it assumes mythic or archetypal dimension in the impostures of the opportunist pro-American Skinners and pro-British Cow-boys; in the repeated allusions to the twin *eminences grises* of Anglo-American espionage, Benedict Arnold and Major André; and in the use of the Neutral Ground as an "America," a landscape and climate, full of hidden niches and crevices and as given to the shadow of night as to day-time military "noises and profusion" (30).

Not without purpose, then, does the novel speak self-indicatingly of "Westchester" as "intersected with roads of every direction." Cooper might well have gone on to write stronger fiction, but *The Spy* achieves its own singularity. For in this first of his American works, the "making" of his country's history stands at one with the "making" of his own fiction — a "double" of a kind with the very themes it seeks to dramatize and whose recognition has indeed long been overdue.

PROPERTY, MARRIAGE, WOMEN, AND FENIMORE COOPER'S FIRST FICTIONS

ROBERT LAWSON-PEEBLES

Shortly after *The Pioneers* first appeared in February 1823, the *United States Gazette* noticed the critical and public acclaim that had greeted the novel, and remarked particularly that it had "excited a sensation among the artists, altogether unprecedented in the history of our domestic literature."[1] The newspaper detailed several of the paintings which were in progress. The first illustration to be published appeared in *The Port Folio* in June 1823. The scene chosen, and its depiction by Gideon Fairman, helps me to introduce my theme, which is about the implications of Cooper's thinking on the relation of property and marriage. Near the close of the novel's thirty-sixth chapter, Elizabeth Temple climbs towards the top of Mount Vision, where her father the Judge had cleared "a little spot ... in order that a better view might be obtained of the village and the valley."[2] On her way she encounters Chingachgook, his face and body streaked with red paint, his ears and nose hung with ornaments, and on his chest the medallion of Washington. It is a sight which "would have terrified a less resolute female" but the ensuing conversation shows that Elizabeth barely lost her "self-possession" (399). In the illustration she seems not to have lost it at all. Chingachgook, seated on a felled tree, occupies the lower right of the frame while Elizabeth, inclining solicitously over him, dominates the center-left. She is portrayed as an exemplar of modern

1. *United States Gazette*, rpt. in *The Port Folio* 15 (June 1823), 520. I would like to thank the British Academy for a Personal Research Grant which made this project possible, and the Huntington Library, San Marino, California, for the congenial circumstances in which it was undertaken.

2. James Fenimore Cooper, *The Pioneers, or the Sources of the Susquehanna; A Descriptive Tale* (1823), eds James Franklin Beard, *et al*. (Albany: State University of New York Press, 1980), 398. Future references to this edition will be cited parenthetically within the text.

female fashion. Indeed it is too modern, for the novel is set in 1793-94, while her "Empire style" clothes commemorate the First French Empire established by Bonaparte in 1804. Her ankle-length white chemise dress is gathered into a waist just below the bust; a shawl is draped loosely but gracefully around her shoulders; she wears elbow-length gloves and a bonnet garnished with a bow; and her attire is completed by a parasol reposing lightly in her right hand. Near the parasol stands a receptacle collecting the sap of the maple-tree which inclines leftwards out of the frame.[3] The illustration, therefore, orchestrates a series of contrasts, between dark and light, nature and culture, depredation and conservation, old and new, masculine and feminine.

It should have been clear where the artist's, and by implication the viewers', sympathies lay. Nevertheless, an accompanying description reinforced the point when *The Port Folio* reissued "Elizabeth conversing with Mohegan" in 1826 as part of a small collection of illustrations of Cooper and Scott novels:

> The time selected by the artist is the period in the conversation at which the aged chief adverts to the loss of his family .... This Indian forms a fine and striking portrait in the *dramatis personae* of the Pioneers. He represents, with barbarous dignity, in his seventieth year, the last remnant of a powerful race over whom his ancestors bore sway. The stubborn, but fallen, power and pride, — the lofty sentiments of personal dignity, — the enduring, uncomplaining patience of ruin and despair, — the feverish and convulsive recurrence to his former state, — the deep sense of his wrong, all softened, though not subdued, by his conversion to christianity, are depicted by Mr. Cooper with a strong and vivid pencil.[4]

---

3. *The Port Folio* 15 (June 1823), opp. 441. Alice Morse Earle, *Two Centuries of Costume in America*, 2 vols (New York: Macmillan, 1903), II, 786-89. For illustrations of the "Empire Style," see James Laver, *Costume and Fashion: A Concise History* (New York: Oxford University Press, 1983), 151-55; and Mila Contini, *Fashion from Ancient Egypt to the Present Day* (London: Paul Hamlyn, 1965), 216-28.

4. *Illustrations from The Spy, The Pioneers, and The Waverley Novels, with Explanatory and Critical Remarks* (Philadelphia: Harrison Hall, 1826), n.p. These comments originated in the review of *The Pioneers* in *The Port Folio* 15 (March 1823), 234.

"Elizabeth conversing with Mohegan." From *The Port Folio* 15 (June 1823), opp. 441 (reproduced by permission of the Huntington Library, San Marino, California).

That strong and vivid pencil was reflected in the chiaroscuro of Fairman's illustration. Its contrasts display, in this instance with a muted sense of conflict, a moment of confrontation between two value systems which would be resolved by the end of the novel, with Leatherstocking trekking westwards, Chingachgook dead, and Templeton occupied by Elizabeth and her new husband Oliver, the son of a Loyalist. The red family had been supplanted by the whites, representatives of a so-called modern "civilization."

Perhaps because their resolution was clear, such moments of confrontation, between "society" and "savagery," fascinated the various illustrators of the novel. Henry Inman, who drew the third of the five illustrations that appeared in *The Port Folio*, shows Chingachgook being interrogated about his beliefs by the Rev. Grant.[5] The fifth, again by Inman, shows the fashion-conscious Elizabeth weeping at the imminent departure of Leatherstocking, while her frock-coated husband vainly offers him "some of the new-fashioned money that they've been making at Albany" (455).[6] The fourth, by Fairman, is a "Vignette Title" (never, as far as I know, to grace a title-page of the novel) with a maple-tree as its foreground, from which are suspended the carcasses of a bear and a deer and the various weapons used in hunting them. In the background can be seen, in the words of the 1826 pamphlet, "a perspective view of Cooperstown, on lake Otsego ... founded by Judge Cooper, — father of the author of the American Tales."[7] Two of the novel's set-pieces inspired a crop of illustrations. The Turkey Shoot in Chapter 17 was engraved by Tony Johannot around 1828-29 for a French edition of Cooper's works, and painted in 1832 by John Quidor and, once again, around 1857 by Tompkins H. Matteson. The Panther Scene in Chapter 28 not only prompted an account in *The Port Folio* of "A Panther Hunt in Pennsylvania," but also oil paintings in 1832 by John Quidor and 1834 by George Loring Brown; an engraving by the Frenchman Alexis Francois Girard; and, most vivid of all, a drawing by Robert Farrier used as the frontispiece for the 1832 London edition, bearing the quotation: "Miss Temple did not, or could not move. Her

---

5. *The Port Folio* 16 (November 1823), opp. 353.

6. *The Port Folio* 17 (January 1824), frontispiece.

7. *The Port Folio* 16 (September 1823), opp. 177. The second illustration in *The Port Folio*, not discussed here, portrayed Edwards showing his wound to Judge Temple. All the illustrations discussed are to be found in Beard's 1980 edition of *The Pioneers*.

hands were clasped in the attitude of prayer, but her eyes were still drawn to her terrible enemy" (309).[8] Taken together, the illustrations surrounded the novel with a complex apparatus of cultural interpretation, while still remaining true to its central message, contained in the epigraph taken from James Kirke Paulding's 1818 poem:

> Extremes of habits, manners, time and space,
> Brought close together, here stood face to face,
> And gave at once a contrast to the view,
> That other lands and ages never knew. (v)

It is worth emphasizing the importance of the female face. In a recent reconsideration of Cooper's heroines, Kay House has shown how powerful a figure is Elizabeth Temple.[9] She undertakes many of the functions of Leatherstocking, linking the past (through her father) with the present, nature with culture, and the white race with the aboriginal. But also, significantly unlike Leatherstocking, she is a figure of authority. The first description of Elizabeth in the novel shows that she is a "dazzling" beauty, but also a "commanding" one (66). She has "female grace" combined with "womanly dignity." She has inherited her mother's beautiful face, "but its expression was her father's." Her intrepid nature is clearly illustrated during the Panther Scene. She never thinks of flight, but rather kneels protectively over the fainting form of Louisa Grant and dauntlessly faces the panther: "Notwithstanding the fearful aspect of her foe, the eye of Elizabeth had never shrunk from its gaze" (310). Her wealth comes from her father, too. When she first arrives at the Judge's mansion he announces her as "the heiress," and

---

8. Anon., "A Panther Hunt in Pennsylvania," *The Port Folio* 17 (June 1824), 494-99. Cooper, *The Pioneers* (London: Colburn and Bentley, 1832), frontispiece. For a discussion of the Panther Scene, see Lawson-Peebles, "Fenimore Cooper's Frontier Comforts," *Revue française d'études américaines* 48-49 (Avril-Juillet 1991), 249-50.

9. Kay S. House with Genevieve Belfiglio, "Fenimore Cooper's Heroines," *American Novelists Revisited: Essays in Feminist Criticism*, ed. Fritz Fleischmann (Boston: G. K. Hall & Co., 1982), 43. Professor House's interpretation, and my own, differ from that of Joyce W. Warren in *The American Narcissus: Individualism and Women in Nineteenth-Century American Fiction* (New Brunswick, NJ: Rutgers University Press, 1984), where Cooper's young women are called "uninteresting nonpersons" (103).

the housekeeper, Remarkable Pettibone, now knows "that her own power had ended" (64, 66). Furthermore, it is clear from the lengthy description of the mansion's interior that Elizabeth will inherit a substantial fortune.

Elizabeth is endowed with such power because she plays a key role in Cooper's thought about property. Throughout his career, Cooper defended the rights of property-owners. He continued the story of the Elizabeth's family in a pair of novels, *Homeward Bound* and *Home As Found* (1838), which were prompted by the Three Mile Point controversy; while the Littlepage Trilogy (1845-46) was a defense of the landlords during the Anti-Rent War. Cooper summed up his position in *The American Democrat* (1838):

> Social station, in the main, is a consequence of property. So long as there is civilization there must be the rights of property, and so long as there are the rights of property, their obvious consequences must follow ....
>
> As property is the base of all civilization, its existence and security are indispensible to social improvement.[10]

I want to suggest that, if Cooper believed that "property is the base of all civilization," its apex was achieved through marriage with an appropriate partner. In other words, women provided the vital link between property and "social improvement." I will develop my argument by concentrating on the period 1818-23 in Cooper's life, first by looking at the sources of what might be called his moral aesthetics of property, and then by examining his two earliest published fictions, *Precaution* and *Tales for Fifteen*.

* * *

Our first view of Templeton is through the eyes of Elizabeth. Cooper devotes almost all of Chapter Three of *The Pioneers* to allowing "Elizabeth to dwell on a scene which was rapidly altering under the

---

10. James Fenimore Cooper, *The American Democrat, or Hints on the Social and Civic Relations of the United States of America* (Cooperstown: H. & E. Phinney, 1838), 77-78, 135. John P. McWilliams discusses the *Homeward Bound / Home As Found* duo and the Littlepage Trilogy in *Political Justice in a Republic: James Fenimore Cooper's America* (Berkeley: University of California Press, 1972), 215-37, 298-339.

hands of man" (40). As James D. Wallace has pointed out, those alterations are viewed critically.[11] The descriptions are either comic or ironic, and the chapter is opened by an epigraph which presents the alterations as a rape:

> Yet man can mar such works with his rude taste,
> Like some sad spoiler of a virgin's fame. (38)

Elizabeth Temple's view of Templeton problematizes two famous moments in Jane Austen's fiction. The first is Elizabeth Bennet's view of Pemberley in *Pride and Prejudice* (1813):

> She had never seen a place for which nature had done more, or where natural beauty had been so little counteracted by an awkward taste.[12]

The second is Emma Woodhouse's view of Donwell Abbey in *Emma* (1815):

> She felt all the honest pride and complacency which her alliance with the present and future proprietor could fairly warrant, as she viewed the respectable size and style of the building, its suitable, becoming, characteristic situation, low and sheltered — its ample gardens stretching down to meadows washed by a stream ... and its abundance of timber in rows and avenues, which neither fashion nor extravagance had rooted up .... It was just what it ought to be, and it looked what it was — and Emma felt an increasing respect for it, as the residence of a family of such true gentility, untainted in blood and understanding.[13]

Part of the description from *Emma* is in the fashionable language of the Picturesque Tour, but the sentences are also studded with moral comments such as "respectable" and "suitable." These comments come to a climax with the two phrases, "It was just what it ought to be, and it

---

11. James D. Wallace, *Early Cooper and His Audience* (New York: Columbia University Press, 1986), 136-38.

12. Jane Austen, *Pride and Prejudice*, ed. Frank W. Bradbrook (1813; rpt. London: Oxford University Press, 1970), 214.

13. Jane Austen, *Emma*, ed. David Lodge (1815; rpt. London: Oxford University Press, 1971), 323.

looked what it was." At first sight they seem tautologous, but in fact they contain two important components of Austen's moral system, fidelity to social station and fidelity of appearance. The ensuing dash and conjunction signal the shift from description to conclusion, the appropriate admiration of the owner. It follows that, in the fullness of time, Emma will marry the owner of Donwell Abbey, just as Elizabeth Bennet had married the owner of Pemberley. It is as well for Cooper's Elizabeth Temple that she is the legatee of the Judge's property. The voluntary act of marrying the owner of that gimcrack building and those felled trees would surely be a devastating comment on her moral status.

Cooper's commentary on the "rude taste" with which Templeton is constructed comes not only from Jane Austen but also from his dubious experience as a landscape gardener. In 1818 his father-in-law, John Peter De Lancey, gave him "Angevine," a small farm at Scarsdale. According to an account published in 1861 by his daughter Susan, Cooper "took very great pleasure in the improvements required by a new place."[14] She noted that "[h]orticulture and landscape-gardening are the growth of an older and much higher civilization than that which flows from commerce alone." At that time, "landscape-gardening was in its very earliest stages in America," and the gardens of the wealthy could barely be distinguished from "those of the laboring farmer who had no leisure for finish of improvement." She then described "Angevine":

> The position of the house was fine, commanding a beautiful view over the farms and woods of the adjoining country, in whose varied groves hickory and tulip-tree, cedar and sassafras, grew luxuriantly; a broad reach of Sound stretched beyond, ... while the low shores of Long Island, with the famous pippin orchards of Newtown, formed the distant background. Planning a lawn, building a ha-ha fence, then a novelty in the country, and ditching a swamp, were the tasks of the moment; while the friends who followed his movement often smiled at the almost boyish eagerness with which he watched the growth of the shrubs, or shook their heads sagely at the size of the trees he was engaged in transplanting.[15]

---

14. Susan Fenimore Cooper, *Pages and Pictures from the Writings of James Fenimore Cooper* (New York: W. A. Townsend and Co., 1861), 14.

15. Susan Fenimore Cooper, *Pages and Pictures*, 14-15. She repeats the account, with slight variations, in "A Glance Backward," *Atlantic Monthly* 49.352 (February

Susan Fenimore Cooper wrote this more than forty years after the event, and her memory in the intervening years seems to have become selective. The view from the garden is lovingly described in detail, but when she comes to the garden itself the description becomes vague, its power no longer vesting in the nouns but rather in the present participles, concentrating on the transformations which her father made to the environment.

Those transformations do not entirely abide by Austenian dicta of taste. As Raymond Williams has pointed out, Austen distinguished between two kinds of improvement: one which made an environment more productive or useful, and one which simply absorbed wealth. Appropriately echoing Austen's language, Williams suggested that she favored the first: "improvement is or ought to be improvement."[16] Indeed, *Mansfield Park* (1814) can be regarded as an extended inquiry into the different kinds of improvement, and the ways that they reflect on the morals of the improver. Cooper does not emerge too well at this stage as a moral gardener. Planning a lawn may be morally neutral, but ditching a swamp is suspect. It could be acceptable if it results in fertile soil, but the garden at "Angevine" is devoted to "leisure." Transplanting trees, we already know from *Emma*, is reprehensible; no wonder Cooper's friends shook their heads sagely. Indeed, Cooper would later, like Jane Austen, regard the felling of trees as an act that was both immoral and in bad taste.[17] The catalogue of misdeeds is completed by the ha-ha. A narrow ditch used as a concealed boundary, the ha-ha was, according to Horace Walpole, a term coined by "the common people ... to express their surprize at finding a sudden and

---

1887), 202. Brief details of the grant of land are to be found in *The Letters and Journals of James Fenimore Cooper*, ed. James Franklin Beard, 6 vols (Cambridge, MA: Harvard University Press, 1960-68), I, 87.

16. Raymond Williams, *The Country and the City* (New York: Oxford University Press, 1973), 116. For an extended discussion of Jane Austen and improvements, see Alistair M. Duckworth, *The Improvement of the Estate: A Study of Jane Austen's Novels* (Baltimore: Johns Hopkins University Press, 1971), particularly 38-55.

17. Susan Fenimore Cooper, "Small Family Memories," in *The Correspondence of James Fenimore Cooper*, ed. James Fenimore Cooper (grandson), 2 vols (New Haven, CT: Yale University Press, 1922), I, 12.

unperceived check to their walk."[18] Walpole approved of ha-has. They served to extend the view from inside the garden, giving a sense of apparent unity with the surrounding country while unobtrusively marking a boundary to the property. Jane Austen may not have liked them. The ha-ha at Sotherton is of a piece with the other proposed fashionable improvements. Furthermore, Austen uses it for ironic effect. It gives the flighty Maria Bertram "a feeling of restraint and hardship," and, quoting the caged starling from Sterne's *Sentimental Journey*, she remarks that she cannot get out.[19] Her vaulting sexuality prompts her to misunderstand the purpose of the ha-ha; it was designed to prevent ingress rather than restrain egress.

Jane Austen's attitude to improvements reflected the views of Edmund Burke:

> [O]ne of the first and most leading principles on which the commonwealth and the laws are consecrated, is lest the temporary possessors and life-renters in it, unmindful of what they have received from their ancestors, or of what is due to their posterity, should act as if they were the entire masters; that they should not think it amongst their rights to cut off the entail, or commit waste on the inheritance, by destroying at their pleasure the whole original fabric of their society; hazarding to leave to those who come after them, a ruin instead of an habitation ....[20]

Burke's belief in the obligations which pass from generation to generation in a "commonwealth" are also to be found in Cooper's description of New York State in the first paragraph of *The Pioneers*:

> [T]he whole district is hourly exhibiting how much can be done ... under the dominion of mild laws, and where every man feels

---

18. Horace Walpole, "The History of the Modern Taste in Gardening," in Isabel W. U. Chase, *Horace Walpole: Gardenist* (Princeton: Princeton University Press, 1943), 25. On the ha-ha, see Simon Pugh, *Garden - Nature - Language* (Manchester: Manchester University Press, 1988), 57-59.

19. Jane Austen, *Mansfield Park*, ed. John Lucas (London: Oxford University Press, 1970), 86-89. Future references to this edition will be cited parenthetically within the text (*MP*).

20. Edmund Burke, *Reflections on the Revolution in France*, ed. Conor Cruise O'Brien (1790; rpt. Harmondsworth: Penguin, 1968), 192.

> a direct interest in the prosperity of a commonwealth, of which he knows himself to form a part. The expedients of the pioneers who first broke ground in the settlement of this country, are succeeded by the permanent improvements of the yeoman, who intends to leave his remains to moulder under the sod which he tills, or, perhaps, of the son, who, born in the land, piously wishes to linger around the grave of his father. (15-16)

In striking contrast, his earlier activities at "Angevine," far from being in the "instinctive good taste" suggested by his daughter,[21] seem instead to resemble the changes made to Sotherton by the thoughtless James Rushworth, or even the proposals for Thornton Lacey by the immoral Henry Crawford:

> "The farm-yard must be cleared away entirely, and planted up to shut out the blacksmith's shop. The house must be turned to front the east instead of the north .... And *there* must be your approach — through what is at present the garden. You must make a new garden at what is now the back of the house .... Then the stream — something must be done with the stream; but I could not quite determine what. I had two or three ideas." (*MP* 218)

Crawford's plans to uproot the environment are interrupted by Edmund Bertram, whose home this will be. Bertram will be satisfied "with rather less ornament and beauty" (*MP* 219). Instead, the premises will be made "comfortable, and given the air of a gentleman's residence without any very heavy expense." That must suffice him and "all who care" about him, including Fanny Price, who will eventually marry him.

It may be that Cooper's "improvements" to "Angevine" were prompted by the circumstances of the gift. He was far from being the farm's "entire master" according to the letter of the law. It was given to him only in trust, so that it could not be "encumbered or alienated by the said James Cooper or subjected to any charge whatever on account of his debts."[22] The farm's trustees were his two brothers-in-law, Thomas James and Edward Floyd De Lancey, with whom Cooper was soon at odds. The argument, recorded in a letter of reconciliation that

21. Susan Fenimore Cooper, *Pages and Pictures*, 14.

22. *Letters and Journals*, I, 87 (footnote).

Cooper wrote in 1822, may have signified a deeper family malaise.[23] Warren Motley has suggested that, although Cooper's marriage to Susan was extremely happy, his relationship with her family was far from easy.[24] A brief comparison of the De Lancey and Cooper families may reveal why this was so. The De Lanceys were an aristocratic Huguenot family who, after arriving in America in 1686, created a network of marital connections that reads like a colonial who's who and includes Sir William Johnson, Cadwallader Colden, William Allen, John Penn and John Jay. Etienne De Lancey began the process by marrying a daughter of Stephanus Van Cortlandt, whose family, according to the historian Thomas Jones, was "then the most opulent and extensive of any in the province."[25] His son, James, became Chief Justice and Lieutenant Governor of New York. He married Anne, daughter of Caleb Heathcote, a leading New York merchant, and niece of Sir Gilbert Heathcote, Lord Mayor of London, a founder of the Bank of England and reputedly one of the richest commoners in England. James De Lancey's eldest sister, Susanna, married Admiral Sir Peter Warren, the victor of Louisbourg in 1745 and another extremely wealthy man, later described by Cooper as an "excellent and efficient officer, than whom there was not a braver in the British marine."[26] One of her daughters married Charles Fitzroy, the first Baron Southampton. Another married Willoughby Bertie, the fourth Earl of Abingdon. A granddaughter married the third Viscount Gage.[27]

In comparison the marriage of James De Lancey's granddaughter Susan must have seemed modest, even unfortunate. Cooper's father was

---

23. *Letters and Journals*, I, 86-87.

24. Warren Motley, *The American Abraham: James Fenimore Cooper and the Frontier Patriarch* (Cambridge: Cambridge University Press, 1987), 51-54.

25. On the De Lanceys, see Thomas Jones, *History of New York during the Revolutionary War*, ed. Edward Floyd De Lancey, 2 vols (New York: New York Historical Society, 1879), I, 154-58, 649-63; and Robert E. Spiller, *Fenimore Cooper: Critic of His Times* (New York: Minton, Balch, & Co., 1931), 60-66.

26. Cooper, *History of the Navy of the United States of America*, 3 vols (New York: G. P. Putnam & Co., 1854), I, 32.

27. Details of the Heathcote and Warren families come from the *DNB* and the *Dictionary of American Biography*. On the wealth of Caleb Heathcote, see Dixon Ryan Fox, *Caleb Heathcote, Gentleman Colonist* (New York: Scribner's, 1926), 275-76.

a self-made man, a jurist and land speculator who died (possibly in odd circumstances) a few months before Cooper declared his love for this "fair damsel of eighteen."[28] The son seemed to have inherited his father's temper and his elder brother's incendiary disposition. William junior had been expelled from Princeton, charged with burning down Nassau Hall.[29] Cooper was rusticated from Yale for blowing up another student's room, with gunpowder. His sister described him as "very wild"; a tutor, with typical reserve, as "rather wayward."[30] A few years at sea had instilled some discipline but had not cured his irritability. Of course, money can indemnify many flaws of character; and Judge Cooper had left each of his six surviving children $50,000 in cash and considerable holdings in land. But the Coopers seemed determined to burn their way through their patrimony, and their profligacy was cut short only by death, and by the declining land values which rendered the residue of the estate unsaleable. By 1820 James Cooper's four brothers had all died, leaving their families, according to William Leete Stone (Cooper's onetime friend), "all but destitute."[31] Cooper, who became the administrator of his father's estate on the death of William junior in 1819, tried to save it by increasingly frenetic and fruitless speculations. In 1822 he left "Angevine" with his family for rented accomodation in New York City, and a year later the sheriff listed their household goods in order to satisfy debts.[32]

In these circumstances the "improvements" to "Angevine" may have seemed to the De Lanceys like a Jane Austen horror story come true: a pretentious attempt to suggest the surface appearance of wealth which only served to undermine its substance further. Yet it was precisely at this time that Cooper began to restore the substance of his life, and also to move towards the Austenian moral aesthetics suggested

28. *Letters and Journals*, I, 17. On Judge Cooper's death, see Alan Taylor, "Who Murdered William Cooper?" *New York History* 72 (July 1991), 261-83.

29. *Letters and Journals*, I, 27, footnote 2.

30. *Letters and Journals*, I, 4-6.

31. William Leete Stone, *The Life and Times of Sa-go-ye-wat-ha, or Red Jacket* (Albany: J. Munsell, 1866), 35.

32. On Cooper's finances, see Beard, ed., Historical Introduction, *The Pioneers*, xxxi-xxxii; Henry Walcott Boynton, *James Fenimore Cooper* (New York: Century, 1931), 68-76; and Wayne Franklin, *The New World of James Fenimore Cooper* (Chicago: University of Chicago Press, 1982), 16-19.

by the opening of *The Pioneers*. He did both by becoming a novelist. His daughter's story that his career started in response to a challenge from his wife is attractive and may well be true at a superficial level.[33] But there were deeper causes. William Leete Stone thought that it was "the loss of property" which "called forth the slumbering energies of his mind."[34] Recently, critics have proposed other reasons. Warren Motley suggested that writing resulted from Cooper's "compulsion to meet ... the issue of authority."[35] Wayne Franklin believed that it "was a part of Cooper's attempt to seize control of his life, to remake or at least reform or rediscover himself."[36] That reformation, I want to suggest, was achieved through an imaginative dilation which made him adopt the point of view of his wife and the longsuffering De Lanceys. The dilation, appropriately enough, was prompted by Jane Austen.

A long time ago it was established that the models for *Precaution*, Cooper's first novel, were *Persuasion* and, to a lesser extent, *Pride and Prejudice*.[37] *Persuasion* must have seemed particularly apposite to Cooper, concerning as it does the romance between a young naval officer with no ship and no money and an aristocratic girl of nineteen. But the sources of *Precaution* are more wide-ranging. James D. Wallace has shown that the moral novels of Hannah Opie and her "School" provided further material from which Cooper could draw.[38] In their turn, the fictions of Austen, Opie and others drew on the "conduct" or "courtesy" books.[39] These had initially been intended for young men;

---

33. Susan Fenimore Cooper, *Pages and Pictures*, 17. The incident is discussed by Anna Mulford, *A Sketch of Dr. John Smith Sage, of Sag-Harbor, N.Y.*, (Sag-Harbor, NY: John H. Hunt, 1897), 28-34; Harold Scudder, "What Mr. Cooper Read to his Wife," *The Sewanee Review* 36 (April-June 1928), 177-79; George E. Hastings, "How Cooper Became a Novelist," *American Literature* 12.1 (March 1940), 20-23; and Wallace, 64-65.

34. Stone, 35.

35. Motley, 51, 40-42.

36. Franklin, 21.

37. See Scudder and Hastings (n. 33 above).

38. Wallace, 69-72.

39. Discussions of Austen's indebtedness to the conduct books are to be found in Frank W. Bradbrook, *Jane Austen and Her Predecessors* (Cambridge: Cambridge University Press, 1966), 20-49; Nancy Armstrong, *Desire and Domestic Fiction: A*

Lord Chesterfield's *Letters to his Son* (1774) is a latter-day example. Increasingly as the eighteenth century progressed, however, they were also aimed at young women. A pair of books published by the English Anglican priest Thomas Gisborne (1758-1846) is typical of the genre. An *Enquiry into the Duties of Men in the Higher and Middle Classes of Society in Great Britain* was first published in 1794 and by 1824 had reached its seventh edition. Many of Gisborne's enquiries are not relevant here, concerning as they do the English aristocracy and professional classes, but his remarks about "private gentlemen" could have been heeded by Cooper with profit. Gentlemen, said Gisborne, must keep their family expenses "within the bounds prescribed," and particularly avoid "that pride and false shame, which sometimes impels men to persist in a mode of life far more expensive than they can afford."[40] Improvements to property, "within due bounds," are good because they provide work for "the labouring poor" and make "the owner attached to his home." But they "should be planned with taste" and the owner should "not be ostentatious and vain of them" (*EDM*, II, 464-65). And as with a home, so also with a wife. Marriage, says Gisborne, is rendered "a scene of misery" if a gentleman chooses his companion "merely for the sake of personal beauty and accomplishments, of a weighty purse, of eminent rank, of splendid and potent connections." A gentleman should look instead for "congruity" with his "own dispositions and habits, and those intrinsic virtues stedfastly grounded on religion" (*EDM*, II, 423-24).

Gisborne's companion volume, *An Enquiry into the Duties of the Female Sex*, was even more popular. First published in 1797, it had reached its thirteenth edition by 1824. In common with other conduct books, Gisborne made a clear distinction, not only between the duties of men and women, but also between their psychologies. Men, he thought, tended to be interested in business, while women were less "serious," endowed instead with "quickness of imagination, and ... of feeling"

Political History of the Novel (New York: Oxford University Press, 1987), esp. 134-60; Duckworth, *The Improvement of the Estate*, 134, 186-87; and Tony Tanner, *Jane Austen* (Cambridge, MA: Harvard University Press, 1986), 30-35. A good account of the conduct books is to be found in Joyce Hemlow, "Fanny Burney and the Courtesy Books," *PMLA* 65.5 (September 1950), 732-61.

40. Thomas Gisborne, *An Enquiry into the Duties of Men in the Higher and Middle Classes of Society in Great Britain*, 2 vols, 2nd edn (1794; rpt. London: D. & J. White, 1795), II, 461. Future references to this edition will be cited parenthetically within the text (*EDM*). A brief life of Gisborne is to be found in the *DNB*.

which could be "aggravated sometimes by familiarity with novels and theatrical productions."[41] Gisborne was particularly unhappy about the influence of the stage, which, he thought, "inculcates pernicious sentiments and maxims" (*EDFS*, 181). He disapproved, too, of "gaming" (*EDFS*, 200). Dancing, in contrast, was "in itself both innocent and salubrious," although appearances at a ballroom "easily excited vanity and envy in the female breast" (*EDFS*, 190). Women were at their best, of course, in the home; and it was there, Gisborne believed, that they exerted their most salutary influence, by "improving the general manners, dispositions, and conduct of the other sex," providing for the "comfort" of husbands and parents, and particularly "modelling the human mind during the early stages of its growth" (*EDFS*, 12-13).

Gisborne's conduct book for men was never published in America, although doubtless copies were shipped across the Atlantic. His book for women appeared in American editions in 1820 and 1825. Other conduct books had a greater circulation. Edward Moore's *Fables for the Female Sex*, first published in 1744, appeared in eleven editions in America between 1787 and 1815. James Fordyce's *Sermons to Young Women* (1766) was brought out in five editions between 1767 and 1809. John Gregory's *A Father's Legacy to his Daughter* (1774) appeared in no less than nineteen American editions between 1775 and 1821, and was only exceeded by Hester Chapone's *Letters on the Improvement of the Mind* (1773), which by 1820 had gone through twenty four American editions. In addition, many of the conduct books were bound together in miscellanies. An example is *The Lady's Pocket Library*, which among other things contained works by Moore, Gregory and Chapone, as well as Lady Pennington's *Unfortunate Mother's Advice to her Daughters* and the essays of Hannah More. The conduct books, therefore, were widely available and widely consulted, and they provided an appropriate context on which Cooper could draw for his first attempts at fiction.

When *Precaution* was first published it was, according to Susan Fenimore Cooper, believed "to have been written in England, and by a woman."[42] She continued: "What American naval officer, it was

41. Gisborne, *An Enquiry into the Duties of the Female Sex*, 4th edn (1797; rpt. London: T. Cadell & W. Davies, 1799), 116-17. Future references to this edition will be cited parenthetically within the text (*EDFS*).

42. Susan Fenimore Cooper, *Pages and Pictures*, 20.

asked, would be likely to write a book so English, and so womanly in tone and execution?" Her answer, that it was an intellectual exercise on Cooper's part, is incomplete. *Precaution* could also be regarded as an attempt to engage his own financial and family problems, and its hero, the Earl of Pendennyss, could be seen as a projection of the author's ideal self.

Well into the latter half of the novel we see the Earl, for the first time, at his home in Caernarvonshire:

> [A] princely mansion, so situated as to command a prospect of the fertile and extensive domains, the rental of which filled the coffers of its rich owner, having a beautiful view of the Irish Channel in the distance.[43]

The prospect is similar to that of "Angevine," as described by Susan Fenimore Cooper. The difference, of course, is that the coffers of the occupant of "Angevine" are not filled by the rentals from the surrounding farms. Cooper looked out on them, but did not own them. Within two pages, he dwells on the vision of wealth by adopting Pendennyss's point of view. It is an anticipation of Elizabeth's view of Templeton, but in a foreign country and without a hint of criticism:

> [H]is eye rested ... on a scene in which meadows, forests, fields waving with golden corn, comfortable farm-houses surrounded with innumerable cottages, were seen in almost endless variety. All these owned him for their lord, and one quiet smile of satisfaction beamed on his face as he gazed on the unlimited view. Could the heart of that youth have been read, it would at that moment have told a story very different from the feelings such a scene is apt to excite; it would have spoken the consciousness of well applied wealth, the gratification of contemplating meritorious deeds, and a heartfelt gratitude to the Being which had enabled him to become the dispenser of happiness to so many of his fellow-creatures. (*P* 297)

The novel gives several instances of the ways in which Pendennyss has assisted his fellow-creatures. His wealth has been well applied on his home, too. Pendennyss's mansion is "irregular, but built of the best

43. Cooper, *Precaution* (1820; rpt. Grosse Pointe, MI: Scholarly Press, 1968), 295. Future references to this edition will be cited parenthetically within the text (*P*).

materials," conveying a unity of past and present, of the "baronial grandeur" of the thirteenth century with the "comforts" of the nineteenth (*P* 295).

Pendennyss, it seems, has been reading Thomas Gisborne:

> To encourage a race of honest, skilful, and industrious tenants, is one of the first duties of a private gentleman; whether he consults his own interest, or the general welfare of the community. (*EDM*, II, 384)

Responding to complaints, common at the time, about absentee landlordism, Gisborne gave detailed advice on supervision of tenants, levels of rent, promotion of "tillage" and repairs to the infrastructure. In all this the gentleman should (as Burke suggested) have an eye to the future; he should "take into consideration ... the benefit of those who are to succeed him" (*EDM*, II, 398). At this point in *Precaution*, however, Pendennyss has no one to succeed him. He is unmarried. But the sight of his property would attract the discriminating female eye, for it resembles Pemberley and Donwell Abbey.

The central plot of the novel is taken up with finding the appropriate partner. Cooper presents an array of characters in search of a mate, either for themselves or their children, and a variety of environments in which the search takes place. The search, significantly, is seen from the woman's point of view, and here too Cooper draws upon Jane Austen and the conduct books. Indeed, when Cooper wishes to make a general observation he falls into the moralizing tone of the conduct books:

> Marriage is called a lottery, and it is thought, like all other lotteries, there are more blanks than prizes; yet is it not made more precarious than it ought to be, by our neglect of that degree of precaution which we would be ridiculed for omitting in conducting our every-day concerns? Is not the standard of matrimonial felicity placed too low? Ought we not to look more to the possession of principles than to the possession of wealth? (*P* 177)

The heroine, Emily Moseley, finds it difficult to distinguish the blanks from the prizes. The metaphor of the lottery occurs several times in the novel, appropriately because it engages its central moral problem, to be found also in Jane Austen's fiction: the relationship between appearance and reality.[44] Soldiers like Colonel Egerton and Captain Jarvis present themselves as winners, while in truth they are morally flawed: the one is a rapist, the other a coward. Fortunately, Emily has an adviser to hand, an aunt, the widowed Mrs Wilson, whom Cooper, drawing on his nautical background, describes as a "kind of Eddystone, to prevent matrimonial shipwrecks" (*P* 243). As George Hastings has pointed out, Cooper's fiction bears here a strong resemblance to *Persuasion*.[45] Both novels, indeed, have the same antecedent, for Lady Russell and Mrs. Wilson are personifications of the conduct books, which present themselves as surrogate parents. Sometimes they did this by removing natural parents. Lady Pennington's *Unfortunate Mother's Advice to her Daughters*, for instance, begins by remarking that "a long train of events, of a most extraordinary nature, conspired to remove you very early from the tender care of an affectionate mother."[46] John Gregory's *A Father's Legacy to his Daughter* dispatches both parents by the most common of methods. The text begins:

> My dear girls,
> You had the misfortune to be deprived of your mother at a time of life when you were insensible of your loss, and could receive little benefit either from her instruction or her example. Before this comes to your hands, you will likewise have lost your father.[47]

Thereby sugaring instruction with tears; no wonder *A Father's Legacy* went through so many editions.

Precaution is more nakedly driven by the demands of the conduct genre than *Persuasion*. Austen makes Sir Walter Elliot a widower; Cooper does not say why Emily, with two living parents, should be raised by Mrs Wilson. An economic imperative is present in the text,

---

44. Alistair M. Duckworth discusses Austen's attitude to games and gaming in "'Spillikins, Paper Ships, Riddles, Conundrums, and Cards': Games in Jane Austen's Life and Fiction," *Jane Austen: Bicentenary Essays*, ed. John Halperin (Cambridge: Cambridge University Press, 1975), 279-97.

45. Hastings, 27-28.

46. Lady Pennington, *Unfortunate Mother's Advice*, in *The Lady's Pocket Library* (Philadelphia: Mathew Carey, 1797), 123.

47. John Gregory, *A Father's Legacy to his Daughter*, in *The Lady's Pocket Library*, 86.

but Cooper does not make the appropriate connection. Sir Edward Moseley inherited an encumbered estate, due largely to the extravagance of his mother. Refusing to sell any land, Sir Edward rents out his London house, withdraws to his country estate, and there institutes "a course of systematic but liberal economy" (*P* 51), taking seventeen years to save his inheritance. During this time Mrs. Wilson's Christian principles instill the proper morals in Emily; and her clear, sometimes sardonic, eye is later able to see the flaws in the men who present themselves as suitors for Emily and the other girls. She has greater difficulty distinguishing between appearance and reality; for Pendennyss, in an attempt to escape the attentions of fortune-hunters, has temporarily shed his title in favor of his family name, George Denbigh. In consequence he is mistaken for a cousin who bears that name. A "masquerade" of errors occurs, to be resolved only after twenty-nine chapters and much heartache (*P* 449). Emily and Pendennyss are reunited. After a brief interlude, during which Pendennyss deals with Napoleon at Waterloo, they retire to his estate, where the concluding scene, with its balanced clauses, echoes Jane Austen and the conduct books: "Every thing spoke society, splendor, and activity without; every thing denoted order, propriety, and happiness within" (*P* 475). Appearances once more "speak" and "denote" realities, and they do so in an appropriate environment, where "the harvest had been gathered, and the beautiful vales of Pendennyss were shooting forth a second crop of verdure."

James D. Wallace has shown that the genteel world of *Precaution* is interrupted on three occasions by "an alien world of mortality and madness"[48]; and that these occasions look forward to Cooper's later fiction, thereby adding further support to Richard Slotkin's myth of regeneration through violence.[49] The novel can also be seen to address some of Cooper's most pressing family and financial concerns. The urging of "principles" rather than "wealth"; a hero who is misunderstood precisely because he tries to follow that course; some thoughts on the proper management of an estate, and a happy marriage on a well-managed estate — all these are issues calculated to gain the approval of the De Lancey family. This is not to say that *Precaution* is

---

48. Wallace, 73.

49. Richard Slotkin, *Regeneration through Violence: The Mythology of the American Frontier, 1600-1860* (Middletown, CT: Wesleyan University Press, 1973).

a *roman à clef*, although one of the novel's minor characters, Admiral Sir Peter Howell, may well be based on his wife's great-uncle by marriage, Admiral Sir Peter Warren. It is to say, rather, that "an ingenious blending of fact and fancy," as Cooper would later put it, allowed him the imaginative space to come to grips with some urgent issues; and in coming to grips with them he adopted a point of view that could have been his wife's.[50]

The woman's point of view is adopted even more clearly in *Tales for Fifteen*, probably written early in 1821 when Cooper had temporarily abandoned work on *The Spy*.[51] The book's title indicates its intended audience, teenage girls, and it was published under the pseudonym of Jane Morgan. Together, intended audience and pseudonym acted as a salutary discipline on Cooper's prolific imagination. *Precaution* had deployed a wide range of characters, not with complete success, in an English setting. *Tales for Fifteen* contains two lengthy stories, each with an identifiably American setting and each with a cast limited by the didactic demands of the plot. Otherwise, the concerns in both texts are similar, with Cooper developing in each story a moral point made in *Precaution*.

At one point in *Precaution*, the Moseleys visit a lending library, giving their creator the opportunity to suggest that "books are, in a great measure, the instruments of controlling the opinions of a nation like ours" (*P* 216). Jane Moseley, Emily's older sister, indulges in "unlicensed and indiscriminate reading," and therefore is an easy prey for the rake Colonel Egerton (*P* 217). Julia Warren, in "Imagination," has the same failing. (Once again, Cooper raided the names of his wife's family for his fiction.) Her close friend Anna Miller writes to her about one Edward Stanley, who is "as delightful as his name" (*TF* 25), and who longs to know Julia. Julia's imagination quickly fleshes out the fellow, gives him the code name "Antonio," and portrays him as Apollo in the uniform of Bonaparte (*TF* 35, 50). During a trip to Albany, Julia imagines that the coachman is Antonio in disguise, one eye romantically covered with a patch. She gets into such a flutter that she cannot attend

50. *Letters and Journals*, IV, 73. Cooper would again use his wife's family when he adopted the name "Heathcote" for the frontier patriarch in *The Wept of Wish-Ton-Wish* (1829).

51. See James F. Beard, ed., Introduction, *Tales for Fifteen*, by James Fenimore Cooper (Gainesville, FL: Scholars' Facsimiles & Reprints, 1959), viii. Future references to this edition will be cited parenthetically within the text (*TF*).

to the beauties of the Hudson Valley. But she is soon brought down to earth with a bump. Anna tells her that "Edward Stanley" is an invention. Antonio becomes mere Tony. His patch covers "a face that was deformed with diseases, and wanting of an eye!" (*TF* 124). And the effluvium from his chewing tobacco hits her shoe and soils her stocking. Suitably humbled, Julia marries the worthy Charles Weston, who fortunately is still waiting for her.

As one would expect, Julia is an orphan. She is raised by a maiden aunt who is virtuous but too modest to undertake "the sacred duty" of preparing Julia properly "for the world in which she was to live" (*TF* 5). "Heart," the second story in *Tales for Fifteen*, treats another problem confronting women of marriageable age, and in doing so develops another element of *Precaution*. One of the sub-plots in Cooper's first novel concerns two brothers, the elder "naturally diffident" and a plain child, whose "doom" is "sealed" by smallpox (*P* 406); while the younger has all the graces. Unfortunately, their parents make the younger their favorite. The elder becomes a melancholic recluse, goes mad, and dies. Male appearance is again an element of "Heart." The setting is New York City, its streets and social gatherings, and the male characters are George Morton, plain but a good samaritan, and Seymour Delafield who (as his name may suggest) is a narcissistic dandy. The two men are seen through the eyes of Charlotte Henley and her distant relative Maria Osgood. Charlotte is a catch: she is beautiful and wealthy but also possesses "that quiet and regulated esteem, which grows out of association and good sense" (*TF* 141). Maria possesses only "youth and health" (*TF* 127), but also has an "unconquerable good nature" (*TF* 142). Unfortunately, she is one of thirteen children in a family whose estate is small. Since this is America, the Osgoods are not saddled with the problem of entail, and society has no "artificial distinctions" (*TF* 149). Yet, "[s]even grown-up daughters was a melancholy sight for the contemplation of the parents, and they both felt like vendors of goods who were exhibiting their wares to the best advantage" (*TF* 150). The echo of *Pride and Prejudice* is clear, and the problem not unlike that which confronts the Bennets. Of course, Delafield pursues Charlotte. Used to being pursued himself, he is "utterly astounded" when she refuses him (*TF* 193). Charlotte loves George, but his good deeds have affected his health, and he dies in her arms. Delafield, chastened, becomes "so much accustomed to the society of Maria Osgood, that at length he felt it was necessary to his comfort" (*TF* 212), and they marry. Charlotte remains unmarried, becoming "a striking instance of female dignity, by exhibiting to the world the difference between affection and caprice, and by shewing how much Imagination is inferior to Heart" (*TF* 223).

* * *

In this discussion of Cooper's earliest fictions and their contexts, I have tried to show how concerned he was about the relationship of property and marriage, and about the central role of women. This is not, of course, the normal view of Cooper's career; one in which the antisocial frontiersman Natty Bumppo dominates. *Precaution* is usually written off as a *jeu d'esprit*, an unsuccessful, overly anglicized first attempt at fiction. *Tales for Fifteen* has, as far as I know, never been discussed at all. Examinations of Cooper's career usually begin with *The Spy*. Why is this? The problem, I believe, begins with *The Pioneers*. Cooper's attempt to provide a balanced discussion between the virtues of natural and civil law were foiled by Natty. He enters the novel as a Shakespearian fool, a grouchy buckskin buffoon with a drip on the end of his nose. He leaves it as a superb marksman, a deeply serious figure who no longer makes wise jokes about society (as befits a Shakespearian fool), but is rather at odds with it. The change in status was fatal for the delicate design of *The Pioneers*, and indeed for the rest of Cooper's career.

Our view of the shape of that career has been influenced, firstly by his daughter's comments, and secondly by a critical tradition which goes back to Francis Parkman. Parkman's article about Cooper in the *North American Review* claimed the novelist as "the most original, the most thoroughly national" of American writers,[52] but staked out the claim in words which say more about Parkman than about Cooper:

> His genius drew aliment from the soil where God had planted it, and rose to a vigorous growth, rough and gnarled, but strong as a mountain cedar. His volumes are a faithful mirror of that rude transatlantic nature, which to European eyes appears so strange and new.[53]

52. Francis Parkman, "The Works of James Fenimore Cooper," *North American Review* 74 (January 1852), 147.

53. Parkman, 147.

This critical tradition has drawn its strength by concentrating on the five Leatherstocking novels. It has also led to particularly narrow interpretations of the Leatherstocking novels themselves. For instance, when Allan Nevins produced his Modern Library omnibus of the novels, rearranged in the order of Bumppo's life, he believed that "for many readers the five novels will become more interesting if love-passages ... not related to the career and character of Leatherstocking and not today very convincing, are shorn away."[54] The novels most affected by the shearing were *The Pioneers* and *The Prairie*; the novels, that is, which deal most fully with the ethics of property and settlement.

However, a revisionist movement seems to be under way. Douglas Anderson has recently suggested that the creation of two antagonistic categories of writers, "serious artists" and "literary domestics," depended on a partial view which ignored their "common enterprise."[55] Jane Tompkins produced an analysis of *The Last of the Mohicans* which suggested that the text, like those of Charles Brockden Brown, "should not be judged by the standards of modern literary criticism but seen as agents of cultural formation."[56] Women played an essential role in the cultural work of Cooper's first fictions. His illustrators recognized the value of that role. So too did Cooper, and it prompted him to identify himself, on the title pages of the early American editions of *The Pioneers*, not as the author of *The Spy*, but rather as the author of the much-maligned *Precaution*.[57]

---

54. Allan Nevins, "Preface" to *The Leatherstocking Saga* (New York: The Modern Library, 1966), x.

55. Douglas Anderson, *A House Undivided: Domesticity and Community in American Literature* (Cambridge: Cambridge University Press, 1990), 5.

56. Jane Tompkins, *Sensational Designs: The Cultural Work of American Fiction 1790-1860* (New York: Oxford University Press, 1985), 119.

57. Cooper, *The Pioneers, or the Sources of the Susquehanna: A Descriptive Tale* (New York: Charles Wiley, 1823), title page; *The Pioneers, or the Sources of the Susquehanna: A Descriptive Tale* (1823; rpt. New York: Collins, Hannay & Wiley, 1825), title page.

NEUTRALIZING THE LAND: THE MYTH OF AUTHORITY, AND THE AUTHORITY OF MYTH IN FENIMORE COOPER'S *THE SPY*

W.M. VERHOEVEN

Fenimore Cooper's treatment of landscape and space has attracted considerable attention in modern critical discussions of his work, so much so that it has more or less become a commonplace in Cooper criticism that space is a major instrument to create meaning in his fiction.[1] For many commentators the most salient aspect of Cooper's use of the spatial element in his settings is the fact that, like the temporal aspect, it is fixed, or frozen — "neutralized" is the phrase most often used, after Cooper's own subtitle to *The Spy*, "A Tale of the Neutral Ground." H. Daniel Peck, for instance, observes — in his *A World by Itself: The Pastoral Moment in Cooper's Fiction* — that in Cooper's "highly structured and formal settings ... a dominant feature of the landscape acts as a moral center of gravity and holds the action of the novel within a tightly bounded perimeter, thereby creating a self-contained world which draws its imaginative power from the qualities of stasis and centrality."[2] In the light of John P. McWilliams's assertion that "All of Cooper's American fictions are laid in a time of social

1. For example, see Donald A. Ringe, *James Fenimore Cooper* (New York: Twayne, 1962), 27-32; Edwin Fussell, *Frontier: American Literature and the American West* (Princeton: Princeton University Press, 1965), 11-18; George Dekker, *James Fenimore Cooper: The Novelist* (London: Routledge, 1967), 33-34; John P. McWilliams, *Political Justice in a Republic: James Fenimore Cooper's America* (Berkeley: University of California Press, 1972), 1-31; Annette Kolodny, *The Lay of the Land: Metaphor As Experience and History in American Life and Letters* (Chapel Hill: University of North Carolina Press, 1975), 89-115; H. Daniel Peck, *A World by Itself: The Pastoral Moment in Cooper's Fiction* (New Haven: Yale University Press, 1977), 91-108.

2. Peck, 91-92.

change,"[3] the neutral ground that is center stage in so many of his fictions can be regarded as the eye of a social, political, and ethnic storm — a moment of ideological equilibrium portending doom, disruption and chaos.

While the centrality of the neutral ground to Cooper's fiction is widely accepted, its purpose is still contested. Whereas Donald A. Ringe, for instance, argues that the neutral ground serves as a "physical and moral no-man's-land" where a character's moral stamina is tested, where the good are distinguished from the wicked, and where moral justice will ultimately prevail,[4] McWilliams believes that Cooper uses the neutral ground — which he identifies as a battleground, the sea, or the forest — "for two distinctly separate purposes."[5] McWilliams goes on to offset his interpretation of the neutral ground against the readings of earlier critics:

> Both Edwin Fussell and George Dekker have pointed out that for Cooper the neutral ground is a no-man's-land adapted from Scott's romances — both a testing ground for heroism and an exciting source of melodramatic action. When Cooper is at his best, however, he endows the neutral gorund with more significance than ciritcs have yet acknowledged. R.W.B. Lewis made the interesting suggestion that "For Cooper the forest and the sea shared the quality of boundlessness; they were the *apeiron* — the area of possibility." Lewis did not emphasize, however, that these two qualities, boundlessness and possibility, are the essence, not only of Cooper's frontier, but of his view of America. In many of Cooper's border tales, the immediate neutral ground, the setting of the action, is deliberately made to stand for the boundless promise of the entire land. Whereas Cooper's ocean is a place of boundless possibility that Cooper deliberately separates from America and its problems, Cooper's forest frontier is America itself.[6]

Peck for his part believes that previous commentators have applied the term "neutral ground" too broadly, failing in particular to do justice to

---

3. McWilliams, 6.

4. Ringe, 28.

5. McWilliams, 9.

6. McWilliams, 9.

"the aesthetic differences among Cooper's works."[7] "The crucial factor," according to Peck, "is that the neutral ground lacks demarcations; it exhibits neither the 'curved lines' that order nature nor the design of civilized space. Further, it is a territory without law, and law is the moral equivalent of geographic demarcation."[8]

It would appear, then, that Cooper's neutral ground has become one of the most visited and best-documented spots in the American literary landscape. Yet, there is, I believe, one aspect of the neutral ground has not so far received the critical attention it deserves. Up to now discussions of Cooper's neutral ground have presented it as a *passive*, descriptive metaphor; in my view, however, Cooper uses the metaphor of the neutral ground as an *active*, creative instrument — that is, the neutral ground is not so much morally and ideologically neutral, as morally and ideologically *neutralizing*.

The distinction may appear to be slight but is actually of considerable importance. Thus it helps to explain why Cooper's tales of the Revolution and the frontier made such an immediate, powerful and lasting impact on his contemporary audience, whose social, cultural and ideological composition belied, if anything, the equilibrium and neutrality of the spatial and temporal setting of Cooper's tales. The significance of Cooper's fiction in terms of national pathos did not and does not derive from his skill in resolving fraternal and paternal conflict or in deciding legal and ecological debates, but from its successfully clearing the scene of his imaginary America of all traces of conflict and discord by projecting those elements of discord and conflict to the transcendent realm of myth. Cooper's neutral ground — to which his work owes its lasting appeal as the nation's "ideal" history — is therefore essentially a *reality gap*, a carefully constructed void that has subsequently been filled by myth in a way that reminds one of Roland Barthes' observation that "The function of myth is to empty reality: it is, literally, a ceaseless flowing out, a haemorrhage, or perhaps an evaporation, in short a perceptible absence."[9]

Cooper's mythical neutral ground may constitute "a perceptible absence," but to regard his myth of America as "history's antithesis"

---

7. Peck, 97 (note).

8. Peck, 97.

9. Roland Barthes, *Mythologies*, selected and trans. Annette Lavers (London: Paladin paperback, 1973), 143 ("*Myth is depoliticized speech*").

(the phrase is used by William P. Kelly in his *Plotting America's Past: Fenimore Cooper and the Leatherstocking Tales*),[10] and therefore as essentially an escapist mode, is to miss, I believe, a key element in the way Cooper's fiction operates as myth. Surely the purpose of a myth is not so much to challenge the process of historical formation as to propose alternative reality concepts. Unlike history, that is, myth does not pretend to represent THE truth but rather tries to communicate a *version* of the truth: a *version* of the truth that — and here lies the true significance of Cooper's fiction — at some point begins to interfere with and to actively participate in the formation of history's "official" truth. The embarrassing inner conflict that Lawrence believed was central to both Cooper's soul and his fiction ("Fenimore, lying in his Louis Quatorze hotel in Paris, passionately musing about Natty Bumppo and the pathless forest"[11]) is therefore not really a conflict at all: Cooper's fictions are located in a space and a time in which such issues as historical truth and historicity simply do not apply. In this way Cooper not only managed to transcend the ideological and ontological indeterminacy which held the nation in its sway at the time he started his career as a novelist, but — once he had cultivated an audience — he was actually able to feed the myth of ideological consensus and national identity back into the historical reality of his day.

Cooper's metaphor of the neutral ground thus ties in with what Sacvan Bercovitch has called the Puritan "ritual of consensus." In his intriguing study *The American Jeremiad*, Bercovitch offers a profound analysis of the cultural and ideological indeterminacy that can be observed in American society from the days of the Founding Fathers onward. According to Bercovitch, this indeterminacy, and the ontological doubt that resulted from it, manifests itself through a ritual of cultural awakening, the emergence of a national ideology during America's formative years, when "the sacred drama of American nationhood" was being staged.[12] Bercovitch convincingly argues that in a sense even the Declaration of Independence and the Constitution can

10. William P. Kelly, *Plotting America's Past: Fenimore Cooper and the Leatherstocking Tales* (Carbondale, IL: Southern Illinois University Press, 1983), 159.

11. D.H. Lawrence, *Studies in Classic American Literature* (1923; rpt. Harmondsworth: Penguin, 1971), 54.

12. Sacvan Bercovitch, *The American Jeremiad* (Madison, WI: University of Wisconsin Press, 1978), 132.

be seen as part of this immanent process toward ideological consensus. In this context he aptly refers to the "notorious paradox" in the Declaration of Independence whereby the promotors of the American consensus "could denounce servitude, oppression, and inadequate representation while concerning [themselves] least (if at all) with the most enslaved, oppressed and inadequately represented groups in the land .... Through the ritual of the jeremiad, the leading patriots recast the Declaration to read 'all propertied Anglo-Saxon Protestant males are created equal' .... [T]hey used the jeremiad to confine the concept of revolution to American progress, American progress to God's New Israel, and God's New Israel to people of their own kind."[13] The ideological consensus that emerged from the ritual of the jeremiad is clearly that of a WASP middle-class, and appeared to be so strong that it could easily absorb all sorts of "un-American" activities and minorities, such as feminists, blacks, Indians, Jews, and Catholics, as long as they were willing to fill their allotted slots in the American Dream. That Cooper was a firm believer in this ritual of national consensus is borne out by his *Notions of the Americans* (1828), in which he observes at one point: "I have never seen a nation so much alike in my life, as the people of the United States, and what is more, they are nor only like each other, but they are remarkably like that which common sense tells them they ought to resemble."[14]

At first sight it may seem somewhat remarkable that Cooper should feel like this, seeing that the two central metaphors in much of his work — the frontier and the Revolution — are preeminently metaphors of conflict, dissent, and alienation: after all, both metaphors bring together in sharp binary oppositions the fundamental tensions that existed in past and contemporary American society, such as civilization versus wilderness; order versus chaos; democracy versus despotism; mobocracy versus natural aristocracy; freedom versus allegiance to imperial power. Yet, in the light of Bercovitch's remarks on the American jeremiad, it is not hard to recognize in his choice of metaphors Cooper's Puritan heritage. Clearly by the time Cooper started writing his popular myths, the Puritan rhetorical inversion — that is, the recasting of the confrontation with the savage wilderness into a holy mission to cultivate the desert — had become standardized and

13. Bercovitch, 153-54, 154.

14. *Notions of the Americans: Picked up by a Travelling Bachelor* (1828; rpt. Philadelphia: Carey, Lea & Blanchard, 1836), II, 108-09.

internalized into popular belief and into the politics of American consensus. And the same thing had happened to the American Revolution. Thus Cooper clearly wrote his myths of the struggle against the haughty foreign oppressors and the glorious spread westward in accordance with the Puritan concept of "process as order and control."[15] That is, Cooper's myths provide an ideological basis for deciding fundamental questions of authority and allegiance, questions that were of course of crucial concern to the young republic. In terms of Bercovitch's argument, the frontier and the revolution have become vehicles of the jeremiad: "to create anxiety, to denounce backsliders, to reinforce social values, and (summarily) to define the American consensus." The frontier and the revolution, then, are in the hands of Cooper only superficially what they once were in historical time: that is, instead of metaphors of conflict, they have become *mythologized* moments of ideological balance, of national consensus.[16]

* * *

As a novel of the Revolution, *The Spy* may serve as an illustration of the points raised above. Though an early work, *The Spy* is in my view a central text in Cooper's oeuvre for at least two reasons. First, it is the first novel in which Cooper consciously set out to make a fictional record of the thoughts and manners prevalent among the Americans of his day.[17] Seeing that the novel became a great popular success (it

---

15. Bercovitch, 164.

16. That this puts Cooper firmly in the Puritan tradition is borne out by a remark made by Henry Cumings in his *A Serman preached at Billerica*. According to Cumings (as quoted by Bercovitch), the republic was "poised in an even balance, between extremes of arbitrary power and despotism, on the one hand, and of anarchy and unrestrained licentiousness, on the other." "*Poised,*" Bercovitch adds, was the jeremiadic *mot juste*. It suggested, as it were in one anxious breath, the cultural ideal and its disastrous alternative. *Despotism* meant the feudal (or quasi-feudal) ways of the Old World; *anarchy*, the dangers of unbridled laissez-faire; and *even balance*, finally ... America's "middle way" (Bercovitch, 137).

17. In contrast to his first novel (*Precaution*), *The Spy* was launched at "an American novel professedly," and in writing *The Spy*, Cooper explicitly took upon himself the "task of making American manners and American scenes interesting to an American reader" (*The Letters and Journals of James Fenimore Cooper*, ed. James Franklin Beard [Cambridge, MA: Harvard University Press, 1960-68], I, 49, 44).

rapidly went through three editions, and was soon translated and adapted for the stage), we may assume that the reading-public at large shared his rendering of the American experience, notably of the early, revolutionary phase. The second reason why I want to call attention to *The Spy* is that despite its seemingly unoriginal and straightforward thematic organization — the very reason why most critics ignore the book — the novel reveals a rhetorical organization that can be considered paradigmatic for Cooper's literary work in general. One does not have to be a historian to see that in dealing with the final years of the War of Independence in *The Spy*, Cooper rearranges the historical complexities of the Revolutionary era into characteristic sets of binary oppositions, one of which is invariably put forward as the ideological ideal — the implied standard being of course the middle-class consensus which Cooper adhered to. The most apparent of these binary oppositions are: the Americans versus the British; Washington versus King George III; West-Chester versus New York; the Highlands versus the lower grounds; the Skinners versus the Cow-Boys; the gentry versus the lower class; Harvey Birch versus Mr Wharton; Frances Wharton versus her sister Sarah; Major Dunwoodie versus Colonel Wellmere. The ideological equilibrium, the moment in historical time at which the tensions between the binary oppositions are temporarily in abeyance, is represented in geographical terms as the "neutral ground," a territory in the country of West-Chester which separates the British forces from the American: a military demarcation-zone that on a symbolical level functions much the same as Cooper's frontier, which separates white civilization from Indian savagery. It is a characteristic setting of the jeremiad: the "neutral ground" is presented as a moral and ideological wasteland; a place where Skinners and Cow-Boys are given every opportunity to loot and murder at will as if they were a god-sent scourge; a place, too, that is infested with turncoats, spies, and deserters; where people are mistrustful, confused and led astray. In short, the neutral ground is a place where immediate and radical choices of allegiance and authority have to be made: political choices, most obviously, but also social, moral, and religious choices. And what the proper choices are, is of course determined by the way in which Cooper and his compatriots wished to remember the Revolution, that is, by their stance toward *contemporary* ideological dilemmas, such as national politics, class, gender, and race. A more detailed discussion of Cooper's treatment of these ideologically sensitive issues will reveal that the transcendent myth which is supposed to assimilate all discordant elements in contemporary American society actually contains a few serious fault lines.

The most apparent of these dialectical tensions involves the political conflict between America and England. Yet although strictly speaking a "Revolutionary novel," *The Spy* does not in the first place concern itself with the political struggle between the British and the Americans; basically, as Cooper explains in his 1849 preface, the book is about the "domestic character" of the American Revolution, which was a conflict "in which the contending parties were people of the same blood and language."[18] Since the Revolution is never represented as a bilateral affair, choices of national, cross-Atlantic political allegiance and authority are, superficially at least, never really an issue: the Americans, it is simply assumed throughout the novel, were in the right, while the few British characters that do make an appearance in the book, are shown to be absurd sticklers for conventions, uninspired and spineless soldiers, and filled with the arrogance of despotic power. Colonel Wellmere, the most explicitly British character, is a case in point; significantly, he simply drops out of the story well before the end of the novel after a final act of double betrayal: first he is only barely prevented from committing bigamy, and then he decides to save his own skin, while he is in a position to prevent the rampaging Cow-Boys from attacking the Whartons and setting fire the their home.

The American Revolution, Cooper insists, was a "family quarrel" (v), and it was no doubt part of Cooper's plan to bring the Revolution into the homes of his popular, middle-class audience when he chose the genteel Whartons and their estate, "The Locusts," as the principles contenders and setting respectively of his version of the War of Independence. Not only is the Locusts situated in the center of the neutral ground between the American and British forces: the very front-line appears to run right through the family. Thus the elder daughter Sarah, one of the most sought-after girls in New York, supports the British cause, while her younger sister Francis, a golden-haired, ardent sixteen-year-old, favors the rebel side, "the cause of the people" (16). Not surprisingly, in such a clear case of "political doubling," the process of moral and ideological ranking is a mere formality: Sarah's flirting with the British officers is shown to be a mild form of treason and after the fiasco of her engagement to Wellmere, she drifts off into a

18. *The Spy; A Tale of the Neutral Ground* (1821; rpt. London: Routledge & Sons, n.d.), ix. All future references to this edition will be cited parenthetically within the text.

state of near-debility and is duly completely forgotten. Frances, on the other hand, turns out to possess the stuff of a staunch American frontier woman; while of course retaining her exquisite feminine delicacy and angelic innocence, she grows into the heroine of the story, who on her own effects the safety of her brother where brave men like Dunwoodie fail — a feat which earns her a personal compliment from Washington, alias Harper, the Father of all Americans: "God has denied to me children, young lady; but if it had been his blessed will that my marriage should not have been childless, such a treasure as yourself would I have asked from his mercy" (387-88). This statement can be seen as the final condemnation of Frances' legitimate father, Mr Wharton, who is pilloried for failing to provide paternal authority and leadership for his family — that is, for not being a responsible, proud American. He has tried to save his estate and his social position by affecting to be politically neutral, but — Cooper emphasizes in retrospect — there could be no true neutrality during the formative era of the American national consciousness.

In fact, to be neutral was even worse than to be on the enemy's side: this seems to be the purport of the curious vicissitudes in the career of Henry Wharton. For though he is strongly on the British side of the conflict and never for a moment wavers as to where he true allegiance lies, Henry is held up as a model of a brave officer and a true gentleman. Significantly, he is never treated with anything of the sarcasm that his father comes in for; whereas Mr Wharton, like his eldest daughter, slides into a state of premature senility (in the words of Lawton, "a crazy, irresolute old man, who doesn't know whether he belongs to us or to the enemy"; 252), his son Henry makes a rather astonishing, last-minute comeback in Cooper's wrap-up chapter as "*General* Wharton" (434; italics added).[19] Apparently it was important

---

19. Susan Fenimore Cooper has commented on the speed with which the characters are "hurried off the stage" in the novel's final chapter (*Pages and Pictures from the Writings of James Fenimore Cooper* [New York: W.A. Townsend and Co., 1861], 35). She claims that this was merely the result of the fact that Cooper's publisher, who had expressed concern over the sheer length the book was getting while it was being printed, had asked Cooper, lest they should both lose their profits, to write the final chapter before he had actually completed the preceding chapters. However, this does not materially detract from the impression that Cooper presents a markedly non-egalitarian society in the final chapter of his novel; on the contrary, the fact that he was under some the pressure to decide who would be elegible for America's golden future and who would not, probably contributed, if anything, to the sincerity of his choice.

for Cooper to receive Henry back into the happy American family, which is strange — to say the least — seeing that Henry is by word and deed an enemy of the American people and persists in calling them "rebels." One gets the distinct impression that although in Cooper's eyes all redcoats are to be despised, some are less obnoxious than others.

This raises questions about Cooper's true political stance in the novel. One begins to wonder whether the symmetrical paradigm — democratic America versus despotic Britain; republican versus royalist — is really as unambiguous as it seems; whether Cooper is not on the sly offering us an alternative to the American consensus. In other words: in how far is Cooper — consciously or unconsciously — undermining the very choices of proper political authority that he seems to offer? This point is thrown into greater relief when we extend Cooper's political stance to include his attitude towards social politics, his ideology of class.

In writing *The Spy*, Cooper was catering for a middle-class audience, which had an implicit faith in the myth of political democracy and social equality. Not surprisingly, Cooper's rendering of the "domestic character" of the Revolution is basically an attempt to play down the seriousness of the political and social differences that existed in American society and that came to a head in the violent conflict. The 1849 preface even goes as far as to state that the "partial divisions [were] small ... in actual amount," and subsequently blames the intensity of the internal conflict on the presence of foreign agitators, that is, the British troops and British spies (vi). History, of course, tells a different story: viz. that there *was* no consensus about what the Revolution was actually all about. Thus for some Americans the Revolution was a struggle for economical independence from the British oppressor, but they very much wanted to retain existing social and political order. For others, the Revolution meant a radical break with traditional forms of government, existing social structures, a repudiation of the traditional elites that had dominated the social and political life in the colonies.[20] Yet despite their radically different ideas about the social and political future of America, both parties glorified the freedom of the people and the leveling and democratic ideal.

Cooper's stance toward this socio-political conflict is well-documented. The son of an aspiring pioneer and wilderness founder,

---

20. See James Madison, Alexander Hamilton, and John Jay, *The Federalist Papers*, ed. Isaac Kramnick (1788; rpt. Harmondsworth, Penguin, 1987), 15.

Fenimore Cooper on the one hand had a strong, if somewhat romantic interest in the taming of the wilderness and the cultural forces at work there, and he was intrigued by the idea of becoming a frontier patriarch who was on a par with his people, and yet their leader — a *primus inter pares*. On the other hand, however, Cooper felt at the same time strongly drawn to the genteel, bourgeois world of such politically prominent and cultured families as the Hamiltons and the Jays.[21] Cooper never really managed to come to terms with the dilemma; while in real life he saw himself primarily as the American gentleman, a man of moral greatness and refined manners, his novels reveal that the conflict between the pioneer and the gentleman in him was actually never resolved. In this sense Cooper did not differ from many of his fellow-Americans, who shared the Jeffersonian duality of being able to believe both in the integrity and good sense of the common man, and in the existence of a "natural aristocracy."

The Spy pre-eminently reflects these ideological tensions. Superficially, Cooper appears to condone the democratic, egalitarian principle. The clearest manifestation of this is his choice of Harvey Birch as his main character. A poor, lonesome peddler, Birch belongs, socially speaking, to the fringe. But he is not merely a social outsider: as a double-agent, he is despised by friend and foe — a pariah in self-imposed exile. And yet it is he who is always there to save and support members of the Wharton family (throwing stones at them with notes of warning attached to them), a guardian angel for those on the proper side of the domestic conflict, but an avenging angel for those on the wrong side (such as the leader of the Skinners, whom he quite stolidly eliminates by turning him over to the bloodthirsty Cow-Boys; 406). Amidst the military and moral chaos of the neutral ground, Birch can be depended on for guidance and inspiration; he is in this, in fact, second only to the Great Father of the nation himself, that ultimate gentleman Washington, whose closest associate Birch is. In *The Spy* the lowest of the low consort with the highest of the high; in this way the novel is ostensibly a manifestation of the American social experiment.[22]

---

21. See Motley, *The American Abraham: James Fenimore Cooper and the Frontier Patriarch* (Cambridge: Cambridge University Press, 1987), chs 2 and 3.

22. Although there is evidence to suggest that at the time peddlers were by no means regarded as mere tramps or ne'er-do-wells, not even by the landowning gentry (they were often an essential link in the spread of information and news), there can be no doubt that Cooper's peddler is meant to be seen as a pariah.

However, Cooper may feign social egalitarianism, but in the final analysis the novel makes a strong plea for the superior status and authority of the middle class. Thus even while Birch is given the status of a lower-class hero and even while he is seen to succeed where some of his social superiors — notably Mr Wharton — fail, Cooper, in accordance with his deep-seated middle-class ideology, sets up a hierarchy of leadership and moral authority that is definitely rooted in social elitism. What it comes down to is that in Cooper's opinion true gentlemen are true leaders, and vice versa. Leadership, Cooper seems to say, is as much a matter of breeding as of talent. This is illustrated by the way in which the highest authority of all, Washington, is described in the scene where Frances has just made her way to the hut where she hopes to find Birch. Instead of Birch, she finds a stranger there, of whom she tries to form an impression:

> Before the fire was a table, with one of its legs fractured, and made of rough boards; these, with a single stool, composed the furniture, if we except a few articles of cooking. A book that, by its size and shape, appeared to be a Bible, was lying on the table, unopened. But it was the occupant of the hut in whom Frances was chiefly interested. This was a man, sitting on the stool, with his head leaning on his hand, in such a manner as to conceal his features, and deeply occupied in examining some open papers. On the table lay a pair of curiously and richly mounted horseman's pistols, and the handle of a sheathed rapier, of exquisite workmanship, protruded from between the legs of the gentleman, one of whose hands carelessly rested on its guard. (381)

The technique of introducing a character by slowly zooming in on it is typically Cooperian: moving from the circumstantial and general to the specific and detailed; from outer appearances to character. First, there an empty stool; then we find that "the occupant of the hut" is sitting on it; then we learn that this person is "a man"; then we are told about his

---

Indeed, his being a social outcast is what makes him "neutral" and what protects him from the aggression of the warring parties; moreover, much of the novel's dramatic and propagandistic effect depends on the close and personal relationship between the Father of the Land and one of his humblest and most despised subjects. For a discussion of the role of peddlers in the late eighteenth and early nineteenth century, see J.R. Dolan, *The Yankee Peddlers of Early America* (New York: Clarkson N. Potter, 1964).

"richly mounted horseman's pistols" and the "exquisite workmanship" of the handle of his rapier; and then, summing up, the narrator concludes that the mysterious person must be "a gentleman." It is only later that he is identified as Harper. The same technique can be observed when Harper is first introduced in the opening chapter. Characteristically, the Whartons immediately take to the stranger simply because his "whole appearance was so impressive and so decidely that of a gentleman" (5). But when shortly afterwards Henry comes in disguised as a poor traveler, we learn that "Mr. Wharton and his family disliked the appearance of this new visitor excessively" (10), and accordingly they treat him as an "unwelcome intruder" (12). In this way *The Spy* quite consistently reflects qualities such as moral integrity and intrinsic leadership in terms of social appearance and status.

In doing so, Cooper to a certain extent of course merely adheres to the literary conventions of the day; he is, to put it differently, faithful to the tastes and social codes of his genteel reading public. And yet Cooper must have been aware of the glaring inconsistencies in his ideology of class, an ideology that on the one hand propagates social egalitarianism and on the other hand calls for a "natural aristocracy." The question that arises here is, How does Cooper fit Washington and his lower-class counterpart Birch into the *one* and the same social framework? Are there, in other words, any places in the text where we can observe Cooper introducing a certain ordering into the rhetorical organization of the text in order to bring his quasi-egalitarian principles in line with his social elitism?

It appears that Cooper is making attempts to smooth out hitches in the novel's hidden ideology from the start. A clear example is his attempt to realign Birch's social status in order to make him a more likely companion for Washington. Thus at one point Cooper intimates that although Birch may have been a peddler from his youth, he is actually somewhat above his class:

> He was a native of one of the eastern colonies; and, from something of superior intelligence which belonged to his father, it was thought they had known better fortunes in the land of their nativity. Harvey possessed, however, the common manners of the country, and was in no way distinguished from men of his class, but by his acuteness, and the mystery which enveloped his movements. (27)

Cooper is clearly making an effort here to establish Harvey both as a man of the people (by firmly establishing him as a peddler and an immigrant), and as a man possessed with *intrinsic* qualities of intelligence and superiority, which raise him above his station. What it comes down to, in fact, is that Birch is established as a gentleman in disguise, and not at all, or not in the first place, as the lower-class hero that we were led to expect. However, this does not quite solve Cooper's problem; for although Cooper hereby "saves" Birch from the masses (to which he belongs professionally), he still cannot incorporate him into the class of true leaders without upsetting the social framework that lies imbedded in the novel.

This leads to a situation where Harvey Birch can no longer be depicted as a mere outcast (for even outcasts are a class of their own): thus he is gradually shown to exist completely *outside* the social framework. In the final analysis Birch is the archetypal *isolato*, or, as he himself puts it at one point, "I am alone truly — none know me but God and *him*" (229) — neither of whom, unfortunately, is in a position to divulge his true character and status.

Warren Motley, following Bewley in this, has argued that the figure of Harvey Birch is a projection of how Cooper saw himself at the time as a budding author: isolated and misunderstood, yet full of great potential.[23] It makes more sense, I believe, to regard Birch as a specimen of the figure of the "hermit-pilgrim" that Elliott has identified in post-Revolution literary: the literary device used by writers to overcome the aversion of the contemporary audiences to overt moralizing. The hermit-pilgrim is

> a wise and learned but humble man who loves his countrymen and wishes to instruct them through his example of simple living and his moral observations. Neither a misanthrope nor a romantic idealist, he has withdrawn to the forest because he is aware that his ideas might seem threatening to others, and he wishes to avoid needless contentions .... In many ways this figure is a forerunner of Cooper's Natty Bumppo.[24]

---

23. Cf. Motley, 43. See also Marius Bewley, *The Eccentric Design: Form in the Classic American Novel* (New York: Columbia University Press, 1959), 78.

24. Emory Elliott, *Revolutionary Writers: Literature and Authority in the New Republic* (New York: Oxford University Press, 1981), 48.

If we see Birch in this light, he becomes the great national reconciler: the isolate, selfless, sexless spiritual leader, who retains his moral integrity while so many others are losing theirs; who does not live, or belong, but who simply *is* — the sublimated spirit of the neutral ground. He exists within a cosmos of his own, which Cooper has purposely created for him. This explains why it is increasingly difficult to conceive of Birch as a realistic character as the story develops. There is something illusive about him; he is often no more than a silhouette in a cosmic landscape, and is said to make miraculous escapes from prison. In fact, he is hardly of this world: he is an archetypal figure, who carries his pack through a primordial forest and across a mythical neutral ground as if he were carrying the burden of the American conscience, the burden of fratricide. He is a Christlike figure, misunderstood by all, but sacrificing himself stoically for the greater good of his people and the reunion of the nation. Years later, when Washington has become "the acknowledged hero of an age of reason and truth" (430), Birch still wanders the country like a guardian angel hovering over the young republic; yet whereas Washington has by then become part of national myth, Birch is still a shadowy, spectral figure. It is only when he dies that Birch finally gains public recognition; and it is only when they find Washington's note on him that Birch is finally given a true identity. Significantly, Birch is allowed to become "real" only in death.

And Birch is not the only character on the fringe of Cooper's social framework that meets with this fate. Thus Captain Lawton makes an astonishing development from a blunt, boorish killing-machine in the early parts of the novel to a defender of the honor of American women and a man subtle enough to have scruples about the fate of a double spy. For a time he even completely eclipses his superior, Major Dunwoodie, outrivaling him both in bravery and leadership. But Lawton, too, is ultimately sacrificed to the mechanical logic of Cooper's ideology of class. First he is glorified as the brave, proud all-American soldier, but ultimately he is not allowed to share the final victory of the American army: he dies in the antepenultimate chapter.

Yet Lawton's fate is rosy in comparison to that of other fringe figures in Cooper's social universe, notably the blacks and Indians. For a novel supposedly dealing with the "domestic" side of the American Revolution, it is remarkably silent on the subject of Indians. Indians are only mentioned once, when an English minister refers to them as murderous and scalping savages — a remark that elicits a sharp rebuke from Lawton, who firmly believes that Indian hostility is the least of the problems besetting the American army, adding that the real savages are to be sought in the ranks of British court and among the treacherous elements within the American army (306-7).

Blacks figure slightly more prominently in the novel, the most conspicuous black character being the Whartons' man servant Caesar Thompson. Cooper's attitude toward blacks appears to be as ambivalent as that toward the British and the lower classes. Adhering to the principles of liberty and equality as defined in the Declaration of Independence, Cooper on the surface seems to be all in favor of racial equality and black self-assertion. Thus Caesar is on several occasions seen to respond vehemently and indignantly when offensive remarks are made about blacks. When Harvey Birch, for instance, expresses himself rather derisively about the southern "niggers," Caesar is quick to retort, "A black man so good as white" — adding, however, "so long as he behave heself" (32). For if one thing does become clear in the course of the novel, it is that in Cooper's ideology there are really *two* kinds of blacks: socially acceptable blacks (of the domesticated kind, like Caesar), and unruly, lawless blacks (all those who are not in the fortunate position to be in the service of civilized middle-class families such as the Whartons): "The race of blacks of which Caesar was a favorable specimen," we are told in an aside, "is becoming very rare. The old family servant, who, born and reared in the dwelling of his master, identified himself with the welfare of those whom it was his lot to serve, is giving place in every direction to that vagrant class which has sprung up within the last thirty years, and whose members roam through the country unfettered by principles, and uninfluenced by attachments" (36). Yet although on the right side of the Constitution, so to speak, Caesar and the other members of his family are never really related to the novel's central concerns. Like Birch, Lawton, Betty Flanagan and others, the blacks move about in a world of their own, and they seem to be mostly there in the novel for comic relief. Caesar for one is presented as a spoiled, quirky child, whom nobody need take seriously (36).

In *The Spy*, then, the historical conflict known as the American Revolution has been neutralized, effaced, and the raw historical data have been recast to form a rendering of the national drama as it never took place, and in which difficult choices of allegiance and authority were decided on the basis of a national ideology that never existed. It is not surprising, therefore, that when Cooper is looking back upon the Revolution in his final chapter (which is set 33 years later), the center of the neutral ground should be occupied by a young Captain Wharton

Dunwoodie, who, as a second-generation son of the Revolution, presumably unities the best of two ancient families and who will no doubt carry the burden of natural authority and leadership as bravely as his ancestors; nor is it surprising to learn that of all the figures that once existed on the fringes of Cooper's broad social spectrum, Harvey Birch is the only one to have made it into this final scene — but, then, he has one foot in the grave, and is conveniently childless ("I am alone in the world!"; 432). While the lesser names are merely commemorated parenthetically, Birch, the novel's token hero, apparently has at least the right to a perfunctory death-scene. But it is the descendents of the Whartons and the Dunwoodies, those upholders of the middle-class consensus, that survive and emerge as the true patriarchs: they are the sole inheritors of Cooper's American Revolution. Despite his flirtation with egalitarianism, Cooper's ultimate stance in the novel is a confirmation of the American consensus. The unruly, libertine Skinners and Cow-Boys have long since disappeared into the mists of the past; the last British troops are being rounded up on the banks of the Niagara; Birch, the lower-class hero, is safely relegated to the realm of myth; but it is the natural aristocracy, "the rule of the best," that remains, simply because it *is* — Cooper intimates — "the rule of the *best*." The decline of all those outside the middle-class consensus has really all along merely served as a foil to the inherent superiority and ultimate ascendency of the gentry, whose final victory on the moral and ideological wasteland of the neutral ground is confirmed by intermarriage, inheritance, and the restoration of genealogy.

The relevance for the contemporary audience of Cooper's attempt to neutralize historical reality and to supplant it by transcendent myth is that his myth works two ways: both regressive and progressive. In creating his private version of the American Revolution, that is, Cooper manipulated the past as it was not only in order to propagate a particular view of the present — *his* present — but also to determine the face of the future; in doing so, he contributed significantly to the emergence of America's present-day myths and of its dominant middle-class ideology.

REVOLT IN MASSACHUSETTS: THE MIDNIGHT MARCH OF LIONEL LINCOLN

JOHN McWILLIAMS

for Donald Ringe

Listen, my children, and you shall hear
Of the midnight ride of Paul Revere,
On the eighteenth of April, in Seventy-five;
Hardly a man is now alive
Who remembers that famous day and year.

. . . .

You know the rest. In the books you have read,
How the British Regulars fired and fled, —
How the farmers gave them ball for ball,
From behind each fence and farm-yard wall,
Chasing the red-coats down the lane,
Then crossing the fields to emerge again
Under the trees at the turn of the road,
And only pausing to fire and load.[1]

I. America's Glorious Morning

For the creating of an American Revolutionary mythology, the crucial historical moment would quickly prove to be the Battles of Lexington, Concord and Bunker Hill, understood as one interconnected episode. A chronological listing of the writers who reflected upon the events of April 19 and June 17, 1775 reads like a sizeable roster of the foremost historians, political orators and men of letters of the entire antebellum

1. Henry Wadsworth Longfellow, "Paul Revere's Ride" (1860), in *Tales of a Wayside Inn*, Vol. IV of *The Poetical Works of Henry Wadsworth Longfellow* (Boston: Houghton, Mifflin & Co., 1886), 24, 28.

period: David Ramsay, Mercy Otis Warren, Jedediah Morse, Edward Everett, George Bancroft, Ralph Waldo Emerson, Robert Rantoul, Henry David Thoreau, Henry Wadsworth Longfellow, James Russell Lowell, John Greenleaf Whittier, Nathaniel Hawthorne, Oliver Wendell Holmes. These names collectively suggest that determining the meaning of Lexington and Concord was very much a Massachusetts affair, a persistent concern of that highly literate, gentlemanly, even patrician group of writers, co-centered around Harvard College and the town of Concord, a group which, as Lawrence Buell has shown, was to become increasingly self-conscious about its assumed role as the torchbearer of new world literary culture.[2] Protestants, libertarians and nationalists all, they repeatedly sought, in writing about Lexington, Concord and Bunker Hill, to uncover the Republic's highest origin in events that had shortly preceded — and presumably caused — the declaring of independence in July of 1776. But they were also men of Massachusetts, not ashamed that their particular state, by being the first place of armed revolt, had provided the source of those local "associations" (Archibald Alison's influential term), from which later generations could and should rekindle the inner spirit of Liberty.[3]

Later writers adding to this commemorative tradition would pay tribute to their literary predecessors either by naming them or, more often, by recalling their climactic phrases (Samuel Adams's "Oh, what a glorious morning for America," Edward Everett's "the countryside rose as one man," Emerson's "the shot heard round the world," Longfellow's "a voice in the darkness, a knock at the door"). Throughout this self-referential body of literature, however, the name of "our national novelist" (Melville's well-known words) remains conspicuously absent. Ephemeral praise for the historical chapters of *Lionel Lincoln* can be found in reviews of 1825 and 1826, but not until George Bancroft wrote his letter for the *Memorial of Cooper* (1852) would there be an informed public acknowledgment that "In *Lionel Lincoln* he [Cooper] has described the battle of Bunker Hill better than

---

2. Lawrence Buell, *New England Literary Culture: From Revolution through Renaissance* (Cambridge: Cambridge University Press, 1986).

3. Archibald Alison, *Essays on the Nature and Principle of Taste* (1790; rpt. Edinburgh: Bell and Bradfute, 1811).

it is described in any other work."[4] Bancroft's praise, however, did not markedly alter the insularity of Massachusetts's self-congratulation.

My purpose here is neither more nor less than to restore *Lionel Lincoln* to its due importance in creating Revolutionary history for the new Republic. Cooper's novel did indeed lie outside the Massachusetts commemorative tradition, not because Cooper the man was a New Yorker who had been raised to suspect Yankee cant, but because Cooper the author was an impartial and accurate historian in fiction. To demonstrate the truth of Bancroft's tribute, we need to recontextualize the historical chapters of Cooper's novel by placing them among the important analagous accounts written by predecessors and contemporaries. Before doing so, however, it is important to define exactly what was at stake in this particular act of political remembrance. Militarily, the three events were inconsequential. The eight colonial militia killed on Lexington Green, the 235 casualties which 1,800 British troops suffered during the retreat from Concord, and the British displacement of Continental forces from Breeds (not Bunker) Hill were of little strategic importance in forcing British General Thomas Gage's withdrawal from Boston, and they were of no military importance to the Revolutionary War as a whole. The confrontations at both Lexington and Bunker Hill ended in retreat for the patriots; the estimated total of American deaths on the 19th of April (about 50) is not dramatically less than the total of British deaths (about 75).

The importance of the three battles lies rather in the sudden historical validation of the patriots' collective identity as oppressed farmers and homespun martyr-heroes, an identity which patriots as diverse as James Otis, Samuel Adams, Ethan Allen, John Dickinson, and even Alexander Hamilton had already begun to cultivate. Once the events of April 19 had occurred, the skirmish at Lexington could readily be seen as the beginning of a just, defensive revolution. The revolution's opening shots had been fired, not by self-seeking rebels, but by invading British redcoats advancing upon farmer-militia who were standing quietly in defense of their Common and their inland village. The Minutemen who, a few hours later, would drive the British from Concord's North Bridge, and then harrass the British troops on their retreat to Boston, could thereby emerge as a gloriously undisciplined people's army. Emerson would later claim in his

---

4. George Bancroft, letter to the Cooper Memorial Committee, in *Fenimore Cooper: The Critical Heritage*, eds George Dekker and John P. McWilliams (London: Routledge and Kegan Paul, 1973), 245.

"Historical Discourse at Concord" that in the gathering of the Minutemen the principle of democracy had come unheralded to the military field, "every one from that moment being his own commander."[5] Hesitant colonials were instantly transformed into vigilant Americans who were willing to endure neither British raids upon their homes, nor the marching of British regulars through their lands. The defiant placing of American forces on Bunker Hill could then show the world who the British truly were — an unpopular invading army shut up in besieged coastal towns, an army whose "victories" could be won only by the inhuman force of superior artillery.

Gone were the vexing issues of whether Crown, Parliament, royal Provincial officials, or the colonists themselves should have the powers to appoint judges, to summon and suspend legislatures, to provide payment for the common defense, to impose import duties and, above all, to assess taxes. To Thomas Paine, it was but Common Sense to recognize that "all plans, proposals &c. prior to the nineteenth of April, i.e. to the commencement of hostilities, are like the almanacks of the last year; which, though proper then, are superceded and useless now."[6] Since that glorious day, America's Rubicon has presumably been crossed, and her War of Independence begun. The controlling value for determining and judging collective behavior could therefore suddenly shift from the adjusting of political powers within an empire to the heralding of those heroic deeds of resistance that were to inaugurate a new age.

Robert Ferguson has recently argued that American expressions of values associated with "The Enlightenment" are especially likely to be shaped by images of a future light glimpsed through the surrounding darkness.[7] From David Ramsay's *History* (1789) to Longfellow's "Paul Revere's Ride" (1860), accounts of April 18 and 19 stress the long night's westward march from Boston to Lexington, the dawn of conflict

---

5. Ralph Waldo Emerson, "Historical Discourse at Concord" (1835), in *The Complete Works of Ralph Waldo Emerson*, ed. E.E. Emerson (Boston: Houghton, Mifflin and Co., 1906), XI, 75.

6. Thomas Paine, *Common Sense*, ed. Isaac Kramnick (1776; rpt. New York: Viking Penguin, 1982), 82.

7. See Robert A. Ferguson's fine reading of "The Star-Spangled Banner" in "What is Enlightenment?: Some American Answers," *American Literary History* 1 (Summer 1989), 249-52.

on Lexington Green (a dawning to which Samuel Adams's famous exclamation "What a glorious morning for America!" is so perfectly suited) and then the long march of the beaten British back eastward through the gathering darkness of a spring afternoon. Here, clearly, was a powerful combination of seasonal, directional and diurnal metaphors ideally suited to the politics of republican progress.

Although *Lionel Lincoln* was the first novel to draw the terms of connection among all three battles, the Massachusetts revolt had been presented as history's new fulcrum long before 1825. Within a few days of April 19, sometime patriot Benjamin Church completed, under Joseph Warren's direction, a short, semi-official "Narrative of the Excursions and Ravages of the King's Troops" that was promptly readied for newspaper and broadside distribution in coastal cities from Salem to Charleston. Church's long opening clause ("On the nineteenth day of April, one thousand seven hundred and seventy-five, a day to be remembered by all Americans of the present generation, and which ought, and doubtless will be handed down to ages yet unborn ...")[8] presupposes that a new ordering of time, as well as a permanent separation of America from Great Britain, has now and forever occurred. By assuming that the British committed "the first fire" both on Lexington Green and at Concord's North Bridge (an unprovable claim now debated), Church characterizes the Minutemen as victimized defenders of local communities. For good reason, his narrative fastens almost exclusively upon doubtful British atrocities ("plundering and burning of dwelling-houses and other buildings, driving into the street women in child-bed, killing old men in their houses unarmed"[9]). Church senses that the alleging of cruel British violations, not of the colonial merchant's purse, but of the American farmer's hearth, was henceforth to be the effective means of persuading the poeple to act. Readers of Church's "Narrative" are challenged to make real the dictum of his final sentence: "And all this because these colonies will not submit to the iron yoke of arbitrary power."[10]

The full retrospective significance of April 19 was first formulated by David Ramsay in his two volume *The History of the American*

---

8. Cited in Arthur B. Tourtellot, *Lexington and Concord: The Beginning of the War of the American Revolution* (New York: W.W. Norton, 1959), 228.

9. Tourtellot, 229.

10. Tourtellot, 230.

Revolution (1789). Perhaps because Ramsay had read Church's "Narrative" with a clear, critical eye, or perhaps because he was from South Carolina and not Massachusetts, Ramsay insisted at the outset that, among enlightened nations, revolutions were henceforth to be won by the pen as much as the sword:

> In civil wars or revolutions it is a matter of much consequence who strikes the first blow. The compassion of the world is in favour of the attacked, and the displeasure of good men on those who are the first to imbrue their hands in human blood.[11]

The significance of the events in Massachusetts during the spring of 1775, Ramsay believes, was presumably what it is now fashionable to call "hegemonic" — a matter of how a dominant cultural belief is formed and sustained. The Americans who fell in action "were revered by their countrymen, as martyrs who had died in the cause of liberty."[12] And this reverence, Ramsay observes, had immediate practical consequences. The skirmishes at Lexington and Concord provided patriot leaders in the Continental Congress and in local Committees of Safety their clear justification for immediately seizing forts (Ticonderoga), for impounding public moneys still in the hands of royal appointees, and most importantly for raising the army which George Washington was to command in Cambridge.

Ramsay's perspective on the contradictory effect of the retreat from Concord remains remarkably acute. On the one hand, the militia's harrassment of British regulars from behind trees and houses proved both the ability of the formerly despised colonial soldier and the advantages of "Indian" (today "guerilla") tactics in a war of self-defense. On the other hand, the humiliation of the redcoats convinced many a patriot leader that the war could somehow be won by relying upon the less costly defensive armament of militia and Minutemen, rather than a properly trained national army. Behind these perceptions lies Ramsay's Southerner's sense of the enormous importance to the American Revolution of New England's ethnic solidarity and comparative equality:

---

11. David Ramsay, *The History of the American Revolution*, (Philadelphia: Aitken & Son, 1789), I, 186.

12. Ramsay, I, 191.

> As arms were to decide the controversy, it was fortunate for the Americans that the first blood was drawn in New- England. The inhabitants of that country are so connected with each other by descent, manners, religion, politics, and a general equality, that the killing of a single individual interested the whole, and made them consider it as a common cause. The blood of those who were killed at Lexington and Concord proved the firm cement of an extensive union.[13]

The words "firm cement" may now seem an unfortunate metaphor but they describe a real historical fact. Eight fathers and eight sons had stood together among the Minutemen on Lexington Green; with one British volley, five father-son bonds were ended in death.

As the allegiances of her name suggest, Mercy Otis Warren's kind of patriotism has precious little of David Ramsay's dispassion. Warren's anger at the Federalists' presumed betrayal of America's libertarian Republic led her, as Lester Cohen has shown, to pen repeated confrontations between the liberty, virtue and humanity of the Patriots, and the power, luxury and cruelty of the British and their Tory minions. Accepting and even heightening the atrocities in Church's "Narrative," Mercy Warren concludes that the British acted throughout the day with such "perfidy and meanness," such "rancorous and ferocious rage," that their "barbarities" left an "indelible stain on a nation long famed for their courage, humanity and honor."[14] Because of the "savagery" of the British grenadiers, within twenty-four hours the whole country rose in arms." Emerson's famous term "the embattled farmers" seems genteel indeed beside Mercy Warren's willingness to praise the Minutemen as "raw inexperienced peasantry, who had ran hastily together in defense of their lives and liberties."[15] The issue of class is, however, more complicated for Mercy Warren than may first appear. When she describes Massachusetts's great "moment of unfading glory," the death at Bunker Hill of her cousin-by-marriage Major General Joseph Warren, (a moment also commemorated in a painting by John Trumbull), she creates a model of virtue that is at once libertarian,

---

13. Ramsay, I, 189.

14. Mrs Mercy Otis Warren, *History of the Rise, Progress and Termination of the American Revolution*, ed. Lester H. Cohen (1805; rpt. Indianapolis: Liberty Classics, 1988), I, 103.

15. Warren, I, 105, 103.

Roman and decidedly elevated: "This heroic officer was the first victim of rank that fell by the sword in the contest between Great Britain and America; and the conflagration of Charlestown, enkindled by the wanton barbarity of his enemies, lighted his *manes* to the grave."[16]

By the time *Lionel Lincoln* was published in 1825, the British presence to America's west had been ended by a second war, the rancor between Federalists and Republicans had died away, and the so-called Era of Good Feelings was beginning to sour into sometimes worried claims for expansion, internal improvements, and Indian Removal. As the 50th anniversary year approached, Cooper was not the only man of letters who sought literary advancement by recalling the increasingly mythic beginning of the Revolution. For the sesquicentennial celebration of April 19, Edward Everett wrote his once famous "Oration Delivered at Concord," an often republished speech which is one of the essential pieces — along with Webster's speeches at Plymouth Rock and on the deaths of Jefferson and Adams, — of republican hagiography during the early national period. Everett gave his audience a vivid narrative of a sequence of events that were clearly already legendary: the lanterns in the North Church, Paul Revere's and William Dawes's Ride, the (supposedly) unprovoked British firing upon the Lexington militia, Sam Adams's exclamation about America's glorious morning, the (supposedly) unprovoked British firing from the North Bridge upon the farmer-militia of Middlesex County, how "the people rose in their strength," and then the long, despairing retreat of the British invaders, ever more exhausted because "[e]very patch of trees, every rock, every stream of water, every building, every stone wall was *lined* ... with an unintermitted fire."[17]

In Everett's view, true understanding of the meaning of April 19 should arouse filiopietistic pride in a citizenry within regions far beyond the local audience before him. Concord Fight was no mere Middlesex County affair, but a moment of cultural definition in which the "national character ... must be formed, elevated, and strengthened from the materials which history presents" ("ODC," 9). If the Lexington militia had laid down their arms, if the Concord townsmen had give up their military stores, "then the Revolution had been at an end, or rather

---

16. Warren, I, 122.

17. Edward Everett, "An Oration Delivered at Concord, April the 19th, 1825" (Boston: Cummings, Hilliard and Co., 1825), 34, 36. Future references to Everett's "Oration" will be cited parenthetically within the text ("ODC").

never had been begun" ("ODC," 5-6). In Everett's time, the power of such seemingly absurd assertions depended upon his contemporaries' assumption that the progress of the western world derived from the perceived connection between the American and French Revolutions. Since April 19, 1775, the power of progressive historical change had begun flowing back from west to east, no longer from east to west, as in George Berkeley's familiar stanzas on the westward course of empire. Because the patriots had acted with no awareness of their own importance, with no ulterior historical motive whatsoever, the Minutemen of Lexington and the farmers of Concord had lifted the curtain upon an age of Liberty and Reason:

> No Washington had appeared to lead, no Lafayette had hastened to assist, no charter of independence had yet breathed the breath of life into the cause, when the 19th of April called our fathers to the field. ("ODC," 51)

The yeomen's ignorance of their historical role is thus transformed into the true sign of their virtue; the silent resolution of the Minuteman becomes his way of declaring as well as embodying the Rights of Man.

The intended reach of Everett's narrative finally transcends even the question of national character. April 19 must be seen as "a day as important as any recorded in the history of man" because "it was one of those great days, one of those elemental occasions in the world's affairs, when the people rise, and act for themselves" ("ODC," 42). All the liberating events of the years 1776, 1783, 1787, 1789, 1794, 1800 and 1815, in America, France and England, have grown steadily from the germ of the Minutemen's deeds at the edge of the world in April of 1775. Seen properly, the blows endured at Lexington and struck at Concord constitute the awakening of a worldwide religion of democratic politics:

> It was the people, in their first capacity, as citizens and as freemen, starting from their beds at midnight, from their firesides, and from their fields, to take their own cause into their own hands. Such a spectacle is the height of the moral sublime; when the want of every thing is fully made up by the spirit of the cause; and the soul within stands in place of discipline, organization, resources .... The people always conquer. They always must conquer .... In defiance of the whole exerted powers of the British empire, the yeomanry of the country rose

> as one man, and set their lives on this dear stake of Liberty. ("ODC," 42-43, 44, 47)

As if he were preaching in church, or looking at a late eighteenth century painting of Roman heroism by Jacques David or Benjamin West, Everett exhorts his audience to join in a communion with a forefathers' spirit that is at once secular and aesthetic. Each revolutionary Massachusetts freeman, he insists, made his decision to resist tyranny as an individual. Considered collectively, however, the Minutemen and yeomanry should now summon up in every reverential citizen's eye a picture, a canvas, a "spectacle" in which one may see "the height of the moral sublime" embodied in the most ordinary of human forms and callings.

II. Mourning Victory

Ramsay, Warren and Everett assumed the long historical view, passing judgment from a universalist, Enlightenment perspective upon the origins of a Revolution which, they believed, could be truthfully understood only through the lens of patriotic values. In writing "this his only historical tale,"[18] Cooper assumed the near view of the participant observor, the man who simply happens to be there. This fictive point of view — so like a Jamesian "reflector" — was not, however, adopted as a license for inaccuracy:

> The battles of Lexington and Bunker's Hill, and the movement on Prospect Hill, are believed to be as faithfully described as is possible to have been done by one who was not an eye-witness of those important events. No pains were spared in examining all the documents, both English and American; and many private authorities were consulted, with a strong desire to ascertain the truth. The ground was visited and examined, and the differing testimony was subjected to a close comparison between the statements and the probability. (7)

Cooper's claim rightly rests on his historical accuracy rather than his historical romance. If one compares the novel's rendering of historical details with the careful sifting of available evidence in Arthur B.

---

18. *Lionel Lincoln; or, The Leaguer of Boston* (1825), eds Donald A. Ringe and Lucy B. Ringe (Albany: State University of New York Press, 1984), 6. Future references to this edition will be cited parenthetically within the text.

Tourtellot's *Lexington and Concord*, the impartiality and accuracy of Cooper's fiction remain remarkable in almost every detail. As Kay Seymour House, Donald Ringe and Lucy Ringe have discovered, Cooper not only examined the ground and consulted knowledgeable individuals;[19] he read extant British narratives (including depositions of soldiers on both sides) that were available in accounts by William Gordon, Charles Stedman and General Burgoyne. He studied, in other words, exactly those kinds of complicating, hard-to-obtain historical sources which Ramsay, Warren and Everett would have dismissed as British prejudice, even if such sources had been known to them.

The informed but never omniscient narrator of *Lionel Lincoln* often writes from the progressivist perspective which Ramsay, Everett, and Mercy Otis Warren had all shared. For example, Cooper's factual, balanced overview of the causes of the Revolutionary War at the end of chapter five begins by claiming that the American Revolution, considered retrospectively as a whole, "established a new era in political liberty and founded a mighty empire" (57). In his fictive plot, as well as his historical observations, Cooper provides sufficient evidence of British ministerial oppression and colonial courage to persuade contemporary reviewers that *Lionel Lincoln* was a novel fully as patriotic as *The Spy*.

The challenge Cooper's novel offers to the commemorative tradition, a challenge still unacknowledged, was his decision to describe the battles of Lexington, Concord and Bunker Hill from a worriedly impartial point of view. By conceiving of the wavering Lionel Lincoln as his title figure, Cooper centered his novel around an American variant of Scott's Edward Waverley. Both protagonists are gentlemen of divided allegiance caught in a rebellion they try not to see as civil war. A major in the Royal 47th, Lionel Lincoln is of aristocratic lineage but patriotic fathering, of American birth but British education, sympathetic to American grievances yet loyal to his king. In all five of the historical chapters, Cooper describes the precipitating incidents of the Revolution from the perspective of the British military, not the Minutemen. Cooper arranges for Lionel to enter into each incident, not as Major Lincoln in charge of royal troops, but as a "volunteer," an "aide," or simply as a "witness." This semi-disengaged point of view achieves two ends. The reader experiences incidents of Revolutionary war as the British military did, but looks at them through the eyes of an objective, sensitive, but

19. See Donald Ringe and Lucy Ringe, eds, Historical Introduction, *Lionel Lincoln*, xv-xxi.

unsure gentleman. Secondly, it prepares the reader for the likelihood that Lionel Lincoln will change his allegiance, thereby justifying the Patriots' cause through character association.

The worth of the fictional rendering of any historical event must depend to some degree on the accuracy of its seemingly incidental details. Cooper rightly shows us that the British troops were given no clear idea of their mission in Concord, and no hint of any confrontation to occur in Lexington. Cooper discovered that the Concord militia, after marching down the Lexington road to meet the British coming toward them, had then turned completely around and had, in effect, escorted the British into their own town. Plunderings of Concord homes, in Cooper's fiction as in historical fact, were real but not numerous. Exactly as Cooper describes, the British sent two or three companies (some 40 men) to guard the North Bridge, while upwards of 400 Minutemen gradually gathered beyond the bridge, and eventually decided to use force, cross the bridge, and defend the town. Cooper wisely omits all mention of the now discredited but then notorious atrocities supposedly committed by the British on their return through Lexington and Arlington.

As Joseph Warren, Benjamin Church and David Ramsay had all perceived from the outset, the determination of who fired first, however insignificant it may have been militarily, was the crucial issue for political persuasion. Because the events of April 19 were always presented as a narrative, whether historical, oral or fictional, the vexing question of rightful powers (were the Minutemen forcibly resisting properly constituted British authority?) would always be secondary to the reader's or listener's sense of who was the victim, who the victimizer, when the bullets first rang out. Tourtellot has concluded that, on Lexington Green, both the British and American forces faced each other with orders to stand firm, but to disperse rather than to fire.[20] At the North Bridge, both sides had received orders not to fire unless fired upon, but no mention had been made of dispersing.[21] On both occasions, one or two desultory shots, fired by no one knows whom, caused the British to fire a volley. On Lexington Green, that volley would make patriotic martyrs of dead Minutemen; in Concord town, it would make martyrs of a few more, but heroes of an entire populace. In neither episode, however, does there seem to have been a

20. Tourtellot, 131.

21. Tourtellot, 164.

deliberate decision on either side to begin battle. If the passing of the Declaration of Independence truly can be ascribed to the rising of the populace after Lexington and Concord, logic compels us to conclude that the reasoned deliberateness of Jefferson's words ("a decent respect to the opinions of mankind requires that they should declare the causes which impel them to the separation"[22]), is a deft verbal plank extended over recent abysses of chaos and confusion.

After a dark and tiring inland march beside the grenadiers, Lionel Lincoln, titular British major but at present a "volunteer," enters "a small hamlet of houses dimly seen through the morning haze" (103). He sees "a small body of countrymen, drawn up in the affectation of military parade"(103). A British major of marines shouts at them "Disperse, ye rebels, disperse!" (104). There are reports of pistol fire from no identifiable source, then an order to fire. Not until six pages later does Cooper inform his reader that the "hamlet" was indeed Lexington, and the major the controversial Pitcairn. Similarly, while Lionel Lincoln is observing grenadiers searching for military stores in some town named Concord, "the report of fire-arms was heard suddenly to issue from the post held by the light-infantry, at the bridge" (112). Cooper then renders "the shot heard round the world" in this offhand manner: "A few scattering shot were succeeded by a volley, which was answered by another, with the quickness of lightning, and then the air became filled with the incessant rattling of a sharp conflict" (112). Such passages suggest the "realist" literary techniques we have long associated with the battle descriptions of Tolstoy, Stephen Crane and Hemingway: the chaotic impressions of war's senselessness, recorded as lived in the moment, not cleaned up as a part of some orderly pattern that can make sense of "history." In this regard, Cooper's modernity stands in startling contrast to the nineteenth-century tradition of the way the events of April 19th should be understood. Mercy Otis Warren claimed to know that, at Lexington, British Lieutenant Colonal Smith had "branded the minutemen with the epithets of rebel and traitor; and before the little party had time, either to resist or to obey, he with wanton precipitation, ordered his troops to fire."[23] For the collective sons of Concord, Everett's rendering of the firing at the North Bridge must have seemed reassuring. Everett somehow

---

22. Thomas Jefferson, *The Portable Thomas Jefferson*, ed. Merrill D. Peterson (New York: Viking Penguin, 1977), 235.

23. Warren, I, 102.

discovered that the British, without any provocation, had simply decided to fire: "the signal for a general discharge is made; a British soldier steps from the ranks and fires at Major Buttrick" ("ODC," 33). Only through such clear instances of just retaliation, Warren and Everett imply, could the patriots ever have been willing to begin their revolution.

If the word "enlightenment" connotes the perceiving of emerging light through retreating darkness, it is little wonder that the Revolutionary war paintings of John Trumbull, like the commemorative rhetoric of later generations, offer us clearly defined tableaux flooded with light, centered in form, and apparent in political meaning. Contrast Lionel Lincoln's scattered impressions of the retreat from Concord:

> On either side of the highway, along the skirts of every wood or orchard, in the open fields, and from every house, barn, or cover in sight, the flash of fire-arms was to be seen, while the shouts of the English grew, at each instant, feebler and less inspiriting. Heavy clouds of smoke rose above the valley, into which he looked, and mingled with the dust of the march, drawing an impenetrable veil before the view .... (115)

The phrase "impenetrable veil" conveys Cooper's suspicion of the phony clarity of historical hindsight. When Lionel Lincoln later describes the Americans' second repulse of the British attack on Bunker Hill, Cooper lowers the impenetrable veil yet again:

> As the uproar of the artillery again grew fainter, the crash of falling streets, and the appalling sounds of the conflagaration, on the left, became more audible. Immense volumes of black smoke issued from the smouldering ruins, and bellying outward, fold beyond fold, it overhung the work in a hideous cloud, casting its gloomy shadow across the place of blood. (186)

Although such battle clouds do not preclude Cooper's final tribute to the patriots' courage, the veiling of heroism in artillery smoke remains the reader's predominant sensual impression. To picture gritty clouds obscuring American triumphs must have been disconcerting to all those patriotic readers whom Cooper had lulled into the usual expectation that the day would bring "an effect not unlike the sudden rising of the curtain at the opening of some interesting drama" (98). In Cooper's novel, the only character who, in the manner of Edward Everett, sees the Battle of Bunker Hill entirely as "a glorious spectacle" is the impulsive and braggardly British General John Burgoyne (180), whose subsequent surrender at Saratoga had discredited him to both sides.

While confronting the guns of the colonists, Lionel Lincoln must also try to resolve a variety of conflicting inner and outer claims: loyalties of origin (his American birth), loyalties of education (Oxford), loyalties of allegiance (the British military), the callous wrongs of British ministerial policies, and, perhaps most important, all the confusions of the recent acts of rebellion. As Lionel arrives from England, he assumes that "the utmost required is what they [the colonists] term a redress of grievances, many of which, I must think, exist only in imagination" (69). Shortly before the march to Lexington, Lionel watches Joseph Warren speak at a Sons of Liberty meeting in Boston. Withholding comment on Warren's politics, Lionel remarks with somewhat surprised approval on Warren's "elegance of style," a manner that shows Warren "to be of a class altogether superior to the mass of the assembly" (74). Near the meeting's conclusion, Warren tries to search out Lionel Lincoln's motives for being there: "Does Major Lincoln meet his countrymen to-night as one who sympathizes in their wrongs, or as the favoured and prosperous officer of the crown?" (75). Answering one pointed question with another, Lionel replies "Is sympathy with the oppressed incompatible with loyalty to my Prince?" (75). Although this reply earns the momentary respect of both Joseph Warren and Cooper's reader, Lionel has assumed a political posture that is likely to lock him into a discomfiting loyalty once violence has begun. Here Cooper both follows and reverses Scott's model for plotting political indecision. Edward Waverley, who long believed his father's ties to George II's ministry to be quite incompatible with his own increasing sympathy for the Jacobites, was saved only when he handily rediscovered his allegiance to the Hanoverian establishment.

Lionel's responses to armed revolt follow a revealing, consistent pattern. At the instant the grenadiers fire on the Minutemen at Lexington Green, Lionel protests "Great God! ... what is it you do? ye fire at unoffending men! is there no law but force!" (104). When he later looks at the writhing bodies of the dying Minutemen, however, "sickening at the sight, he turn[s], and walk[s] away by himself." Soon thereafter he understandably concludes that "the power of Britain is too mighty for these scattered and unprepared colonies to cope with." As Lionel watches the grenadiers break into Concord homes, he reflects on "the insults and wanton abuses of a military inroad," during which "no place was held sacred from the rude scrutiny of the licentious soldiery" (112). But once Lionel knows that the countryside has risen in revenge, he rides up to Lieutenant Colonel Smith and asks to fight alongside the retreating British troops, "having lost every other sensation in youthful blood, and the pride of arms" (114).

At the Battle of Bunker Hill, Lionel Lincoln once again remains an onlooker until the British are threatened with total defeat. Even though he has twice been impressed by the courage of the Americans under fire, especially by the bravery of Joseph Warren, Lionel rushes up to Sir Henry Clinton and demands to go to the field: "Until this moment the feelings of Lionel had vacillated between the pride of country and military spirit, but losing all other feelings in the latter sensation, he looked fiercely about him, as if he would seek the man who dare exult in the repulse of his comrades" (184). When Waverley had felt similar impulses of military spirit, he had joined the Highland rebels, rather than the Hanoverian grenadiers who, in Cooper's novel, will become history's losers, not its winners.

At each of these three moments of personal crisis, Lionel Lincoln senses that his own "countrymen," the Americans, are in the right, yet his personal decision is always to rejoin his British "comrades." Nothing that Lionel witnesses at Lexington, Concord or Bunker Hill leads him even to consider adopting Waverley's growing neutrality, a neutrality that ends in quiet defection. Cooper does not, however, criticize Lionel's instinctual British loyalty by labeling it a "Tory" failure of personal courage or a "Tory" lack of political integrity — as Mercy Warren or Edward Everett would surely have done. The similar phrasings in the two preceding quotations — "having lost every other sensation" (118) and "losing all other feelings in the latter sensation" (184) — suggest that Lionel's loyalty is a present psychological necessity. Cooper has immersed his reader in the experience of battle in order to show why, amid the murk of killing, a young man's "pride of arms" or "military spirit" (evidently bred in him by institutional training) must finally control his actions. Waverley's prudential considerations, Cooper implies, must at such moments be secondary whether they should be or not.

One may of course respond to this argument by insisting that an instinctual response during the heat of battle may be one thing, but the aftermath of a reasoned decision is quite another. Here too, however, Cooper frustrates the reader's expectations for a comforting political conversion. Despite all the collective patriotic pressures placed on Lionel Lincoln (his American heritage, the cruelties of his family's pride in aristocratic lineage, and the colonists' evident courage in 1775), Cooper never allows Lionel a quiet hour to think through a possible change of allegiance. (We are allowed to see Waverley throughout whole days of reflection.) Perhaps Cooper had simply developed an understanding awareness of Loyalist feelings because of the collective misfortunes of his De Lancey in-laws. Perhaps Cooper believed, as Benedict Arnold's then current reputation would suggest, that honorable military officers do not shift sides. Perhaps Cooper wished to challenge Scott. Perhaps Cooper wished, at the end of the novel, to remove all traces of British nobility from American soil. Or perhaps he had become sufficiently skeptical of Massachusetts legendizing that he wished to restore the historical complexities of the three battles, thereby challenging their much touted influence in changing every true man's allegiance. It was, after all, John Adams who had estimated that, at the outset of the Revolutionary War, one third of the colonies' population had been Loyalists while another third had remained neutral.

The full import of Cooper's divided but impartial vantage point emerges in his portrayal of the British assaults on Bunker Hill. Unlike the Battles of Lexington and Concord, in which the reader experiences skirmishes at ground level through Lionel Lincoln's eyes, the Battle of Bunker Hill is seen as an unexpectedly murky panorama from atop Copp's Hill. Because this vantage point at last affords Lionel an overview, Cooper provides his reader, in one ringing sentence, perhaps the most concise summary in American literature of the way antebellum Americans wished to remember the Revolutionary patriots:

> ... [I]gnorant of the glare of military show; in the simple and rude vestments of their calling; armed with such weapons as they had seized from the hooks above their own mantels; and without even a banner to wave its cheering folds above their heads, they stood, sustained only by the righteousness of their cause, and those deep moral principles which they had received from their fathers, and which they intended this day should show, were to be transmitted untarnished to their children. (177-78)

In the cumulative parallel rhythms of contemporary oratory, Cooper's four opening phrases lay claim to the qualities most prized in the revolutionary father: plainness, diligence, domesticity, self-sufficiency and self-reliance. The sentence's exact center are the two simple words — subject and verb — "they stood." The strong rhythmic accents upon these two words reinforce the virtue most essential to Revolutionary self-justification: the silent public witness of an inner political principle. (Emerson's "Concord Hymn" would repeat the same trope with the same rhythmic emphasis: "Here once the embattled farmers stood / And fired the shot heard round the world."[24]) Cooper's long concluding clause urges the sons to be worthy of their fathers' heritage in the same terms that Webster or Everett customarily used when placing the burden of filiopietism on the sons sitting before them.

Cooper's sentence pictures the Patriot heroes at the precise moment when Lionel Lincoln, having climbed Copp's Hill to gain a prospect, first sees them preparing for defense. After the first two British assaults on Bunker Hill are repulsed, a "hideous cloud, casting its gloomy shadow across the place of blood" can then serve to obscure (186), but not to efface, the reader's memory of Cooper's tribute. Nonetheless, Cooper does not end his Bunker Hill sequence by any return to reassuring pictures of the virtues of the farmer-militia. Instead, he describes the courageous and tragic deaths of British Major Pitcairn and American General Warren, and then ends the chapter by tersely observing that "nothing further remained for the royal lieutenants but to go and mourn over their victory" (188).

The fictional narrative in Cooper's Bunker Hill chapter also ends in a complicating reversal. After Bunker Hill has been retaken by the British, Lionel Lincoln is suddenly and senselessly shot by a patriot whose desire for vengeance has remained unsatisfied: "At this instant the trappings of his [Lionel's] attire caught the glaring eye-balls of a dying yeoman, who exerted his wasting strength to sacrifice one more worthy victim to the manes of his countrymen. The whole of the tumultuous scene vanished from the senses of Lionel at the flash of the musket of this man" (188). Lionel here experiences a momentary glimpse behind the impenetrable veil. Consistent with Cooper's troubling characterizations of Ralph and Job Pray, the patriotic ardor of this "dying yeoman" is revealed to be inseparable from the "glaring eye-balls" of insanity. Cooper's decision to have Lionel wounded in such a manner suggests one more reason why neither author nor protagonist need contemplate the morality of changing one's allegiance.

Cooper closes out his historical scenes with this haunting glimpse of Patriot insanity. In Hawthorne's view, despite all the intervening efforts of Revolutionary commemoration, the lasting significance of Concord Fight would rest almost entirely upon such a glimpse. While living in the Old Manse, Hawthorne became increasingly troubled by an incident which Concord's patriots still preferred to ignore. After the fighting at

---

24. "Concord Hymn," in *Poems*, Vol. IX of *The Complete Works of Ralph Waldo Emerson*, ed. E.E. Emerson (Boston: Houghton Mifflin, 1906), 58.

the North Bridge had ended, a local farm boy had come upon a British officer lying wounded beside the road. Whether driven by zeal, fear or both, the would-be Minuteman had impulsively axed the British officer in the head. This image of crazed, unnecessary violence, Hawthorne wrote, "has borne more fruit for me than all that history tells us of the fight."[25]

Hawthorne's morbid and ahistorical response to Concord Fight is as far removed from Cooper's perception of divided loyalties as it is from Everett's relentless glorifying. By the 1840s, Hawthorne had good reason to wish to dismiss "all that history tells us." The kinds of doubts expressed through Cooper's research and Lionel's British perspective had formed no part of the intervening regional record. No matter that *Lionel Lincoln* was to be reprinted in three languages, seven editions and twenty-two reimpressions by 1850. Within the state of Massachusetts, the novel was conveniently and tacitly forgotten after 1825.[26]

The commemorative tradition, however, continued to flourish: two addresses by Emerson, poems by Emerson, Whittier, Lowell and Longfellow and, perhaps most influential of all, Robert Rantoul's 1850 "Oration Delivered at Concord on the Celebration of the Seventy-Fifth Anniversary of the Events of April 19, 1775." On that four hour occasion, Rantoul spoke before an audience of at least 8,000 people including the Governor, Lieutenant Governor, two brass bands, delegations from three cities and eight towns, and, of course, the state's major newspaper editors. Although Rantoul had risen politically by the appeal of his mildly anti-industrial and anti-corporate rhetoric, he knew that most of the state's dignitaries, like himself, had come to town by the newly completed Concord and Fitchburg Railway. Rantoul told the assembled crowd what they surely expected and probably wished to hear: "the site of the old North Bridge at Concord is the pivot on which the history of the world turns."[27] On April 19, 1775, in Concord

---

25. Nathaniel Hawthorne, "The Old Manse," in *Mosses from an Old Manse*, Vol. X of *The Centenary Edition of the Works of Nathaniel Hawthorne*, eds W. Charvat, R.H. Pearce, C.M. Simpson and J.D. Crowley (Columbus: Ohio State University Press, 1974), 10.

26. Donald A. and Lucy B. Ringe, eds, Textual Commentary, *Lionel Lincoln*, 391.

27. Robert Rantoul, "An Oration Delivered at Concord on the Celebration of the Seventy-Fifth Anniversary of the Events of April 19, 1775" (Boston: Dutton & Wentworth, 1850), 46.

Massachusetts, the entire western world rejoiced in the arrival of the deity who would forever end monarchy and inaugurate the *Novus Ordo Saeclorum*:

> The fair enchantress Liberty has waved her potent wand; prosperity and happiness crown all the hills, and cover the plains; on every waterfall, a city rises like an exhalation; the iron horse, the missionary which science despatches to lead the van of advancing refinement, snorts over prairies scarcely abandoned by the disappearing buffalo.[28]

Once the light of Liberty dawned in Concord, Franklinian reason, technological power and the people's independent spirit all coalesced into one glorious, indomitable force that is evidently shaping our prosperous yet refined nation. The history made by revolution, Rantoul blithely declares, has just gone on brightening ever since: "It was the electricity developed in our revolutionary atmosphere that burst, in thunder, on slumbering France. Awakening France awoke the world."[29]

Throughout the long literary history of Lexington Green and Concord Fight, the accounts most influential in America were also the ones most imbued with regional and national self-congratulation. Many more patriots and their children read Church's broadside, heard Rantoul's oration, and recited "Paul Revere's Ride," than reflected upon available texts with a different perspective. Surely the undeniable fictional flaws in *Lionel Lincoln* in no way explain why Cooper's novel retained its public far longer in Europe than in America. During the year Robert Rantoul eulogized the inauguration of Liberty's reign, the Compromise of 1850 was passed. During the year Longfellow published "Paul Revere's Ride" (1860), the United States of America dissolved in civil war. Blessedly few poets and orators, however, have ever tried to glorify the "rocket's red glare" that burst over Fort Sumter. Perhaps if post-Revolutionary generations had attended more closely to Fenimore Cooper's spirit of mourning a victory, and less to Samuel Adams's proclaiming of America's glorious morning, the national night might have been neither quite so long nor quite so brutal.

---

28. Rantoul, 68-69.

29. Rantoul, 70.

MODE AND MEANING IN *THE LAST OF THE MOHICANS*

DONALD A. RINGE

There can be no need at this late date to defend the literary value of *The Last of the Mohicans*. The time is long past when even so knowledgeable a critic as James Grossman could dismiss the book as an almost pure tale of adventure "in which in an arbitrarily simplified world everything happens for the sake of the excitement of the action."[1] Many readers have, no doubt, read the book on only this level, for *The Last of the Mohicans* is without question a thrilling frontier narrative. But beginning with the Afterword by James Franklin Beard to a 1962 edition of the novel, where he sees *The Last of the Mohicans* as raising "the question of the efficacy of human effort to control irrational forces at work in individual men, races, and nations,"[2] critics have shown that the book contains much of literary interest, and they have analyzed in detail its structure and meaning. Their sophisticated studies have placed it in a variety of contexts: historical, mythic, literary, and even social;[3] and we have come to recognize that, as Beard suggests, the novel "can be read with pleasure

---

1. James Grossman, *James Fenimore Cooper* (New York: Sloan, 1949), 43.

2. James Franklin Beard, ed., Afterword, *The Last of the Mohicans*, by James Fenimore Cooper (1826; rpt. New York: New American Library, 1962), 426.

3. See, for example, Thomas Philbrick, "*The Last of the Mohicans* and the Sounds of Discord," *American Literature* 43 (1971), 25-41; Michael D. Butler, "Narrative Structure and Historical Process in *The Last of the Mohicans*," *American Literature* 48 (1976), 117-39; H. Daniel Peck, *A World by Itself: The Pastoral Moment in Cooper's Fiction* (New Haven: Yale University Press, 1977), 109-45; William P. Kelly, *Plotting America's Past: Fenimore Cooper and the Leatherstocking Tales* (Carbondale: Southern Illinois University Press, 1983), 45-84; Jane Tompkins, *Sensational Designs: The Cultural Work of American Fiction, 1790-1860* (New York: Oxford University Press, 1985), 94-119; John P. McWilliams, "Red Satan: Cooper and the American Indian Epic," *James Fenimore Cooper: New Critical Essays*, ed. Robert Clark (Totowa, NJ: Barnes and Noble, 1985), 143-61.

on many levels."[4] It is both adventure story and profound commentary on the American experience.

What is missing in these commentaries, however, is any extended treatment of Cooper's style. By focusing on thematic concerns, the critics have paid relatively little attention to Cooper's modes of expression. As a result, Yvor Winters' condemnation of the novel for its stylistic excesses has gone largely unanswered.[5] Cooper's language, it must be admitted, is at times rather extreme. Some of his descriptions are lurid, and the chivalric language employed by Duncan Heyward and others is on occasion heightened almost to the absurd. But instead of condemning such expressions, one might better assume that Cooper knew what he was about in writing them and seek the reasons for their inclusion. Such passages, we should recognize, are appropriate to the Gothic and mock heroic modes, both of which Cooper consciously uses — and sometimes even exaggerates — to develop his themes. The dominant mode is of course, the Gothic — so much so that *The Last of the Mohicans* can be read as a Gothic novel — and it appears first in the book.[6] But the mock heroic also has a major role to play in its development, as do the comic, the authentically heroic, and the elegiac. All contribute to the meaning that Cooper wanted to express.

Cooper introduces the Gothic as soon as the white characters become aware of their precarious situation and begin to experience fear. Charged with the duty of escorting Alice and Cora Munro to Fort William Henry, Major Duncan Heyward foolishly trusts Magua, who bears a grudge against their father, Colonel Munro, to guide them by an out-of-the-way trail. Heyward's suspicions are aroused when they travel all day and do not reach their destination, and his fears are confirmed when he encounters Hawkeye and his Mohican companions, Chingachgook and Uncas, who recognize Magua as an enemy. They convince Heyward that Magua is playing him false, and the Huron flees when the young man tries to secure him. The foresters pursue him, Hawkeye fires, but he escapes. Night is falling fast, and since the party cannot travel in the dark through woods that are filled with hostile

---

4. Afterword to *The Last of the Mohicans*, 427.

5. Yvor Winters, *Maule's Curse: Seven Studies in the History of American Obscurantism* (Norfolk, CT: New Directions, 1938), 36, 42, 44.

6. Although a number of critics have noted Gothic elements in the novel, the fullest discussion of the subject is by Donald A. Ringe, "*The Last of the Mohicans* as a Gothic Novel," *James Fenimore Cooper: His Country and His Art* 6 (1987), 41-53.

Indians, they must, instead, change their position quickly and, as Hawkeye puts it, "in such a fashion, too, as will throw the cunning of a Mingo on a wrong scent, or our scalps will be drying in the wind in front of Montcalm's marquee, ag'in this hour to-morrow."[7]

Struck by "this appalling declaration" and anxious for the safety of his charges, Heyward begins to misperceive the reality that surrounds him. His situation is entirely new, and he does not know how to cope with it. For the first time he becomes aware that matters are beyond his control. The gloom of night is settling among the trees, shadows that his vision cannot penetrate, and he fears that, "cut off from human aid," the girls will "soon lie at the entire mercy of those barbarous enemies, who, like beasts of prey, only waited till the gathering darkness might render their blows more fatally certain" (45). Heyward's imagination is aroused, and "deluded by the deceptive light," he converts "each waving bush, or the fragment of some fallen tree, into human forms, and twenty times he [fancies that he can] distinguish the horrid visages of his lurking foes, peering from their hiding places, in never-ceasing watchfulness of the movements of his party." Heyward succumbs to Gothic insecurity and fear, a psychological state that will not be relieved until he reaches the fort and believes — mistakenly — that he and the girls are once again in safety.

The rest of his party too feel "secret terror" when he informs them of their situation, and the emotion is intensified when Uncas and Chingachgook kill David Gamut's foal, for this act of apparent, but necessary cruelty "fell upon the spirits of the travellers, like a terrific warning of the peril in which they stood, heightened, as it was, by the calm though steady resolution of the actors in the scene" (47). When the characters approach Glens Falls to secrete themselves for the night in its caves, the ominous landscape adds to the Gothic mood: "All beneath the fantastic limbs and ragged tree-tops, which were, here and there, dimly painted against the starry zenith, lay alike in shadowed obscurity" (48). Nearing the falls, they become enclosed by the "dark and wooded" banks, while before them "the water seemed piled against the heavens, whence it tumbled into caverns, out of which issued those sullen sounds, that had loaded the evening atmosphere." Though Alice and Cora at first imbibe "a soothing impression of security as they

7. *The Last of the Mohicans: A Narrative of 1757* (1826), eds James A. Sappenfield and E.N. Feltskog (Albany: State University of New York Press, 1983), 45. All further references to this edition will be cited parenthetically within the text.

[gaze on the] romantic, though not unappalling beauties" of the secluded spot, they are soon recalled "to a painful sense of their real peril" (49).

The caves in which the characters take refuge are, of course, the wilderness counterparts of the castles, rooms, and subterranean labyrinths familiar from Gothic fiction, and they are lighted in the usual fashion. The dark chambers are illumined only by the fitful glare of torches which transform even the familiar into the strange. Hawkeye himself takes on the appearance "of romantic wildness" as he sits in the cave "holding a blazing knot of pine" (52). Small wonder then that under the influence of the dark enclosures and the flickering light, the whites become the victims of their own misperceptions of sight and sound. Alice shrieks and Cora is startled when "a spectral looking figure [stalks] from out the darkness ... and seizing a blazing brand, [holds] it towards the further extremity of their place of retreat" (54). Though it is only Chingachgook painted for war, his presence adds to the Gothic tone of the scene, even after he is recognized as their friend. When he sits "within the circle of light" of the fire, they cast "frequent, uneasy glances" at his countenance in an attempt "to separate the natural expression of his face, from the artificial terrors of his war-paint" (56).

Shortly thereafter the entire party encounters a terrifying phenomenon that fills them with insecurity and fear. They hear a frightful cry that appears to be "neither human, nor earthly" (59). It penetrates "not only the recesses of the cavern, but to the inmost hearts of all who [hear] it." Neither Hawkeye nor the Mohicans, who have spent years in the wilderness and are familiar with its manifold sounds, can identify the cry, but they are certain that it is not a sound made by their enemies to intimidate them. When they hear it a second time, even the firmness of Hawkeye begins "to give way, before a mystery that seemed to threaten some danger, against which all his cunning and experience might prove of no avail" (61). Because the cry is a phenomenon that he does not understand, he believes it comes from a supernatural source, and he leaves the cave to go out into the open. He would consider himself "wicked unto rebellion against [God's] will" should he remain under cover "with such warnings in the air" (62). Hawkeye is prepared for battle with the Hurons, but he has "heard that when such shrieks are atween heaven and 'arth, it betokens another sort of warfare."

The episode is especially important because it shows that even Hawkeye, experienced as he is in the wilderness, can succumb to Gothic fear when he encounters a phenomenon which neither he nor the

Mohicans can explain. The other characters are equally at a loss and, on following him from the cave, cast "anxious and eager looks" at "the opposite shores" searching for "signs of life, that might explain" the strange occurrence, but they are "baffled by the deceptive light" and see only the "naked rocks, and straight and immovable trees" (63). When they hear the cry a third time, rising as it seems "from the bed of the river" and "undulating through the forest, in distant and dying cadences," Hawkeye remains convinced that it does "not belong to 'arth." Heyward, however, can now identify it. The sound deceived him when they were confined in the caverns, "but in the open air [he knows] it too well to be wrong." The cry is "the horrid shriek that a horse will give in his agony; oftener drawn from him in pain, though sometimes in terror." His steed, he believes, "is either a prey to the beasts of the forest, or he sees his danger without the power to avoid it."

The "momentary weakness" of Hawkeye disappears "with the explanation of a mystery, which his own experience had not served to fathom" (64), and he immediately regains his equilibrium. Though he knows the situation is perilous, he is prepared to act "with the energy of his hardy nature." His apprehension vanishes, never to return in the ensuing action, no matter how dangerous the situation may become. Not so with Heyward and his companions, who remain the victims of Gothic terror. Unaccustomed to frontier warfare, Alice shrieks and Cora starts upright "in bewildered horror" when the Hurons attack with "a tumult of yells and cries," and Heyward feels as if "the swift currents of his own blood" have been driven back "into the fountains of his heart" (66). He thinks only of flight and listens "with intense anxiety" for Hawkeye to bring the canoe. When he looks at the river and sees only the empty waters, he fancies that he and the girls have been "cruelly deserted by the scout." The flash of Hawkeye's rifle and the shriek of a dying Huron, however, soon reassure him, and during the battle he acquits himself well. But when it is over, he can scarcely accept the events as having really happened (81).

Duncan and the sisters continue to experience Gothic fear, when, rescued by Hawkeye and his companions from the Hurons, who had taken them prisoner at Glens, they take shelter in a ruined blockhouse. Hawkeye tells them of a battle he once fought there and informs them that the dead lie buried under the hillock on which they are sitting. All three instantly rise "from the grassy sepulchre," and the girls cannot "entirely suppress an emotion of natural horror" (126). The Gothic fear is intensified later that night when a group of Hurons approaches the spot while those within watch in silence. "In such a moment of painful suspense," Heyward can only grasp "his rifle more firmly, and [fasten] his eyes upon the narrow opening, through which he [gazes] upon the moonlight view with increasing anxiety" (131). Two of the Indians approach even nearer but soon discover the mound under which the fallen warriors lie buried. They speak in low tones "as if influenced by a reverence that was deeply blended with awe" (132), and as they draw "warily back," they keep "their eyes riveted on the ruin, as if they expected to see the apparitions of the dead issue from its silent walls." The whole Huron party then quietly retires from the spot.

In the midst of this Gothic scene, Cooper introduces briefly a second mode of expression that will become dominant when the characters reach the fort. Through it he presents an aspect of Heyward's character which causes him to misinterpret his true situation in the wilderness. The victim of Gothic fear at both Glens Falls and the blockhouse, Heyward exudes self-confidence in his own milieu and is proud of his position as major in the Royal Americans. This attitude first leads him astray when he trusts in the good faith of Magua, and it makes him treat David Gamut with great haughtiness when the singing master wants to join his party. Assuming that Gamut is a military instructor, he interrogates him rather pompously as to his area of competence (24). Heyward is also inclined to interpret his wilderness experience in conventional military terms, describing the cave at Glens, for example, as a "fortress" (60) that is "fortified, garrisoned, and provisioned" (50). Though certainly a competent soldier in eighteenth-century warfare involving European armies, he possesses a bent of mind and a system of values that are irrelevant to the situation in which he is placed.

These qualities are revealed when the characters settle down to catch some rest in the blockhouse, and the major, who has already once fallen asleep at the falls when he sought to be vigilant (65), volunteers to remain on guard while the others sleep. Hawkeye tries to dissuade him, pointing out that no matter how trustworthy he might be in a military camp, only an Indian can maintain a proper watch in the wilderness. He urges Heyward, therefore, to sleep while Chingachgook stands guard. Hawkeye believes at last that he has prevailed and is soon asleep. But Heyward is obdurate, and although he pretends to comply with Hawkeye's advice, he posts "his back against the logs of the block-house, in a half-recumbent posture" and resolutely determines, "in his own mind, not to close an eye" until he delivers Alice Munro to her father (129). For a while he succeeds. He remains alert for many minutes, "alive to every moaning sound that [rises] from the forest. His vision [becomes] more acute, as the shades of evening [settle] on the place," and he can make out the forms of his sleeping companions and the watching Chingachgook, upright and motionless as the surrounding trees.

But Heyward cannot long remain awake. As he slowly nods off, Cooper describes the process as the young man experiences it, his drowsiness gradually overcoming his attempts to stay alert: "the mournful notes of the whip-poor-will, became blended with the moanings of an owl; his heavy eyes occasionally sought the bright rays of the stars, and then he fancied he saw them through the fallen lids. At instants of momentary wakefulness, he mistook a bush for his associate sentinel; his head next sunk upon his shoulder, which, in its turn, sought the support of the ground; and, finally, his whole person became relaxed and pliant, and the young man sunk into a deep sleep" (129). At this point, Cooper introduces the new mode he intends to develop. Heyward dreams that he is "a knight of ancient chivalry, holding his midnight vigils before the tent of a re-captured princess, whose favour he did not despair of gaining, by such a proof of devotion and watchfulness." Through this means, Cooper mocks the heroic fantasies that arise in Heyward's mind while he sleeps in the wilderness, fantasies by which he will live when they reach the fort.

Heyward is embarrassed when, on being awakened by Chingachgook, he realizes what he has done, and his shame is made all the more intense by Alice's praise of him for having watched the night in their behalf and by her refusal to accept his confession of weakness. Because Cooper makes clear at this point the hollowness of Heyward's pretensions to heroism, the reader is alert to the significance of the language of chivalry when he introduces it a second time. Once the party arrives at Fort William Henry, Heyward leaves the girls to be taken in by their father while he joins his troops in repulsing the French, and for several days he is absent from them while he performs his military duties. When he does encounter them, Cooper strikes again the mock-heroic note. Alice greets Heyward in the language of his dream: "Ah! thou truant! thou recreant knight! he who abandons his damsels in the very lists! ... here we have been days, nay, ages, expecting you at our feet, imploring mercy and forgetfulness at your craven backsliding, or, I should say, back-running — for verily you fled in a manner that no stricken deer, as our worthy friend the scout would say, could equal!" (149).

Alice surely intends this only as banter, but the archaic language and the attitude it signifies, recalling, as they do, the earlier passage, establish the mode for the next two chapters. Cooper's language does not, of course, continue in so extravagant a vein. He uses a diction more appropriate to the highly cultivated eighteenth-century world of the French and British officers, but the attitude of mind that the language reflects is the same. The Gothic wilderness recedes, and in its place the landscape, under the influence of a truce, takes on a tone of almost pastoral calm as the French soldiers fish in the lake or sport on the mountainside (147-48), activities that belie the true situation of enemy forces confronting each other deep in the wilderness and ready for mortal combat. The Mohican warriors disappear from the action, Hawkeye is present only briefly as a captive of the French, and the Hurons are merely observers who ominously watch the white men's activities from the surrounding forest. Within the fort Munro and Heyward are preoccupied with military etiquette and a code of social behavior that are as irrelevant to their situation as are the major's chivalric fantasies.

A proud Scotsman, Munro is so concerned with the trappings of chivalry that he repeatedly questions the claims of Montcalm to gentility. His title, Munro believes, must be of too recent a date to deserve respect. "I would venture, if the truth was known," he remarks to Heyward at one point, "the fellow's grandfather taught the noble science of dancing!" (151), and in language that echoes that of Heyward's dream, he later adds: "A pretty degree of knighthood, sir, is that which can be bought with sugar-hogsheads! and then your two-penny marquessates! The Thistle is the order for dignity and antiquity; the veritable 'nemo me impune lacessit' of chivalry!" (157). Indeed, when Montcalm pledges his word for the safety of Heyward and Munro while they meet under a flag of truce, the colonel is distrustful, for, in his view, the French "patents of nobility are too common, to be certain that they bear the seal of true honour" (163). Through speeches like these, Cooper reveals the absurd attitude of Munro, who asserts his superiority to Montcalm at the very time that the French marquis has invested the fort and is on the point of compelling its surrender.

Even as they negotiate during the truce, both the French and the British are greatly concerned that the proper ceremonies be maintained and the forms of courtesy strictly adhered to. When Montcalm invites Munro to meet him between the lines, the colonel declines lest he appear "to show ... undue solicitude" (152). But because he does not wish to be "outdone in civility" by the Frenchman, he sends Heyward, "an officer of rank," in his stead. Since the major, however, is only "the representative of the commandant of the fort, the ceremonies which should have accompanied a meeting between the heads of the adverse forces, were of course dispensed with." When Heyward and Montcalm meet, they converse in French, and although they engage in a duel of words, both are careful to maintain the appropriate forms. Indeed, their language becomes so elevated as to approach the absurd (154). Heyward is so pleased with a compliment he receives from the French commander that he bows low in acknowledgment of it, and he returns to the fort "favourably impressed with an opinion of the courtesy and talents of the enemy's captain" (155). It is as if they were performing an elaborate minuet.

Once it becomes apparent that the fort cannot be held, the main concern of the British is with their honor. When Munro meets with Montcalm he learns that the French have intercepted a letter from General Webb at Fort Edward informing the colonel that he is not coming to his relief. Faced with the bitterness of this betrayal, Munro thinks only that it "has brought dishonour to the door of one, where disgrace was never before known to dwell" (164). Heyward rashly exclaims that since they yet retain the fort and their honor, they should return to it and die in its defense, and Munro agrees with him. Montcalm, however, will not permit so absurd an act. Although he must seize and destroy the fort, he does not intend to dishonor his enemies. For them, "there is no privilege dear to a soldier that shall be denied" (165). Heyward is quick to enumerate those things which he values: their colors and arms, which Montcalm permits them to keep, and the ceremony of the surrender, which Montcalm assures them shall "be done in a way most honourable to yourselves." Because of these concessions, Munro and Heyward believe that their honor has been preserved (166).

The folly of their attitude is shown by what ensues, for in placing their trust in the forms of the chivalric code, they fail to recognize the threat they face in the wilderness. They act from a false sense of security. The surrender does indeed take place "under all the observances of military etiquette" (171), and Munro is so filled with pride in his profession that he abandons his daughters to be with his troops. When Heyward learns of this, he goes at once to the girls and is quick to reassure them that though the fort be lost, Munro's "good name" has not been tarnished by the surrender (172). His pride too makes him believe that he must join his unit, and the only provision he makes for Cora and Alice is to leave them in the care of David Gamut, whose duty, Heyward tells him, is to protect them from any "insult or taunt at the misfortune of their brave father" (173). Should any Indian or straggler intrude, he goes on to say, "you will remind them of the terms of the capitulation, and threaten to report their conduct to Montcalm. A word will suffice." Heyward is still living the chivalric fantasies that were revealed in his dream.

The massacre that ensues should enlighten Heyward to the absurdity of these instructions, especially since Montcalm, a man of "generous sentiments, high courtesy, and chivalrous courage" (180), does nothing to stop it. Colonel Munro is crushed by the event and sinks into an apathy that eventually destroys him. But Heyward, who, leading the van of the withdrawing British, seems not to have seen the massacre (174), learns less than he should have from the experience. Three days later when he, Munro, and Hawkeye's party return to the scene, he still places his trust in the white man's code of values. Uncas kills an Oneida Indian who tries to shoot Chingachgook, for the Oneidas, though they also serve the British, are enemies of the Mohicans. When Hawkeye claims that he would have done the same, Heyward is concerned that he would have broken a treaty (196), and he even believes that "the authority of Colonel Munro" would protect them should any of the slain man's tribe seek revenge (202). Indeed, Heyward is still enamored of false heroics, for he wants to remain upright, as an officer of rank should, and not lie down in the canoe when they come under attack on the lake.

But these are the last times that Cooper mocks the absurd attitudes and behavior of the British officer. Immediately after the massacre, Cooper turns again to the Gothic mode in the desolate landscape he draws around "the ruins of William Henry" (190), in the sharp contrasts of light and shade, and in the ominous sounds that come from the encircling blackness. "The shades of evening had come" when Heyward and the others arrive at the fort. "Within the bosom of the encircling hills, an impenetrable darkness had already settled, and the plain lay like a vast and deserted charnel-house, without omen or whisper, to disturb the slumbers of its numerous and hapless tenants." Though the wind has fallen, black masses of clouds have gathered at "the horizon, while the lighter scud still hurried above the water, or eddied among the tops of the mountains, like broken flights of birds, hovering around their roosts." Only fitful rays of light illumine the ominous scene. "Here and there, a red and fiery star struggled through the drifting vapour, furnishing a lurid gleam of brightness to the dull aspect of the heavens." The glimmering campfire of the little party completes the Gothic scene.

The function of the mode in this passage is precisely the same as it was in the first half of the book: to reveal the uncertainty and insecurity of the uninitiated. Here, however, it is only Heyward who experiences it. He stands "for many minutes, a rapt observer" of his surroundings (191). His eyes rest "long and anxiously on the embodied gloom, which lay like a dreary void on that side of him where the dead reposed." Before long, he fancies that he hears "inexplicable sounds [rising] from the place, though so indistinct and stolen, as to render not only their nature, but even their existence, uncertain." Heyward is ashamed of his apprehensions and tries to focus his attention on other things, but he continues to hear the sounds and to fear a lurking danger. "At length, a swift trampling seemed, quite audibly, to rush athwart the darkness." Heyward can no longer "quiet his uneasiness" and calls Hawkeye to the spot. The scout seems unconcerned with what to the young soldier is a source of great disquiet, for, as Hawkeye soon reveals, it is only wolves, emboldened by hunger, that have approached the ruined fort to feast on the dead (192).

But if Heyward imagines danger where none exists, he is also unable to perceive it when it is present. Hawkeye hears another sound that focuses his attention, and by secret signs — the hoot of an owl and the hiss of a snake — summons Uncas and warns both him and Chingachgook of impending danger. Uncas disappears before Heyward is aware he is gone, and the young officer remains "a deeply interested and wondering observer. It appeared to him as though the foresters had some secret means of intelligence, which had escaped the vigilance of his own faculties" (195). Heyward can only look on in "admiration and wonder" (194) as a rifle shot strikes the fire near Chingachgook and fills the air with sparks while the Mohican chief vanishes. A rustle is heard in the bushes as the wolves scamper away. Then the plunge of a body into the lake and a second rifle shot ends the incident. All of these events are inexplicable to the young officer until Uncas explains that he has killed and scalped a single enemy. Heyward is unable to read correctly the reality that confronts him and so becomes the victim of Gothic insecurity and fear.

In the ensuing action, Heyward's misperceptions continue to cause him problems. As the party approaches the Huron encampment, Heyward is briefly left alone at the edge of the forest while his companions reconnoiter. Once again his senses deceive him. He mistakes a colony of beavers for the Indian village and is alarmed to see what he takes to be Hurons advancing toward him on all fours. He even mistakes the captive David Gamut, who is nearby, for a hostile warrior until Hawkeye comes up to undeceive him. When Heyward does at last approach the Huron camp, he again misreads what is before him. In "the doubtful twilight" (230), he beholds a group of forms rising from the tall grass and sinking again below it. "By the sudden and hasty glimpses that he caught of these figures, they seemed more like dark glancing spectres, or some other unearthly beings, than creatures fashioned with the ordinary and vulgar materials of flesh and blood. A gaunt, naked form, was seen, for a single instant, tossing its arms wildly in the air, and then the spot it had filled was vacant; the figure appearing, suddenly, in some other and distant place, or being succeeded by another, possessing the same mysterious character" (231).

This time it is Gamut who can explain the phenomenon. Because as a prisioner of the Hurons he has been living in their camp, he knows that the forms are only Indian boys engaging in idle antics. Informed of the truth, the embarrassed Heyward suffers "his lip to curl, as in mockery of his own superstition" (231). Both here and at the beaver pond, Cooper adds an element of comedy to his rendering of the Gothic scene, for the reader can only smile at Heyward's ludicrous misperceptions that convert beavers into men and Indian boys into specters. Comedy has, of course, been present in the book since the entrance of David Gamut, the ungainly Connecticut Yankee who is blood brother to Washington Irving's Ichabod Crane. His role is apparent from the initial description of disproportioned body and odd attire (16-17), and is reinforced by his appearance as he rides his mare through the woods to catch up with Heyward's party, his tall form rising and falling in the saddle with the motions of his horse (22-23). He even supplies a grotesquely comic element during the massacre when he raises his voice in a psalm to test "the potency of music" in taming the passions of the savage warriors (177).

In the later episodes of the book, however, the comedy is centered on Heyward and Hawkeye as well. When Heyward determines to attempt the rescue of Alice from the Huron encampment, Hawkeye and Chingachgook transform him into "a natural fool" with the Indian's paints (228). Chingackgook gives him a look that suggests "a friendly and jocular disposition" (229); he sacrifices "every appearance of the warrior, to the masquerade of a buffoon." With his knowledge of French, Heyward intends to "pass for a juggler from Ticonderoga." He enters the Indian village at nightfall, and although the scene, with its lurid fires fitfully illumining the darkness, has all the elements of the

Gothic,[8] it is the comic that Cooper eventually brings to the fore. Heyward pretends to be "a man that knows the art of healing," sent to "the red Hurons of the Great Lakes, to ask if any are sick" (235). An Indian woman is indeed ill, and Heyward is taken to a cave where she lies dying to attempt to cure her. At this point Cooper introduces a series of comic episodes centered on Hawkeye, who has also entered the camp and is disguised in an Indian conjurer's bearskin.

At first neither Heyward nor the reader realizes the truth. When the young man approaches the cave with his Indian guide, he takes the bear to be real and tries to avoid it. The animal, however, follows him, growls "at his heels, and once or twice [lays] its enormous paws ... on his person" (253). Heyward is understandably unnerved by the animal, which follows him into the chamber where David Gamut is already attending the dying Indian. As the singing master finishes a hymn, he is startled to hear "the dying cadence of his strains ... repeated behind him, in a voice half human and half sepulchral. Looking around, he [beholds] the shaggy monster seated on end, in the shadow of the cavern, where, while his restless body swung in the uneasy manner of the animal, it repeated, in a sort of low growl, sounds, if not words, which bore some slight resemblance to the melody of the singer" (253-54). The scene presents, in Cooper's words, "a strange blending of the ridiculous, with [the] solemn" (255). David, struck with wonder, hurries from the cave, the Indian leaves Heyward to work his magic, and when they are alone, Hawkeye removes the bear's head while his whole body shakes with laughter.

Heyward's fear is dispelled by the comic situation, which, in itself, reveals the security Hawkeye feels in the middle of the enemy's camp. He is in control. He not only defeats and ties up Magua when the Huron comes upon them, but also rescues Alice and Uncas, both of whom are being held prisoner. The scenes are highly comic. Heyward retrieves Alice from another part of the cavern, and to get her out of the village, he wraps her in Indian clothes. Accompanied by Hawkeye, who once more masquerades as the bear, he carries her past the Indians waiting outside the cavern. He tells them that "the disease has gone out of her; it is shut up in the rocks. I take the woman to a distance, where I will strengthen her against any further attacks" (263). When the girl's father would go into the cave to fight the spirit, Heyward warns him not to, lest the spirit enter him or return to his daughter. He instructs the

8. For a discussion of the Gothic in this section of the novel, see Ringe, 49-50.

Hurons to "wait without, and if the spirit appears, beat him down with clubs" (264). As the Indians draw around the entrance, poised to do battle with the imaginary spirit, Heyward and Hawkeye bear Alice away.

The picture of the Hurons waiting with poised tomahawks outside the cave is certainly comic, but it is nothing compared to the rescue of Uncas. Hawkeye returns to the village, locates David Gamut, and uses him for another subterfuge. Since Gamut is believed by the Hurons to be insane, he has the run of the camp, and he visits the tent where Uncas is held prisoner, accompanied by Hawkeye, still in the bearskin of the Indian conjurer. Once inside, Uncas puts on the bearskin while Hawkeye and Gamut exchange clothes. Gamut bravely takes Uncas's place in the lodge, while Hawkeye, wearing Gamut's glasses and carrying his book and pitch pipe, walks with Uncas out into the camp. Hawkeye draws "up his tall form in the rigid manner of David, [throws] out his arm in the act of keeping time, and [commences] what he [intends to be] an imitation of his psalmody" (274). The two proceed through the Huron camp in this ludicrous fashion and escape to the woods. When the Hurons discover the deception, Gamut is in real danger, but thinking his death is imminent, he too breaks into song, and the Hurons, reminded of his presumed mental infirmity, do not harm him.

By this point in the action the comic mode has served its purpose in dispelling the Gothic fear that has dominated so much of the book. It has reduced the Huron warriors, who were the source of that fear, from a frightening threat to the comic butt of Hawkeye's deceptions. The scout is in complete control, and under his tutelage, Heyward, whose false heroics have been consistently mocked, learns to use subterfuge to attain his goal of retrieving Alice from the camp of their enemies. The way is opened, therefore, for the authentically heroic to be celebrated in the person of Uncas. The young Mohican has from the beginning been presented as one who has mastered the wilderness. He is the most capable of the three foresters, yet he remains humble in the presence of his elders, and he is truly chivalrous in his treatment of Cora and Alice. Now he comes to the center of the action. He asserts his proper authority in the Delaware camp, and he rigidly abides by Indian law in allowing Magua to depart with the captive Cora. He then incites the Delawares to war on the Hurons and leads them to an overwhelming victory.

The white characters, too, join in the struggle. Cured at last of his absurd heroics, Heyward assumes a modest role. Though offered the command of a Delaware war party, he declines, preferring instead "to serve as a volunteer by the side of the scout" (323). Uncas, Hawkeye, and Chingachgook are the appropriate leaders, and it is Hawkeye who lays out the plan of the attack. Colonel Munro awakens briefly from his lethargy to strike a blow for the rescue of his daughter, and even David Gamut joins in the action. Hawkeye doubts at first that he would be of any help since he knows "not the use of any we'pon" (327). But like his Biblical namesake, whom he has followed in singing psalms, he possesses a sling, an "ancient instrument of war" that he had practiced with in his youth, and he gathers his ammunition "from among the pebbles of the brook" (328). All the characters unite in a common purpose, and for one brief period they follow the noble Uncas into battle. The heroic mode, however, is not to last. Though the Delawares succeed in defeating the Hurons utterly, both Cora and Uncas are killed and the episode comes to a tragic end.

It is entirely appropriate that the heroic section should be so brief and come to a somber conclusion, for Cooper is not celebrating the birth of a culture, but its death. By 1757, the Delawares have already been driven from their ancestral lands. To be sure, the New York wilderness is only just being entered by the white men, but a process has begun that can end only with the destruction of the Indians. Indeed, the strife between Delaware and Huron both repeats the history of the red men and forecasts their future. While tribe fights tribe, the whites encroach on both and will eventually supplant them. Thus, Uncas's heroic moment must come to a quick end. There is no future for him as a Mohican warrior, nor can one conceive of a possible life that he and Cora might live. The long elegy that comprises the final chapter,[9] therefore, is intended not only for them. The death of Uncas foretells the fate of all the Indians. Though it is only 1757 and a continent remains to be crossed, the tribes are already doomed. Tamenund has the final word: "The pale-faces are masters of the earth, and the time of the red-men has not yet come again" (350).

The tone of this final chapter is vastly different from that of the rest of the book, yet it is a fitting conclusion to the modal development of the romance. The Gothic mode of the first half connotes the fear and anxiety of the white characters when they enter the forest and discover that their fates are beyond their control. The mock heroics of Heyward, especially during the interlude at the fort, reveal the absurdity of the

9. McWilliams sees this chapter as "clearly influenced by the twenty-fourth book of *The Iliad*," where similar lamentations are presented (156).

white man's code of behavior in the wilderness, and the return of the Gothic after the massacre shows once again his insecurity and fear, even as Hawkeye and the Mohicans demonstrate the skill with which they pursue their enemies. The grotesquely comic means used by Hawkeye once they are in the Huron camp reveal his mastery of the situation as he extricates Alice and Uncas. Even Heyward shares in the triumph, and with his newly discovered confidence, the Gothic fear vanishes. What remains is a kind of coda to the action: the brief heroic episode in which Uncas defeats his enemies but meets his death, and the long lament that follows, an elegy not only for him and Cora, but also for the Delawares, and by implication for all the Indian nations.

"IN THE LAND OF HIS FATHERS": COOPER, LAND RIGHTS, AND THE LEGITIMATION OF AMERICAN NATIONAL IDENTITY

SUSAN SCHECKEL

The Pioneers, as suggested by its subtitle, "Sources of the Susquehanna," is in many respects a book about origins. Most immediately, for Cooper it is an account of personal origins based upon the story of his father's founding of Cooperstown, where James Fenimore Cooper spent much of his childhood. More generally, it is a story about national origins, exploring the meaning of the Revolution through which America's national identity originated and describing the process of settlement by which the new nation took possession, from the Indians, of the vast territory it now claimed as its own.

In its examination of American origins, *The Pioneers* looks both forward and backward. One strain of the plot centers upon new beginnings — the building of a new settlement, the progress of a new nation, and the founding of a new line of Americans who will be the legitimate heirs of America's future — while another examines the new nation's relationship to its past. It is significant that the book's final scene occurs in a graveyard. Elizabeth Temple and Oliver Effingham, now married and firmly established as the progenitors of this new line of Americans, discover Natty, lying upon the ground above the graves of Chingachgook and Major Effingham, enacting a graphic display of mourning for these representatives of America's Indian and English past. This final scene encapsulates ideas developed throughout the rest of the book: the new order is built upon the graves of the old, and it is through mourning that the transition between past and future is stabilized and legitimized.

Benedict Anderson, in *Imagined Communities: Reflections on the Origin and Spread of Nationalism*, argues that nationalist imagining, like religious imagining (and like mourning, I would add), is concerned with death and immortality. It entails the attempt to establish a sense of continuity and meaning in the face of historical change: "If nation-states are widely conceded to be new and historical, the nations to which they give political expression always loom out of the immemorial past and, still more important, glide into a limitless future."[1] While Americans of the early nineteenth century, with their optimistic faith in progress, would have had little trouble imagining a "limitless future" for the nation, where were they to ground a sense of continuity with the "immemorial past"? They might have looked toward America's Indian past for a sense of "primitive" origins. But grounding America's national history in its Indian heritage was problematic given the violence and coercion that characterized the history of Indian-white relations. It would be difficult, without a deep sense of patricidal guilt, to claim as forebears those whom Americans were in the process of destroying. Similarly, America's relationship to its English heritage was complicated by the violence of the Revolution. Envisioning the English as historical forebears would again lead to a sense of patricidal guilt and national illegitimacy, for a patrimony (of nationhood) gained through violence against the fathers can not be considered legitimate. While Americans could locate an historical moment of origination in the age of the Revolution and define themselves as the heirs of the founding fathers, this still left them without that sense of connection to the "immemorial past" which Anderson sees as so crucial to national identity. In fact, the Revolution, itself, defined as a quintessential act of discontinuity with the past, provided not a sense of historical continuity, but what many Americans feared would be a legacy of instability and discontinuity — the threat of repeated revolution.

Cooper was not the only American of his day who grappled with the difficulties of establishing a sense of national identity and legitimacy in the face of the nation's complex and conflicted relationship to its historical origins. In *The Pioneers*, this struggle is most clearly articulated in terms of the central question that runs throughout the book: Who has the right to own and govern the land originally possessed by Indians? In 1823, the year that *The Pioneers* was published, the Supreme Court addressed this same question in the case of *Johnson v. McIntosh*. In his attempt to write a legitimating narrative defining the basis of American claims to the land, Chief Justice Marshall confronted many of the same problems that Cooper dealt with in *The Pioneers*. In addressing these problems, both men turned to the past — Cooper constructing lines of loyalty and inheritance to legitimate

1. Benedict Anderson, *Imagined Communities: Reflections on the Origin and Spread of Nationalism* (London: Verso, 1983), 19.

the present by virtue of its ties to the past, Marshall seeking historical precedent to define and justify present rights. In both instances, legitimacy depended in part upon the kind of story told about the past. In my examination of *The Pioneers* and *Johnson v. McIntosh*, I do not suggest a direct relationship, in terms of influence, between these two texts. Rather, I attempt to illuminate, from two very different angles, a set of historically defined problems regarding American national identity and Indian policy, and to shed light upon the larger question of how "the stories a culture tells about itself" work to shape its sense of history and national identity.[2]

* * *

In the case of *Johnson v. McIntosh*, the Supreme Court debated "the power of Indians to give, and of private individuals to receive, a title which can be sustained in the Courts of this country."[3] In his landmark opinion, Chief Justice Marshall reviewed the history of Indian-white

---

2. Brook Thomas, *Cross-Examinations of Law and Literature: Cooper, Hawthorne, Stowe, and Melville* (Cambridge: Cambridge University Press, 1987), 5. Critics such as Brook Thomas and Charles H. Adams (*The Guardian of the Law: Authority and Identity in James Fenimore Cooper* [University Park: Pennsylvania State University Press, 1990]) have recently examined the meaning of the law in Cooper's work. Through their readings of Cooper, these critics explore the condition of and attitudes toward law in nineteenth-century America. While I am not concerned primarily with the meaning of the law, like Thomas I see literature and law sharing certain basic concerns and strategies: both respond to the historical situation and seek ways to resolve social contradictions through a process of narration; both reflect "the stories a culture tells about itself."

Informing their work, and my own is a long critical tradition of viewing Cooper's work as it reflects or engages contemporary political and social issues. See, for example, Robert E. Spiller, *Fenimore Cooper: Critic of His Times* (New York: Minton, Balch, & Co., 1931); John P. McWilliams, Jr., *Political Justice in a Republic: James Fenimore Cooper's America* (Berkeley: University of California Press, 1972); Wayne Franklin, *The New World of James Fenimore Cooper* (Chicago: University of Chicago Press, 1982); Philip Fisher, *Hard Facts: Setting and Form in the American Novel* (New York: Oxford University Press, 1985); and Mark R. Patterson, *Authority, Autonomy, and Representation in American Literature* (Princeton: Princeton University Press, 1988).

3. *Johnson and Graham's Lessee v. McIntosh*, [21 U.S. (8 Wheaton) 543 (1823)], rpt. in Wilcomb E. Washburn, *The American Indian and the United States: A Documentary History* (New York: Random House, 1973), IV, 2537. Future references to Washburn's book will be cited parenthetically within the text (*AIUS*).

relations in America and engaged in a broad examination of the status and rights of Indians in the United States. In the process, he implicitly helped to define the character of the new nation itself. To determine the nature and extent of Native American rights, the Court found it necessary to enquire into the basis and legitimacy of Euro-American claims to the land. This enquiry reached far beyond the narrow limits of Indian-white relations, ultimately raising questions regarding the nature (and implications) of America's relationship to England and the extent to which Americans were upholding the ideals that had legitimated the break from England.

As the Court interpreted the history of Indian-white relations in America, it determined that Indian title could be extinguished only by the government of the nation claiming sovereignty over Indian lands. European claims to sovereignty rested upon the rights of conquest and the "Doctrine of Discovery."[4] By imagining direct ties of political kinship and inheritance between the United States and England, Marshall could claim that, with the Revolutionary War, the rights of Great Britain devolved upon the new nation: "The British government, which was then our government, and whose rights have passed to the United States, asserted a title to all the lands occupied by Indians, within the chartered limits of the British colonies" (*AIUS*, 2544). In this account of history, the new nation's right to the American land derived from European principles transmitted intact from "Old" world to "New," inherited from England by virtue of the Revolution.

It is not difficult to see how such a vision of history might complicate Americans' sense of national identity. Claiming that the United States inherited its rights from England (*AIUS*, 2543, 2545), often placed the new nation, defined politically by its separation from England, in a rather awkward position. For example, the Court found itself upholding as precedent British colonial policies, such as the Proclamation of 1763 (*AIUS*, 2548), which the Revolutionary generation had denounced — and which had, in fact, been cited as a just cause for rebellion. In addition, many elements of British Indian policy, which the United States now claimed as its own, seemed to contradict basic principles of "natural right" that lay at the heart of American

4. Marshall defines this "doctrine" as the principle "that discovery gave title to the government by whose subjects, or by whose authority, it was made, against all other European governments, which title might be consummated by possession" (*AIUS*, 2538).

democratic ideology.[5] Even as he delivered his opinion, Marshall betrayed discomfort with its moral and ideological implications:

> However extravagant the pretension of converting the discovery of an inhabited country into conquest may appear; if the principle has been asserted in the first instance, and afterward sustained; if a country has been acquired and held under it; if the property of the great mass of the community originates in it, it becomes the law of the land, and cannot be questioned. So, too, with respect to the concomitant principle, that the Indian inhabitants are to be considered merely as occupants, to be protected, indeed, while in peace, in the possession of their lands, but to be deemed incapable of transferring the absolute title to others. However this restriction may be opposed to natural right, and to the usages of civilized nations, yet, if it be indispensible to that system under which the country has been settled, and be adapted to the actual condition of the two people, it may, perhaps, be supported by reason, and certainly cannot be rejected by Courts of Justice. (*AIUS*, 2547)

Marshall seemed to admit here that the denial of Indians' full rights to the lands they possessed was a convenient fiction that could not be rejected by the Courts of a nation whose very existence and future expansion depended upon it. While he suggested that "it may, perhaps, be supported by reason," Marshall did not entirely succeed in justifying it.

In *The Pioneers*, James Fenimore Cooper also addressed the question of who legitimately may claim title to the American land. Like Marshall, Cooper attempted to construct a narrative that would legitimate Euro-American claims in the face of the challenge posed by prior Native American claims to the land. For Cooper, as for Marshall, the rights of the new nation did not originate with the Revolution but were transmitted from the past according to the principles of inheritance. But Cooper's fiction, while no less convenient than

---

5. Speculators who wished to acquire Indian lands unhindered by government regulation often justified their actions through an appeal to the Indians' natural rights, drawing specific parallels between these rights and the principles of natural right that informed Revolutionary rhetoric and documents such as the Declaration of Independence. For further discussion of the debate over natural right as it arose in relation to questions of land rights, see Robert A. Williams, Jr., "Jefferson, The Norman Yoke, and American Indian Lands," *Arizona Law Review* 29.2 (1987), 178-91.

Marshall's, achieved a stronger sense of moral resolution. In this essay, I will examine the strategies by which Cooper dealt with elements of conflict and contradiction (arising from America's history of conquest and revolution) that complicated the nation's sense of legitimacy. By constructing a model of kinship and inheritance that included the prior "owners" of the American land--both the Indians and the English — as ancestors willingly conveying their authority and property to their rightful American heirs, and by invoking an attitude of mourning to define America's relationship to these historical forebears, Cooper enacted, in *The Pioneers*, a symbolic affirmation of Americans' legitimate claim to the land and to the legacy of nationhood.

* * *

The first scene of conflict in *The Pioneers*, an argument over who may claim ownership of a recently killed buck, introduces many of the central issues Cooper will develop throughout the rest of the novel. The Judge, believing that his shot has killed the deer, good-naturedly argues his case in mock-legal terms: "I would fain establish a right, Natty, to the honor of this death; and surely if the hit in the neck be mine, it is enough; for the shot in the heart was unnecessary — what we call an act of supererogation, Leather-Stocking."[6] When Natty insists that the buck was actually killed by the shot of his young companion Oliver Edwards (later identified as Oliver Effingham), the Judge offers to purchase the buck, but the young man refuses to sell his property. In a later discussion of the incident, the Judge's cousin Richard links ownership of the buck to ownership of the land: "Well, 'duke, you are your own master, but I would have tried law for the saddle [of the deer], before I would have given it to the fellow. Do you not own the mountains, as well as the valleys? are not the woods your own? what right has this chap, or the Leather-stocking, to shoot in your woods, without your permission?" (93). Richard, continuing the debate with himself, expands the issue of ownership rights even further when he raises the question of Indian rights to the land: "There is Mohegan [Chingachgook], to-be-sure, he may have some right, being a native; but it's little the poor fellow can do now with his rifle." Thus, this brief, fairly light-hearted

6. *The Pioneers, or The Sources of the Susquehanna; A Descriptive Tale* (1823), eds James Franklin Beard *et al*. (Albany: State University of New York Press, 1980), 23. Further references to this edition will be cited parenthetically within the text.

controversy over the ownership of a buck anticipates what is to become the central source of conflict in *The Pioneers*: establishing who has the legitimate right to own and govern the land upon which Americans (here under the guidance of Judge Temple) are building new cities in the wilderness.

In this scene, Natty challenges the authority of the Judge (and the law he stands for) on the basis of his own version of "natural law." According to Charles H. Adams, the debate over the buck illustrates Natty's "persistent rejection of Temple's institutional and historical law in the name of a self-government on transcendental principles."[7] Many critics have seen the conflict between Natty and Judge Temple, interpreted variously as a conflict between natural and civil law or between individual freedom and the constraints of society, as one of the book's central concerns.[8] While I agree that this conflict is important in ways that I will discuss at greater length later, I wish to emphasize here that it is Oliver's challenge, based upon the rights of inheritance, rather than Natty's challenge, based upon natural law, to which Judge Temple responds and finally succumbs. The plot of *The Pioneers*, in fact, centers upon tracing Oliver's efforts to regain his lost inheritance — the land now claimed by Judge Temple. Justice, and resolution, are finally achieved in the novel not by the power of civil law nor by the moral authority of Natty's natural law, but by virtue of Judge Temple's personal loyalty to Oliver's father and his respect for the principles of inheritance.[9] By making loyalty and inheritance the determinants of

---

7. Adams, 55.

8. See, for instance, McWilliams, *Political Justice in a Republic*; Thomas, *Cross-Examinations of Law and Literature*; and Catherine H. Zuckert, *Natural Right and the American Imagination: Political Philosophy in Novel Form* (Savage, MD: Rowman and Littlefield, 1990).

9. For an alternative reading of the resolution that occurs when Judge Temple reads his will aloud in front of the cave, see Adams, 73-74. While he acknowledges that Temple acts because of private feeling rather than public law, Adams emphasizes that it is finally "a legal resolution" that the book achieves (73). Judge Temple's will, a legal document, returns legitimacy to the law. The "renewed legitimacy" of the law, Adams argues, "is synonymous with Edwards' rebirth from anonymity to authority" (74). Since Edwards serves as symbolic heir and father to the nation, the law becomes "'parent' to the nation."

My reading differs from Adams' in placing more stress upon motivation. The fact that the Judge writes the will and thus enacts justice in spite of the law, denying himself the rights (to the land) that the law sanctions — both Oliver and

who may own and govern the American land, Cooper links legitimacy to the assertion of continuity with the past. The unusual nature of Oliver's ties to the past adds force to this resolution.

The reader fully understands the basis of Oliver's claim only near the end of the novel, when it is revealed that Oliver is the grandson of Major Effingham, who is himself the adopted son of Chingachgook. The land upon which Templeton now stands was first given to Major Effingham by Chingachgook's tribe as a sign of friendship and gratitude after Major Effingham saved the chief's life. With the outbreak of the Revolutionary War, Oliver's father, a loyalist, left the family's property in the hands of his friend Marmaduke Temple. When loyalists' property was confiscated and sold after the war, Temple purchased the Effingham lands — an action that Oliver sees as a breach of loyalty and a violation of his hereditary claim to the land.

By playing upon Oliver's adopted relation to Chingachgook, Cooper finds a way to bring together in one family lineage America's Indian and English forebears — something not so easily accomplished outside the realm of fiction. In *Johnson v. McIntosh*, for example, Chief Justice Marshall, attempting to explain European (and American) denial of Indian property rights, bases his argument upon what he sees as the absolute impossibility of uniting Indians and whites as "one people":

> Although we do not mean to engage in a defense of those principles which Europeans have applied to Indian title, they may, we think, find some excuse, if not justification, in the character and habits of the people whose rights have been wrested from them.
>
> The title by conquest is acquired and maintained by force. The conqueror prescribes its limits. Humanity, however, acting on public opinion, has established, as a general rule, that the conquered shall not be wantonly oppressed, and that their condition shall remain as eligible as is compatible with the objects of the conquest. Most usually, they are incorporated with the victorious nation, and become subjects or citizens of the government with which they are connected. The new and old

---

Judge Temple specifically comment upon the fact that Temple's title to the land is perfectly legal — makes it difficult for me to see the will serving to legitimize the law. The Judge may be redeemed by the will, but the law is not. The stable principles that guide the Judge toward this act of justice — principles of loyalty and inheritance rather than legal principles — are the principles, I would argue, that Cooper valorizes as the basis of stability and legitimacy.

> members of the society mingle with each other; the distinction between them is gradually lost, and they make one people. Where this incorporation is practicable, humanity demands, and a wise policy requires, that the right of the conquered to property should remain unimpaired ....
>
> When the conquest is complete, and the conquered inhabitants can be blended with the conquerors, or safely governed as a distinct people, public opinion, which not even the conqueror can disregard, imposes these restraints upon him; and he cannot neglect them without injury to his fame, and hazard to his power.
>
> But the tribes of Indians inhabiting this country were fierce savages, whose occupation was war, and whose subsistence was drawn chiefly from the forest .... What was the inevitable consequence of this state of things? The Europeans were under the necessity either of abandoning the country, and relinquishing their pompous claims to it, or of enforcing those claims by the sword, and by the adoption of principles adapted to the condition of a people with whom it was impossible to mix .... (*AIUS*, 2546)

Unable to include Indians in the American "family" or to justify European or American policies toward them on the basis of "natural right," Marshall finds himself defending "conquest" and "force" as the principles upon which American claims to the land are ultimately founded. Marshall's references to "public opinion" and the demands of "humanity" reflect his discomfort with this position; the relationship he posits between "fame" and "power" indicates how important he considers public sentiment regarding the justice and morality of American Indian policy.

During the second quarter of the nineteenth century, bitter partisan power struggles, efforts of reformers, the drama and pathos of the Cherokees' struggle against removal all helped to focus public attention upon the political and legal battles through which American Indian policy was being defined.[10] As Michael Rogin writes of the Jacksonian

10. In pamphlets and periodicals, in the halls of Congress and courts of law, battles to sway public sentiment were waged. When the Cherokees tried to resist forced removal in the 1830s, they wrote appeals directly to the American people and went on extensive speaking tours through the East in an attempt to move public sentiment. During the year preceding the 1832 election, Anti-Jacksonites did everything in their power to inflame public sentiment against Jackson and his Indian policy. For an account of the 1831-1832 publicity campaign against Jackson,

period, "Indians had not mattered so much since the colonial settlements. They would never matter so much again."[11] Indians "mattered" during this period, I contend, not primarily as a physical or political threat to the American nation, but as a threat to Americans' sense of themselves as a moral and legitimate nation — a threat, in short, to American national identity. The most important battles with Indians were waged, during this era, in the realm of public policy rather than on the field of military action. In this "war," public sentiment became an important weapon that both sides fought to control.

In their attempts to write legitimating narratives defining the basis of Euro-American claims to the land once possessed by Native Americans, both Cooper and Marshall can be seen as participating in this ideological "war." Cooper, examining questions of Indian policy within the framework of fiction, is able to address the moral problem posed by Indians with greater freedom and flexibility than is possible for Marshall in his position as official apologist for American policies. For example, Cooper is able to include Indians, the British, and Americans in one "family" lineage because this kinship remains purely metaphoric.[12] Cooper does not directly defend the moral basis of

---

see Ronald Satz, *American Indian Policy in the Jacksonian Era* (Lincoln: University of Nebraska Press, 1975), notably 47-50.

11. Michael Paul Rogin, *Fathers and Children: Andrew Jackson and the Subjugation of the American Indian* (New York: Knopf, 1975), 4.

12. Elsewhere in the Leatherstocking series, Cooper makes his attitude toward the actual mixing of races clear. In *The Last of the Mohicans*, for example, Cooper raises the issue of miscegenation only to suppress it vehemently. Cora, with her fraction of black blood, is rejected as an unsuitable mate for Duncan Heyward. Cooper rejects the possibility of marriage between an Indian and a white woman even more forcefully. He seems able to imagine that only a "white" woman such as Cora, who is already racially impure, could be attracted to an Indian. Furthermore, he never explicitly refers to the possibility of a union between Cora and Uncas until after both characters have died, and then it is represented as a misguided notion of the Indians.

The characterization of Natty also reflects Cooper's desire to imagine Americans' metaphorical kinship with Indians at the same time that he denies the possibility of actual kinship through the mixing of Indian and white blood. While Natty embodies the best qualities of both cultures, he is "a man without a cross" who repeatedly insists upon the importance of maintaining the "natural" distinctions between red and white gifts and, even more importantly, between red and white blood. Similarly, political rhetoric of the day employed metaphors of kinship — describing Indians as "our red brothers" or "children of the Great Father" — at the

American actions and "rights." Throughout *The Pioneers*, in fact, Cooper gives voice to severe criticism of Judge Temple's claim to the land — criticism that would seem to apply to the claims of the American nation in general. By transforming the question of Indian rights to the land into a question of inheritance rights, however, Cooper diminishes and deflects the real significance of the Indians' dispossession while expanding the symbolic significance of Oliver's status as legitimate heir. The often imperceptible gap between real and symbolic meaning in the novel helps to create a "safe" narrative space in which protests are at once voiced and dismissed.

Throughout the novel, Oliver speaks proudly of his Indian lineage; Natty and Chingachgook both call him Young Eagle, son of an Indian chief, and the townspeople believe that his bitter complaints against Judge Temple's injustice are based upon his sense of the Indians' violated rights. Thus, through the statements of Oliver and those who speak for his rights, Cooper seems to question Americans' treatment of Indians and the moral legitimacy of American claims to the land once owned by Indians. At one point the minister, Mr. Gant, openly expresses doubts regarding white Americans' rights to the land: "I know not, that he, who claims affinity to the proper owners of this soil [the Indians], has not the right to tread these hills with the lightest conscience" (142). Chingachgook responds by suggesting a solution that most Americans would be reluctant to apply, in practical terms, to the more general problem of Indian rights in America: "... he [Judge Temple] will cut the country in two parts, as the river cuts the low-lands, and will say to the 'Young Eagle,' Child of the Delawares! take it — keep it — and be a chief in the land of your fathers."[13]

At first, Cooper seems to suggest that the violation of Indians' rights will lead to violence. On Christmas Eve, as Chingachgook is drinking and singing of his past, Natty frames the issue in the language of conflict, defining Judge Temple as the "enemy." Natty asks,

---

same time that Indians were excluded from real political, social and economic membership of the American "family."

13. In a later discussion with Elizabeth, even Oliver agrees with her when she says that it would be foolish — and impossible — to "convert these clearings and farms, again, into hunting-grounds, as the Leather-stocking would wish to see them" (280). Although both Oliver and Elizabeth express regret over the fate of the Indians, neither one is willing to question the law of progress which informs visions of America's bright future, a future which they will inherit.

> "Why do you sing of your battles, Chingachgook, and of the warriors you have slain, when the worst enemy of all is near you, and keeps the Young Eagle from his rights? …
>
> And why have you slain the Mingo warriors? was it not to keep these hunting-grounds and lakes to your father's children? and were they not given in solemn council to the Fire-eater [Major Effingham's Indian name]? and does not the blood of a warrior run in the veins of a young chief, who should speak aloud, where his voice is now too low to be heard?" (165)

Chingachgook responds to this reminder of his injuries by reaching for his tomahawk, which, fortunately for the Judge, he is too inebriated to use.

But even as Cooper briefly flirts with the threat of violence, he is already framing the conflict in terms that contain that violence; through displacement, he defuses the more radical implications of the questions he raises regarding the justice of American Indian policy. Natty's account of the series of crimes committed by the Indians' "worst enemy of all" actually moves the focus of attention gradually away from Indian rights per se. First, Natty notes Judge Temple's violation of the Delawares' ability to preserve the land for future generations (of Indians, the reader would naturally assume). Next he suggests that Temple has compromised the tribes' act of giving the land to Major Effingham. By the end of the passage, Oliver has replaced Chingachgook as the wronged party, the one whom Natty chastises for his complacency; he is the "young chief" whose voice should be raised against the injustices he has suffered at the hands of Judge Temple.

Later in the novel, Cooper expands this logic of displacement from a personal to a broader historical dimension. Just before he dies, Chingachgook explains to Elizabeth Temple the nature of the injury he feels he has received at the hands of the whites — an injury he associates with the general decline of his people:

> "John [Chingachgook] was young, when his tribe gave away the country, in council, from where the blue mountain stands above the water, to where the Susquehanna is hid by the trees. All this and all that grew in it, and all that walked over it, and all that fed there, they gave to the Fire-eater — for they loved him. He was strong, and they were women, and he helped them. No Delaware would kill a deer that run in his woods, nor stop a bird that flew over his land; for it was his. Has John lived in peace! Daughter, since John was young, he has seen the white man

> from Frontinac come down on his white brothers at Albany, and fight. Did they fear God! He has seen his English and his American Fathers burying their tomahawks in each other's brains, for this very land. Did they fear God, and live in peace! He has seen the land pass away from the Fire-eater, and his children, and the child of his child, and a new chief set over the country. Did they live in peace who did this! did they fear God!" (401)

Once again the crime against the Indians is defined as a violation of the rights of inheritance: the transmission of the land from the Fire-eater (Major Effingham) to his children and to his children's children. Once again, this right is premised upon the Indians' right "to g[i]ve away the country, in council." This is one Indian "right" that most Americans were quite willing to acknowledge.[14] Chingachgook imagines the transfer of property in terms that Americans would find quite appealing: the granting of Indian land to Major Effingham is represented as a willing act of love and appreciation, and once they have given the land to the white man the Indians respect his absolute ownership of the land and everything on it.[15] In this passage, the only violence associated with the loss of the Indians' land and the violation of his rights is not violence between Indians and whites but violence among whites themselves, conceived in broad historical terms: fighting between the French and English and between the Indian's "English and American fathers."

---

14. One notable exception was Andrew Jackson. As early as 1817, while serving as military commander in the South, Jackson had denounced the treaty process because it implied that the Indian "nations" had the right to give (or not give) their lands to the U.S. government. According to Jackson, "Congress had[d] full power, by law, to regulate all the concerns of the Indians," including the right to occupy and possess their lands whenever national interest, broadly defined, made it necessary (*The Correspondence of Andrew Jackson*, II, 279-81, cited in Francis Paul Prucha, *American Indian Policy in the Formative Years: The Indian Trade and Intercourse Acts, 1790-1834* [Cambridge, MA: Harvard University Press, 1962], 234).

15. Cooper never specifies whether Major Effingham's title was obtained privately or with the British government's approval and regulation, but he fact that Oliver's father, Edward, appealed to the Crown to reimburse him for the loss of his lands during the Revolutionary War suggests that Major Effingham's title was officially sanctioned by the Crown.

Near the end of the novel Cooper finally makes clear that the true object of criticism (voiced by Oliver, Natty and Chingachgook throughout the novel) is Judge Temple's purchase of the Effingham lands after the Revolutionary War under conditions that Oliver interprets as a breach of loyalty and honor between two white men. Thus, the Judge's right of purchase is challenged here not by Indian but by English prior rights to the soil, and the crucial event underlying the conflict has nothing at all to do with Indians, but is strictly a matter among whites: as Cooper ingeniously constructs the plot, the American Revolution (fighting between the Indians' "English and American fathers") becomes the ultimate source of the conflict over who legitimately may own and inherit the American land.

* * *

America's revolutionary origins complicated, in many ways, the new nation's attempts to establish a sense of national identity and legitimacy. As I have suggested, the Revolution could be seen as an act of patricidal violence tainting the legitimacy of the nationhood thus acquired. But even for those who accepted the moral validity of the Revolution as a founding act, the question of national legitimacy was far from being settled. As George Forgie has pointed out, many Americans of the post-Revolutionary generation experienced anxiety regarding their legitimacy to claim and ability to preserve the inheritance of nationhood bequeathed them by the founding fathers.

During the 1820s, the nation became widely aware that the founding fathers soon would be gone — by 1826 only one signer of the Declaration of Independence remained alive — and became increasingly concerned with the implications of this fact.[16] As long as the founding fathers lived on, America's national identity, born of the founders' military and political actions, and America's national character, guaranteed by their morality and integrity, were embodied in the founders themselves. But how were Americans of the post-Revolutionary generation to prove their worthiness to claim the authority of the fathers and their ability to preserve the new nation they inherited?

16. George B. Forgie, *Patricide in the House Divided: A Psychological Interpretation of Lincoln and His Age* (New York: W.W. Norton, & Co., 1979), 52.

In answering this question, Forgie invokes a narrowly construed model of repetition: by repeating the actions or traits upon which the father's authority is based, Forgie suggests, the son might attempt to manifest his right to that same authority. But, as Forgie goes on to argue, America's Revolutionary origins complicated the task of imitation: repeating the revolutionary action by which the fathers gained their authority would endanger the very inheritance the sons hoped to preserve; even imitating the virtue of the fathers was difficult since virtue may be proven only through action, and the task of preservation in prosperous times did not provide many opportunities to display the kind of heroic virtue upon which the founding fathers' authority rested. In the absence of an appropriate field of action, Forgie concludes, those with strong ambitions to imitate the fathers would find themselves being pulled toward a patricidal course.[17]

In this analysis, Forgie sees virtue and action as inextricably intertwined: in their attempts to imitate heroic virtues, Americans would be drawn toward heroic actions, which, in an unheroic age, become dangerous. But attitudes toward the heroic virtues and actions of the founding fathers were not as consistent as Forgie's analysis would suggest. Although Americans might embrace and desire to imitate the virtuous character of the founding fathers, they might, at the same time, be less eager to embrace as a national legacy the kind of revolutionary actions associated with the founders. Cooper, in fact, expresses such ambivalence regarding America's Revolutionary origins. In *Notions of the Americans* (1828), he describes a visit to George Washington's home with the reverence of a pilgrim at a holy shrine.[18] When he writes about the Revolution itself, however, he betrays a deep discomfort with the nation's revolutionary origins. At one point he goes so far as to deny, essentially, that a revolution ever took place. According to Cadwallader, Cooper's representative American spokesman in the book,

> We [Americans] have ever been reformers rather than revolutionists. Our own struggle for independence was not in its aspect a revolution .... We have never been in a hurry to make unnecessary innovations. Reform marches with a dignified pace

17. Forgie, 63-71.

18. *Notions of the Americans: Picked up by a Travelling Bachelor*, 2 vols (1828; rpt. New York: Ungar, 1963), II, 185-97.

> — it is revolution that is violent. The States continued the practice of the colonies.[19]

Cooper, of course, does not deny the historical event of the American Revolution, but radically redefines its meaning. By distinguishing between reform and revolution, Cooper is able to accept the radical change occasioned by the Revolution while still stressing the value of political and social stability. In Cooper's reformulation, the Revolution is neither violent nor disruptive of an essential continuity between (English) colonial and (American) national "practices." Like inheritance, reform is a process of gradual change based upon unchanging principles, a process that is ultimately conservative rather than revolutionary.

In *The Pioneers*, too, Cooper attempts to redefine the meaning of the Revolution in America's history. In place of models that imagine the new nation originating out of a revolutionary rupture with the past, Cooper offers a model in which continuity with a more distant, pre-Revolutionary past becomes the fundamental principle underlying America's national identity and legitimacy. In Cooper's version of history, American claims to the land, and to the legacy of nationhood, itself, are not legitimated through imitation of the founding fathers, who violently wrested from England both nationhood and the land which the English in turn had seized from the Indians. Nor does Cooper, like Marshall, simply base American rights upon principles and policies "inherited" intact from England. Rather, Cooper purifies inheritance of the violence and guilt that threaten American legitimacy in Marshall's narrative. For Cooper, legitimacy is achieved through a process of mourning the ancestors, both English and Indian, who willingly bequeath their authority and property to the new nation.

In rewriting the meaning of the Revolution, Cooper edits out the violence of conflict: none of the major characters in *The Pioneers* actually fought in the Revolutionary War. Judge Temple, founder of Templeton, is the closest approximation to a "founding" father represented in the book. Although his Quaker beliefs prevent him from actually fighting, he does gain possession of his lands as a result of the Revolutionary War, through the purchase of lands confiscated from loyalists. Like other American founding fathers, he presides over his newly acquired lands, occupying a position of moral and political leadership. By the end of the novel, Judge Temple's authority and

19. Cooper, *Notions of the Americans*, I, 269; II, 33.

property have been transferred to Oliver, a representative of the post-Revolutionary generation, claiming an authority untainted by violence, originating in the pre-Revolutionary past, and founded upon principles of inheritance that encompass both Indian and English prior rights.

Although Oliver plays an important symbolic role as representative inheritor of the American land, Natty emerges as the hero of *The Pioneers*. Natty, more than any other single character, helps to bring about the resolution of the book's central conflicts and to neutralize the guilt and anxieties that threaten to undermine the legitimacy of the post-Revolutionary generation's claim to the legacy of nationhood. While it may seem odd that Natty, the hero, remains outside of the various narratives of inheritance by which legitimacy is affirmed in the novel, I will argue that much of his effectiveness and power as a hero depend upon his remaining outside of the very processes he facilitates.

Throughout the novel, Natty repeatedly challenges the moral authority of Judge Temple — when he questions the Judge's claim to the buck that Oliver has killed, when he expresses opposition to the Judge's game laws, and perhaps most dramatically in the famous pigeon hunt when Natty's restraint illustrates by contrast the weakness of Judge Temple's claims to moral and social authority.[20] Here Judge Temple, in spite of his repeated assertions that he will use the law to protect and preserve the resources of nature from the wastefulness of the settlers, joins the other settlers in what Cooper describes as the "wasteful and unsportsmanlike execution" of pigeons (245). When Natty reminds him of the immorality of such waste, still the Judge is unable to control himself: "Even Marmaduke forgot the morality of Leather-stocking as it [the flock] approached, and, in common with the rest, brought his musket to a poise" (249). Notwithstanding his supposed commitment to rational, morally responsible use of nature's resources, the Judge is overwhelmed by the sheer excitement of such dramatic enactment of mastery over nature — which is, as Natty repeatedly suggests, the final

20. Critics frequently note that Judge Temple seems to violate his stated moral principles during the pigeon hunt. Kelly finds Temple characterized in this scene as a man whose impotence and moral failings disqualify him as an agent of American change (23). McWilliams cites it as evidence for Cooper's belief that strong civil laws are necessary when even men such as Judge Temple are capable of violating moral laws in which they believe (121). Motley analyzes at length how shifts in narrative perspective throughout the scene force the reader to "witness the difficulty of transferring Natty's way of seeing nature to democratic society en masse" (92).

goal to which the Judge, as a settler, is ultimately committed. Judge Temple's authority, based upon his association with the law and social order, is seriously called into question here: he is unable to control even his own passions, much less bring order and moderation to others; nor is he able, despite his protestations, to escape the negative aspects of the historical process of settlement in which he participates. Natty, in contrast, by shooting only the single pigeon he needs for food, reasserts his commitment to the "natural laws" that he believes should govern the use of nature, and becomes in this scene the sole voice of morality and restraint. In opposing his own notion of "natural law" to the civil laws that Judge Temple represents, Natty raises questions regarding the moral basis of these laws and points toward a more general problem: the difficulty of maintaining the essential connection between civil law, operating in the world of historical expediency, and the universal, unchanging principles of "natural" or divine law meant to inform and guarantee the justice of civil law.

In the McIntosh decision, Chief Justice Marshall also grapples with the difficulty of reconciling natural and civil law. In his introductory comments, Marshall writes, "It will be necessary, in pursuing this inquiry, to examine, not singly those principles of abstract justice, which the Creator of all things has impressed on the mind of his creature man, and which are admitted to regulate, in a great degree, the rights of civilized nations, whose perfect independence is acknowledged; but those principles also which our own government has adopted in the particular case, and given us as the rule for our decision" (*AIUS*, 2538). Marshall articulates here a clear distinction between natural law (universal and unchanging, bestowed by God upon all men) and civil law (historically determined, devised by particular governments for "particular case[s]"). Ideally these two laws should coincide, the laws of God should "regulate, in a great degree, the rights of civilized nations." But Marshall's later comments reveal his difficulty in reconciling, in this particular case, the universal principles of natural law with the historically determined forces shaping civil law: while he must admit that the denial of the Indians' full rights to the land indeed "may be opposed to natural right, and to the usages of civilized nations," still, from a practical, historical viewpoint, he finds it "indispensible to that system under which the country has been settled" (*AIUS*, 2547). Elsewhere, Marshall explicitly resists attempting to justify America's policy toward the Indians through the "abstract principles" of natural or divine law: "We will not enter into the controversy, whether agriculturists, merchants, and manufacturers, have a right, on abstract principles, to expel hunters from the territory they possess, or to contract their limits. Conquest gives a title which the Courts of the conqueror cannot deny, whatever the private and speculative opinions of individuals may be, respecting the original justice of the claim which has been successfully asserted" (*AIUS*, 2545). Instead of appealing to universal, unchanging principles, Marshall allows his judgment regarding Indian and American rights to the land to rest upon purely historical terms — the history of conquest. Such a solution, needless to say, does not resolve, in moral terms, the troubling conflict between natural and civil law.

While one of the central aims of legal rhetoric is to reconcile action and principle, Cooper, working within the realm of fiction, is under no such constraint. Thus he is able to negotiate the conflict in ways that Marshall could not. In *The Pioneers*, Cooper embraces Natty's morality unreservedly but does not fully embrace the actions that follow from it. In practical terms, Cooper represents Natty's opposition to the laws of Templeton as a threat to social order. When Natty finally violates the game laws by killing a deer out of season and then defies the warrant to search his hut, the sheriff proclaims, "[H]e has set an example of rebellion to the laws, and has become a kind of out-law" (355). Still, Natty remains the book's hero, for as the conflict between Natty and the law reaches a climax, Cooper redefines Natty's resistance in terms that contain its dangerous implications. By the time a posse arrives to take Natty to jail, he has already ceased to be a threat. As he stands amid the dying embers of the hut he has burned in order to protect it from their intrusion, he tells the posse, "I come to mourn, not to fight" (357).

At this moment, Natty achieves his full stature and meaning as hero. With this pronouncement, Natty, himself, contains the threat he had represented more completely than the law possibly could (as emphasized by the fact that Natty breaks out of jail after only a few hours). In burning his hut — the one structure that had stood on the land before the settlers arrived, and the place where Natty had continued to live according to pre-settlement values even as the settlement grew around him — Natty in effect acknowledges the essential incompatibility of these two world visions and removes himself from the society he threatens; both literally and figuratively, he now has no place in the world of Templeton. With his adoption of an attitude of mourning, Natty's challenge to the civil laws that regulate life in the settlements, his allegiance to values associated with the past and his resistance to "progress" have not disappeared but have been transferred from the realm of action to that of sentiment.[21]

Here, in the realm of sentiment, I have suggested, the most important "battles" with Indians were waged during the second quarter of the nineteenth century; and it is here, in the realm of sentiment, that Natty performs his most important heroic role. Once defined in terms of mourning, Natty's resistance no longer threatens but actually serves the cause it would overtly seem to resist. The mourner's expression of resistance is, at the same time, an assertion that all resistance is futile, since we mourn that which we admit to be lost beyond our power to regain. In his role as representative mourner of the past, then, Natty opens a safe channel through which opposition to change can be vented under conditions that obviate the need to translate this opposition into action.

Cooper was not the first American to recognize the power of mourning as a means of expiating guilt. Mourning was often invoked in writings about the Indian. In fact, from the Revolutionary era through the middle of the nineteenth century, writings lamenting the passing of the "Vanishing American" were so widespread and popular that they created what Brian Dippie has termed a national "habit of thought."[22] *The Last of the Mohicans; A Narrative of 1757*, Cooper's next installment in the Leatherstocking series, falls within this genre. As indicated by its title, the novel represents the extinction of the Indians as an already determined event, accomplished in the past (1757 in this

---

21. According to Brook Thomas, "When Natty removes himself from society, he exists as a continual reminder of the inability of man's written laws to coincide with the higher laws of nature" (41). I agree that Cooper never fully resolves the conflict between natural and civil law, but would add that he no longer really needs to once he moves Natty gradually away from the realm of historical and social reality represented by Templeton and toward the realm of sentiment represented by the state of mourning. This, I would argue, is the crucial moment of Natty's "removal" from the world of Templeton and all that it represents. It is a removal to a different scheme of values and a different plane of action. By the time that Natty actually leaves Templeton at the end of the book, his physical removal seems natural and inevitable, the outward manifestation of the essential change that has already occurred. Thus the ending has a certain resonance, a feeling of completion, that conveys a sense of resolution in spite of the fact that Natty's departure should represent, as Thomas argues, Cooper's absolute failure to resolve the conflict between natural and civic law.

22. Brian Dippie, *The Vanishing American: White Attitudes and U.S. Indian Policy* (Middletown, CT: Wesleyan University Press, 1982), 15.

case) — a sad but inevitable fact that the reader can mourn but cannot resist. In the political realm, too, the attitude of mourning was commonly adopted as a response to the "Indian problem." The following passage from Andrew Jackson's Second Annual Message to Congress (1830) illustrates how mourning (and inheritance) could be invoked as a rationale for Indian removal:

> Humanity has often wept over the fate of the aborigines of this country, and Philanthropy has been long busily employed in devising means to avert it, but its progress has never for a moment been arrested, and one by one have many powerful tribes disappeared from the earth. To follow to the tomb the last of his race and to tread on the graves of extinct nations excite melancholy reflections. But true philanthropy reconciles itself to these vicissitudes as it does to the extinction of one generation to make room for another.[23]

Describing the dispossession of the Indians in terms of generational change erased both violence and responsibility from the process. In this model, removal became something "natural" and inevitable; the Americans who inherited the Indians' estate could not resist, but could only mourn, the passing of the generation whose "extinction" made room for their expansion.

What exactly is being mourned in *The Pioneers* becomes clear when Natty speaks of his hut, now in ashes. When Elizabeth attempts to comfort Natty by suggesting that the hut can be rebuilt, Natty replies,

> "Can ye raise the dead, child! ... [C]an ye go into the place where you've laid your fathers, and mothers, and children, and gather together their ashes, and make the same men and women of them as afore! You do not know what 'tis to lay your head for more than forty years under the cover of the same logs, and to look on the same things for the better part of a man's life." (386)

In mourning the loss of the hut, Natty mourns in part a way of life he now accepts as incongruous with the forces of "progress" which have overtaken him. But he also mourns something beyond this personal loss, something he associates in these lines with a loss of family. The larger

23. *Papers and Messages of the Presidents*, ed. James D. Richardson (Washington, DC: United States Congress, 1897), II, 520-21.

loss Natty alludes to here becomes clear by the end of the novel, when the site of the hut literally has been transformed into a graveyard. Where the hut once stood, now lie the graves of Major Effingham and Chingachgook, representatives of America's English and Indian origins, fated to become part of America's past as the new nation achieved independent national identity.

These two men had formed part of the odd "family" that had resided in Natty's hut, a family held together through a complex web of loyalties revolving around the aged Major Effingham, who, in addition to being the adopted son of Chingachgook, was once the master and benefactor of Natty. Through their interconnecting bonds of loyalty, Major Effingham, Chingachgook and Oliver, representatives of America's past and its future, come together in Natty's hut, setting the scene for a transition between past and future envisioned in terms of continuity — of inheritance through an unbroken family lineage — rather than the discontinuity of dispossession and revolutionary rupture. Before constructing this new model of national origins, Cooper must lay to rest the guilt associated with the latter more violent model.

Natty's hut (and later the cave), where the transition between past and future occurs, is associated, in the minds of the townspeople, with a vaguely defined guilt and the threat of social disorder. Imagining that Natty and his friends are conducting secret mining operations there, the sheriff is "burning with a desire to examine the hidden mysteries of the cave" (399). It comes to represent for the townspeople "a secret receptacle of guilt" where they locate all "that was wicked and dangerous to the peace of society" (425, 426).

When the contents of the cave are finally revealed, it becomes clear that the guilt associated with the cave is not Natty's but the nation's. Through the series of extended misunderstandings surrounding Judge Temple, Cooper has repeatedly raised questions regarding American injustice toward the Indians and betrayal of loyalty to England. At the moment of revelation in front of the cave, Cooper presents what would seem to be the most incriminating evidence of Judge Temple's (and the nation's) guilt. We discover that the cave holds the corpse of Chingachgook, who received fatal injuries during the recent forest fire, and the rapidly declining Major Effingham — the dispossessed and dishonored remnants of those old orders whose authority and property have been usurped by the new American order.

At this very same moment, however, Cooper reveals the innocence of Judge Temple and thus clears the way for a vision of national identity based upon the legitimate transmission of authority through inheritance. Cooper exonerates the Judge by showing that his adherence to principles of continuity, such as loyalty and inheritance, transcends the disruptive power of revolutionary change. As the explanations pour forth, we discover that the Judge, in spite of the misunderstandings and difficulties caused by the Revolutionary War, did not betray the trust of his friend, as Oliver believed, but instead has been a caretaker preserving Oliver's inheritance for him. In this context, the Revolution becomes not a rupture with the past nor an occasion of betrayal, but a test allowing the American to display the depth of his loyalty to and continuity with the past.

The cave, then, is a place not only of death but also of birth; it is both grave and womb, where the new order is born out of the death of the old. With the revelation of the dying Major Effingham, Oliver's true identity is established, allowing him to assume his proper station in society and assert his hereditary right to the land. This revelation eliminates the supposed differences in race and class which had complicated the developing romantic interest between Oliver and Elizabeth. With his marriage to Elizabeth, Oliver will unite (at least metaphorically) English, Indian and American claims to the land to become the legitimate heir of all his fathers: his biological (grand)father Major Effingham, his adopted (great-grand)father Chingachgook, and his father-in-law Judge Temple. The union between Oliver and Elizabeth, then, marks the beginning of a new line of Americans whose legitimacy is beyond question.[24]

In making inheritance the basis of a legitimate claim to the American land, Cooper shifts emphasis away from the Revolution as the crucial defining moment in America's national history. In *The Pioneers*, in fact, the Revolution is represented not as the basis of Americans' legitimate claim to the land, but as the event that complicates efforts to establish who has the right to own and govern the land. It is also important to note that Oliver's authority does not derive directly from his relationship to or "imitation" of Judge Temple, the book's representative founding father. The authority and property (half of the Temple estate) he receives directly from the Judge was really already his own by virtue of inheritance; the transfer represents simply a restoration of Oliver's former rights. Oliver acquires the rest of the Temple property not directly from the Judge but through marriage to

---

24. Thomas Philbrick notes that Oliver's double lineage makes him heir both to his father's legal claim and the Indians' moral claim to the land ("Cooper's *The Pioneers*: Origins and Structure," *PMLA* 79 [1964], 593).

Elizabeth, another representative of the post-Revolutionary generation. Thus, the new nation's legitimacy, represented by Oliver's legitimacy as heir to the land, is not imagined as something new, originating with the Revolution, but as the resumption of former rights, the evidence of continuity rather than rupture with the past. Similarly, in his non-fiction, Cooper preferred to imagine the Revolution not as a war for independence from the king, but as a fight to regain constitutional rights violated through legislative usurpation of power.[25]

The ending of the book re-emphasizes the important role of mourning in stabilizing and legitimizing the transition between past and future out of which the new nation is born. In addition to exonerating guilt, mourning serves as an assurance of continuity and stability in the face of change — an assertion that there are bonds (of love, loyalty, kinship) that remain in spite of loss, bonds strong enough to transcend the disruptive power of time. But even as it provides a sense of continuity with the past, the end of mourning is finally to commit what is past to memory, to allow the mourner to move beyond it. While in the *process* of mourning, however, the mourner exists somewhere between past and present, in a state of emotional transition.

In his role as representative mourner, Natty remains always in the process of mourning, performing the work of mourning for other characters in the book and for the reader, but never moving beyond it himself. While Natty helps others to commit the past to memory (as history) and move beyond it into the future, he exists somehow outside of time, embodying the site of emotional and historical transition itself. Natty remains frozen in time, unable to move forward with history, while Oliver, although ostensibly committed to many of the same values as Natty, is free to move ahead into the future. It is Oliver, after all, who oversees the dramatic progress of Templeton described in the opening pages of the book. Similarly, readers might identify with Natty in his attitude of mourning, thus affirming their respect for the past and denying complicity in the process of change, without actually abandonning their commitment to the values of progress or changing the policies responsible for the very "losses" they mourn.

The final scene of the novel, appropriately set in the graveyard now established upon the site where Natty's hut once stood, helps to elucidate more precisely the meaning of Natty's role. When Elizabeth

25. Mike Ewart makes this point, based on references to Cooper's *History of the Navy*, *Switzerland*, and *Notions of the Americans*, in "Cooper and the American Revolution: The Non-Fiction," *Journal of American Studies* 11 (1977), 63.

and Oliver discover Natty, he is lying on the ground above the graves of Major Effingham and Chingachgook. These two representatives of America's dual origins have found their final resting place, firmly located in the past, lying next to each other but pointing in opposite directions. Natty asks Oliver to read for him the inscriptions on the headstones, the histories into which their lives have been transformed.[26] On Major Effingham's headstone, Natty finds his own name engraved, as the "servant" whose "enduring gratitude" and loyalty to his master will be remembered. Natty does not become part of the past with a headstone and historical meaning of his own; he is simply the "servant" who enables the history of others to be written. It was Natty, after all, whose initial act of loyalty ensured that Major Effingham did not die forgotten and unmourned. When Oliver reads Chingachgook's headstone, Natty detects a mistake in the spelling of Chingachgook's name — a serious matter since, as Natty notes, "an Indian's name has always some meaning in it" (452). Cooper here seems to suggest that the writing of the Indian into America's history inevitably entails an element of violation. In correcting the mistakes on Chingachgook's headstone, Natty again acts as the servant of a history not his own.

Natty, lying above the ground, is no more part of the present than those lying beneath it. With the burning of his hut, and its subsequent transformation into a graveyard, he no longer has a place in the living, present-day world of Templeton. But unlike those who lie buried on the site of his hut, he cannot be located firmly in the past as part of America's history.[27] Nor is he to be included in America's future

---

26. Thomas Hill Schaub performs an extended analysis of the grave scene, focusing on the thematic implications of the distinction between the written and spoken word as illustrated here. See his "'Cut in Plain Marble': The Language of the Tomb in *The Pioneers*," in *The Green American Tradition: Essays and Poems for Sherman Paul*, ed. H. Daniel Peck (Baton Rouge: Louisiana State University Press, 1989).

27. In *The Prairie* (1827), which Cooper at the time envisioned as the last of the Leatherstocking series, Natty finally is laid in the grave. As Richard Slotkin argues persuasively, at the time that Cooper was writing *The Prairie*, it was generally believed that the end of the frontier had been reached: the Great Plains seemed to represent a permanent barrier to further agrarian expansion and the Far West had not yet been opened for American settlement (*The Fatal Environment: The Myth of the Frontier in the Age of Industrialization, 1800-1890* [Middletown, CT: Wesleyan University Press, 1985], 111). Once the historical process of settlement, which Natty served even as he resisted it, has come to an end, Natty's existence and

(represented here by the new order born of the union between Elizabeth and Oliver); he refuses their offer to build him a new home, choosing instead to drift ever further west "towards the setting sun — the foremost in that band of Pioneers, who are opening the way for the march of the nation across the continent" (456). In these final words of the novel, Natty's paradoxical relationship to history is evident. With his eyes fixed steadily on the past, Natty opens the way to the future, carrying forward the process of historical change through his very attempt to escape it.[28] He is a servant of time, ushering in the new order as he ushers out the old, yet belonging to neither, bringing into being, through no will of his own, a morally purified vision of American history, a history from which he is excluded.

---

function become part of history. It is fitting that Natty is buried among the Indians on the "Great American Prairies," which, Cooper believed, would also be "the final gathering place of the red men" (*The Prairie; A Tale* [1827; rpt. New York: Signet, 1964], vii); for Cooper, this is the place where the closing of the history of American expansion occurs.

28. Natty's exclusion from actual participation in the march of "progress" helps to preserve the moral purity that adds to his authority as hero. Philbrick discusses the ways in which Judge Temple's "position [of authority] is undercut by the principle of change that his whole life has served" (592). Unlike the Judge, who actively presides over (and is somewhat tainted by) a period of rapid change, Natty serves more as a catalyst, enabling change without being touched by the process himself.

COOPER AND THE FRONTIER MYTH AND ANTI-MYTH

JOHN G. CAWELTI

James Fenimore Cooper has always been something of a scandal as a great writer. His style was often ponderous and artificial and his dialogue sounds like a parody of some combination of Samuel Richardson and Jane Austen. His favorite subject was the dynastic romance — that is the courtship and marriage of the offspring of great aristocratic families — and this relationship is as boring in *The Spy* and *The Pioneers*, as it is in *Satanstoe*. His social and political views, though expressed with great vigor and conviction, were marred by the sort of snobbism which made him believe that only a cultivated gentry class — his own, of course — could possibly save American democracy, and by a profound inability to distinguish between the fate of the nation and that of his own pocketbook. His greatest and most popular accomplishments, most notably the character of the Leatherstocking and his Indian companions, were conceived of as minor figures, and only the tremendous public reaction to them made Cooper turn them into central figures. In fact, as Henry Nash Smith pointed out long ago, it is only in the fourth of the Leatherstocking series to be written, *The Pathfinder*, that Cooper made Natty Bumppo a true protagonist and even there he is to some extent upstaged by a romance between the woman he loves and another character.

But Cooper's flaws are an old story and have already been more effectively presented (and the power of his influence acknowledged) in parodies by many writers including Mark Twain and Bret Harte. Yet, in spite of this, the brilliance of Cooper's greatest inventions made him one of the most popular writers of the nineteenth century, outselling in some cases even his great rival Sir Walter Scott. Even until after World War II when Cooper became a figure of the American literary establishment, he was still widely read by American young people who had been persuaded to read him outside the high-school or college curriculum. I can remember reading the Leatherstocking saga back in the late 1930s and early 1940s simply because it was known to be a good read. The legion of Cooper's followers and successors in the romanticization of the American wilderness — the "Sons of Leatherstocking" as Smith calls them — have continued until recently to be an important part of popular culture both in America and in Europe. In fact, one of the most successful recent attempts at a cinematic adaptation of the Leatherstocking tales was a video series produced by the BBC, which was presented in England as popular entertainment, while, as showcased in America it was given the high cultural treatment complete with a place on public television in "Masterpiece Theater" and an introduction by Alistair Cooke, both deep symbols for Americans that something of great cultural distinction is taking place.

But what exactly did Cooper invent that he should so obviously be the continuing inspiration for the mythical treatment of the American West. He was certainly not the first American to write about the wilderness. As Richard Slotkin has shown in *Regeneration through Violence*, a popular literature featuring settler-Indian skirmishes and captivity narratives began in the seventeenth century and flourished in the eighteenth. But what this literature most lacks is the element which Cooper added to the romantic adventure saga of the American wilderness, a complex myth of the frontier. This myth, which gains some of its richness and complexity from the anti-myth which it barely contains within itself, is what I think of as Cooper's most significant contribution to the history of literature and, in the remainder of this paper, I will try to define some of the central dimensions of this myth.

I

First of all, Cooper's most striking creation was his hero, the Leatherstocking. Though based in part on the life of a historical frontiersman such as Daniel Boone, Cooper's Natty Bumppo became, in the course of the Leatherstocking saga, a unique protagonist for the mythical American frontier. The qualities of Cooper's hero were those of a "Lone Ranger," the title accorded one of his much later avatars, the masked Western hero of radio, film, and television. Leatherstocking is utterly alone in the world, except for his longtime Indian companion (I use the word companion because it seems a bit strange to refer to the rather ritualistic relationship between Hawkeye and Chingachgook as friendship). He is an orphan, and has himself no progeny. Though raised by the Indians, he does not consider himself in any way Indianized. He is a man "without a cross" — i.e. pure white — and has "different gifts" from the redskins. Indeed, in some of his statements about Indian ways, particularly with reference to the followers of such demonic characters as Magua in *The Last of the Mohicans*, he seems as racist as the most anti-Indian of the other white characters.

Significantly, though we do not know the exact social background of Bumppo's parents, it is clear that he is not a lost heir of some great aristocratic family, like the Oliver Edwards (Effingham), whom he befriends in *The Pioneers*. On the contrary, he is a virtually nameless, or rather name-shifting product of a frontier classlessness which stands in striking contrast to the hierarchical, gentrified, culture which Cooper felt was the appropriate social form for a more settled American democracy.[1] And not only is he alone, he is also a ranger, who, in the course of the Leatherstocking series not only moves many miles across the wilderness in pursuit of, or escaping from, the Indians, but also moves across the continent from central New York State to the plains of Missouri. However, unlike most Americans his mobility is purely geographical. Socially, he does not rise or fall, succeed or fail. In fact, with respect to his ranging, we might say that the Leatherstocking uses his mobility not to get further into the business of society, but to elude it, and that in this he is the cousin or godfather of several of the most important American literary creations, for instance Rip Van Winkle, the Thoreau of Henry David Thoreau's *Walden*, the Walt of Walt Whitman's *Song of Myself*, and Huckleberry Finn. Leatherstocking's many names seem to symbolize this; his name frequently changes as if to make it impossible to *address* him and thereby pin him down geographically and socially. Moreover, most of his names are given to him by Indians, thereby suggesting that he really belongs to a society which he cannot feel part of, or rather that he doesn't belong to society at all.

Years ago Leslie Fiedler pointed out that many of those male figures who seemed most representative of American literature had their closest personal relationship with a male of another race, usually either Indian or Black. Cooper's Leatherstocking was surely the creative origin of this important fictional and mythical pattern, but the nature of Natty's connection to Chingachgook was significantly different from Huckleberry Finn's relationship with Jim. For one thing, *Huckleberry*

---

1. Though Natty Bumppo's many names are familiar, it was Theo D'haen (whose essay "Dis-placing *Satanstoe*" appears elsewhere in this volume) who made me see just how central name-shifting is to Cooper and how ambiguous his treatment of Natty's many names is in terms of his social consciousness, which stresses the continuity of family names.

Finn is, in an important sense, about the development of Jim and Huck's relationship. Twain is specifically concerned with the deep conflict between Huck's humanity and the racism he has inherited from his culture, and to represent this conflict he must show how Huck's feelings toward Jim develop from Huck's acceptance of his culture's characterization of Jim as an inferior animal and, therefore, as property, to his struggle with his "conscience" over his inability to return Jim to his owner. Cooper, on the other hand, shows us almost nothing about the development of the relationship between Chingachgook and Hawkeye. It is already full-blown in *The Deerslayer* and doesn't seem to change significantly over the next several decades, though of course it ends with the death of Chingachgook in *The Pioneers*. That this relationship begins in the last of the series to be written and ends in the first suggests that it has nowhere to go. Both Hawkeye and Chingachgook are symbols of a state outside of society — a "territory" or "wilderness" which cannot last, the "virgin land" which must inevitably give way to the maturity of civilization. Perhaps to emphasize this inescapable fate, Cooper made Hawkeye's Indian companion one of the last survivors of a vanishing race, the noble tribe of the Mohicans. The relationship between them can be nothing but barren and Cooper killed off the only offspring for either character, Chingachgook's son Uncas, in the second-written volume of the series. Both Leatherstocking and Chingachgook enact that moving elegiac myth of the Vanishing American, whose mysterious power must yield to the further development of civilization. Is it possible that Twain, unable to see how the relationship between Huck and Jim could develop any further in the society he knew, resorted to Cooper's solution of the "territory" to keep at least its possibility alive?

The central paradox of the Vanishing American is that while he in the process of trying to find new "territory" he becomes the savior and leader of the pioneers whose primary mission is to settle and transform the existing "territory." The central symbolic question which Cooper posed in the first-written volume of the Leatherstocking series is whether that seduction of the virgin wilderness results in a wedding or a rape.[2] In *The Pioneers*, the answer the surface plot clearly insists on is a wedding, the dynastic reunion of the Effinghams and the Temples

2. I am greatly indebted for this perception to Joke Kardux of Leiden University, whose paper "Cooper and the Idea of Femininity in the Leatherstocking Tales," presented at the 1989 Cooper Conference at the University of Groningen, develops this idea.

through the marriage of Oliver Edwards (Effingham) and Elizabeth Temple. However, on the level of imagery, and of incident, Cooper also portrays the movement into the wilderness as a rape and a devastation. Never again, in the four Leatherstocking novels he wrote after *The Pioneers* did Cooper deal so explicitly with the negative ecological consequences of pioneering, perhaps because he hoped that the development of an American gentry class might lead to a balance between the interests of the ecology and the needs of the pioneers, just as Judge Temple seeks to balance these interests in *The Pioneers*. Therefore, it would be overdoing it to credit Cooper as a precursor of the ecological and wilderness movements in America. However, Cooper's literary vision of the American wilderness was as important to the development of an American mythology as his conception of the Leatherstocking hero.

II

Cooper's myth of the wilderness was greatly influenced by such romantic conceptions as the myth of nature as pervaded by spirit and the aesthetic ideal of sublimity, which also interested many of his poet and painter friends. However, Cooper's particular notion of the wilderness was also shaped by what he had come to believe about the American Indian and his relationship to the land. Although Cooper thought that "property is the base of all civilization" and that the "existence and security [of property] are indispensable to social improvement," and also that "[property] is desirable as the ground work of moral independence, as a means of improving the faculties, and of doing good to others, and as the agent in all that distinguishes the civilized man from the savage,"[3] he was obviously fascinated by the idea that the American Indian did not believe in ownership of the land. Though Cooper's conception of Native American attitudes toward the land and the idea of property have been seriously questioned by some anthropologists and historians, it has been widely accepted as *the* Indian view of nature, even by Indians themselves. The essential components of this view are the following:

1. Nobody owns the land; it was put there by the Great Spirit to be used by all;

3. *The American Democrat; or, Hints on the Social and Civic Relations of the United States of America* (Cooperstown, NY: H. & E. Phinney, 1838), 135, 140.

2. The land should be used only for personal survival needs and not exploited for profit or speculation;

3. There is danger that the land and its flora and fauna can be destroyed by greed and rapacity; those who do not respect the land may end up by destroying it and themselves;

4. The wilderness is full of Spirit and should be reverenced as the expression of the Great Spirit or Manitou.[4]

If nothing else about this version of Native American attitudes toward the land might give us pause, its remarkable similarity to European romantic ideologies of Nature and even to Marxian versions of the ideal state after the revolutionary destruction of capitalism, should make us suspicious. However, as a pastoral critique of modern European and American civilization, the wonderful myth of the American Indian's deep dedication to communal ownership, to the religious veneration of the land and to a sort of proto-ecological consciousness, has been a remarkably powerful literary and cultural device.[5] A famous advertisement of a couple of decades ago showed an American Indian who resembled the traditional figure on the penny coin with tears in his eyes from air pollution. This was a striking modern

---

4. This ideology, which makes Native Americans to be the original ecologists, would require a much longer note than this to treat it adequately. The central problem, as I understand it, is twofold. First of all, to say that American Indians had a single attitude toward anything is, given the extraordinary diversity and richness of their many cultures, at the very least dubious. It seems highly unlikely, for example, that the attitudes toward nature of the Iroquois confederacy in the Northeast, the settled cities and even empires of the Southeast and Central America, and the migratory buffalo-hunting Plains Indians could possibly have been the same. Secondly, to translate Native American attitudes into the terms of white culture (such as individual property vs. communal possession) really does more to obfuscate the actual philosophy of the Native Americans than to clarify it. In my view, these communal and ecological fantasies of Native American culture rather reflect white ambiguities than that they result from an understanding and appreciation of Native American cultures.

5. Leo Marx has been particularly important in showing us the great significance of the pastoral critique in the mythology of American culture. His *Machine in the Garden*, which made us aware of the many dimensions of the pastoral critique, shaped the ideas of at least two generations of American Studies scholars. In fact, when we look at the way in which ideas about America have been shaped by the work of Frederick Jackson Turner through his commentator Henry Nash Smith, and then through Smith's student Leo Marx, and Marx's follower Richard Slotkin, one realizes how important the intellectual and cultural influence of scholarly inheritances can be.

instance of this very effective formula, though like the original it never, so far as I know, stopped anybody from polluting the air, no more than Cooper's brilliant representation of the noble savage and his relationship to the sublimity of nature prevented anyone from dispossessing the Native American and from expropriating the "wilderness."

Yet Cooper's myth of the wilderness did give the idea of the frontier a mythical significance which has influenced our basic conception of the American character and of the uniqueness of American culture. Almost half a century after Cooper published the last volume in the Leatherstocking series, *The Deerslayer*, Frederick Jackson Turner's "Significance of the Frontier in American History" helped to establish the myth of the frontier as the first half of the twentieth century's most fundamental interpretive ideology of American history, society and culture.[6] Further canonized through Hollywood's exploitation of the western adventure as popular culture, the American myth of pioneers, cowboys, and Indians on the frontier has become an international epic in the twentieth century, influencing the development of popular culture in countries as diverse as Italy and Japan. Thus, Cooper's creation of the wilderness and its hero have become as significant in their way to world mythology as the adventures of Odysseus, the struggles of Rama, or the voyages of Marco Polo and Columbus.

III

The original American myth of the frontier, as many scholars have shown, originated with the Puritan "errand into the wilderness" to bring light and Calvinist Christianity into the heathen darkness.[7] This myth was transformed into the epic of the pioneers bringing law and order to a savage land. During the nineteenth century, this myth developed a further set of meanings which had dire consequences for the future. In this version of the frontier myth, the romantic ideology of nature as a source of regeneration and rebirth, became perverted into a myth of the frontier as creating an epic moment in modern history where civilized man once again encountered his savage and barbarian roots and, by

6. Frederick Jackson Turner, "The Significance of the Frontier in American History," ed. Harold P. Simonson (1893; rpt. New York: Ungar, 1963).

7. Cf. the work on American cultural history of such scholars as Perry Miller, Henry Nash Smith, and Richard Slotkin.

engaging in savage violence, recovered the original potency which he had lost in the process of civilization. In the later nineteenth century, this myth of "regeneration through violence" became in Theodore Roosevelt's version of the "Winning of the West," a return to Anglo-Saxon roots, and it can be further traced into the twentieth-century nightmare of the American quest for regeneration and the recovery of lost world power through the invasion of Asia and South America.

Cooper must have accepted some aspects of this myth of the frontier as a place where civilized man could recover lost potency through learning anew how to live with violence. To a certain extent, his aristocratic heroes, the Temples, Heywards, and Middletons enact a version of this myth. But, even from the beginning of the saga, which in the paradoxical chronology of the Leatherstocking tales is actually near the end, Natty is never fully embedded in that version of the myth. Actually, after he has initiated his aristocratic "dudes" into the code of the West, Natty seems a rather pathetic figure in Cooper's plot of dynastic reconciliation and aristocratic recovery on the frontier. This Natty is the one who, at the end of *The Pioneers* tells the young aristocratic couple that he is terribly pleased to be memorialized as the faithful servant of his master. But there is obviously another Natty, the one whom D. H. Lawrence in his own bitter and rebellious way recognized as a true killer. This is the Hawkeye whose rescue of the young aristocratic couple who represent the future of society is far less important than his own instinctive flight from civilization. This Hawkeye knows that he and everything else he holds dear has no future, but he still persists in looking for the conditions of wilderness where alone he can be his true self, in "lone ranging," in isolation, in movement, in never being possessed by the property he owns, in never being addressed.

Thus, Cooper's anti-myth, which resides rather uncomfortably side by side with the epic of the pioneers and the "Winning of the West," is the story of the hero's flight from civilization, which he comes to recognize as totally destructive of nature and spirit. It is not, as some believe, a vision of ecological balance, for in the portrayal of escape, the hero is running away from both society and the idea of a balance between society and nature. In this very American saga, Cooper's Leatherstocking is one of those typical American heroes who seeks himself where alone he can find himself — away from civilization in the deep forests (Leatherstocking), or in sleep (Rip), at Walden Pond (Thoreau), on the great river (Huck), or the road (Walt Whitman-Jack Kerouac), or, in desperate finality, in the sea (Kate Chopin's *The*

Awakening). These are visions of the isolated individual who can never get far enough from civilization, and Cooper's Natty Bumppo — childless as he was — was their progenitor. The presence of this anti-myth has been a vitalizing influence not only in the most powerful examples of the western genre like Owen Wister's *The Virginian*, or A. B. Guthrie's *The Big Sky*, and in the great western films of John Ford, but also in other areas of American popular culture like the Hawkeye Pierce and Trapper John of M*A*S*H, and, most importantly, in the great traditions of American literature where the Leatherstocking has his many avatars in such figures as Faulkner's Ike McCaslin, Saul Bellow's Henderson and Augie March, and Thomas Pynchon's Tyrone Slothrop. Whatever Cooper's shortcomings as a realist and a stylist, his creation of the ambiguous American epic of the frontier and its deeply divided hero was one of the most important mythical creations in the history of American culture.

FROM LEATHERSTOCKING TO ROCKETMAN: COOPER'S LEATHERSTOCKING TALES AND PYNCHON'S *GRAVITY'S RAINBOW* RECONSIDERED

JAN BAKKER

The opening sentence of Thomas Pynchon's *Gravity's Rainbow* (1973), "A screaming comes across the sky,"[1] has already achieved some fame as expressing most dramatically the dying cry of Western civilization, "this old theatre" (760), as Pynchon calls it, which at the end of the novel seems on the point of being destroyed by the Rocket hovering over its tarnished beauty.

It could also easily have been the sentence introducing James Fenimore Cooper's Leatherstocking Tales, and would then no doubt have signified the desperate war-whoop of the Red Indians, heralding the disappearance of their independent existence on the North-American continent.

As Pynchon's novel deals with the one major event of the twentieth century — the final subjugation of Western man to such revolutionary technologies as nuclear physics and rocketry — so Cooper's Tales have as their subject the one major event of nineteenth-century America: the final subjugation of a race, the Red Indians, to white dominance, an event in which technology, regarded by some as a historical force, can also be said to have played a crucial role.

These are not the only correspondences that suggest themselves. In both Cooper's and Pynchon's work the setting is predominantly one of conflict, war. In the Leatherstocking Tales the conflict is between the French and the English, in actuality a transference of political troubles from Europe to the American colonies, with the Indians in a subsidiary role of useful allies. In *Gravity's Rainbow* the conflict is World War II, or more precisely the end of World War II and its chaotic aftermath, a war once again waged between the major powers of the world, but this

1. Thomas Pynchon, *Gravity's Rainbow* (New York: Viking Press, 1973), 3. Future references to this edition will be cited parenthetically within the text (*GR*).

time brought to a head on the continent where it started, Europe, with also in a subsidiary role a conquered race, the black Hereros from Africa.

The locale of Cooper's Tales is the region of the Great Lakes — in those early days the frontier, the neutral territory between civilization and the wilderness, a region gradually shifting westwards, in *The Prairie* nearly as far as the Rocky Mountains.

In Pynchon's novel the locale has attained global dimensions, encompassing not only the United States and Europe, but also Africa, South America, Japan, Russia and Central Asia. But the main action takes place in the "Zone," that region of war-ravaged Europe where towards the end of the fighting no one is in control yet, where there are no longer distinct patterns, only the potential of new ones, no certainties, and where everybody and everything is adrift, a region, in short, sharing striking characteristics with Cooper's frontier.

More correspondences can still be discerned. In *Gravity's Rainbow* Pynchon reverts again to his favorite plot device, the conspiracy, and in a writer who firmly believes that everything is related to everything else, this need hardly surprise us. But Cooper, too, employs this device, and in a manner no less fantastic.

In dealing with the great social events of their time, Pynchon as well as Cooper have in fact abandoned the realm of realistic fiction and resorted to the fantastic and surrealistic. Cooper's Tales may have a semblance of realism, but as his conception of the frontier, his Indians and the endless series of improbable events that string his Tales together clearly show, it is a kind of realism as distorted as the kind one encounters in Pynchon's work. What it conveys is a world that exists somewhere on the edge of reality and the realm of dreams, symbol, and the archetypal, and the difference between the two writers here is merely that in Pynchon's novels this world has immeasurably expanded, accurately reflecting the development over the past hundred and fifty years of such fields of human interest as philosophy, sociology, psychology, physics, rocketry, literature, and the popular arts.

In the work of these two writers it is therefore pointless to try and invest action with historical truth, character with personality. The truth of action is determined by the particular medium of the authors' minds rather than by historical time and circumstances, and what Cooper said of Natty Bumppo, also applies to Tyrone Slothrop, one of the main characters of *Gravity's Rainbow:* both are "creations," that is, the vehicles of a writer's deepest thoughts, longings, and anxieties — and here remarkable correspondences force themselves again to the surface.

Cooper's Leatherstocking Tales not only stand at the beginning of the rise of American literature, they also present us with America's first cultural hero, Nathaniel Bumppo, Leatherstocking, Hawkeye, Pathfinder, trapper, or Deerslayer, as he is variously called in the five tales that make up the series. We may meet him in *The Pioneers* (1823) as an ungainly, quarrelsome old man living in a squalid cabin on the outskirts of a settlement, and take our leave of him in *The Deerslayer* (1841), where he has been transformed into a young frontier hero of radiant mythic dimensions, but he is and remains the same character: a stoic philosopher of a generous and chivalric disposition, a man, however, who is also a killer, but who during a life time spent on the dangerous frontier has nevertheless managed to preserve his moral integrity, without becoming as "hard and intact" as D.H. Lawrence made him out to be.

Pynchon's novel, published a hundred and fifty years later, not only stands at the zenith of American literature, it also presents us with a character, Tyrone Slothrop, whose life story shows, in a symbolic sense, a remarkable resemblance with that of Cooper's hero. We may meet Tyrone as an intelligence officer in the American army stationed in London, but like a modern Pathfinder he spends most of his time in the Zone, where he too tries to keep his integrity "hard and intact," even though he expresses his moral anxieties by cracking a joke or composing a bawdy song rather than treating us to what makes of Natty Bumppo more often than not a sententious bore.

What motivates Tyrone to flee to the Zone in escape of his pursuers, and the Leatherstocking figure to retreat to the wilderness in flight from the settlements, is also basically the same: fear, the fear of loss of self, of autonomy, or to use Pynchon's favorite term, paranoia.

In Natty's case this fear is given its most dramatic expression in *The Pioneers*. Cooper's first Leatherstocking Tale is no doubt about the birth of a settlement, but as such it is also the novel in which we are already made to witness what in Pynchon's novel becomes the overriding concern: the emergence of a bureaucracy, the "System," as Pynchon calls it. In *The Pioneers* it is — in its emerging shape — represented by the early settlers; in *Gravity's Rainbow* — in its most advanced form — by "The Firm," that is, in concrete terms the world-wide organization of huge corporations and cartels like General Electric, IBM, Siemens, Shell, I.G. Farben, the great multi-nationals, in fact, which can ignore national boundaries, in a geographical as well as in a political sense.

The System's chief aim is, as we learn from both novels, "to do business," to which everything and everyone in the realm of human activities must be subservient. It therefore cannot and will not allow the individual to be in control of his own life.

In Templeton, Natty Bumppo, the frontiersman, is constantly watched, spied upon, and hounded by men who, as he himself remarks, are troubled with "longings after other people's business,"[2] longings which also include their greed to lay their hands on a treasure of silver Natty is suspected to have hidden in his cabin.

In *Gravity's Rainbow*, Tyrone is watched, spied upon, and hounded by men of the "White Visitation," an Allied agency controlled by The Firm, because he too is suspected of hiding a secret, the secret of being able to predict the whereabouts of the German V-2s, the "treasure" The Firm wants to lay its hands on.

Neither the townspeople of Templeton, nor the White Visitation — purposely set up to increase control over individuals — can ever acquiesce in the individual having secrets. The townspeople because it might deprive them of what they consider their rightful share in material gain; the men of the "White Visitation," headed by Dr Pointsman, a fanatic behaviorist, because it deprives them of their belief in cause-and-effect logic, The Firm's chief weapon in exercising control.

To Natty, however, property, money, means nothing, honor and loyalty (the "treasure" he hides in his cabin is old Effingham) everything — an attitude resented by the settlers. To them the right to property and the concomitant right to accumulation is everything, justifying in their eyes the deprivation of others and nature, notions which the Leatherstocking figure deeply detests. But instead of making him exemplary, he comes to be looked upon as dangerous to the peace of society, a view also taken by Pointsman with regard to Tyrone.

Tyrone's odd secret not only insults Pointsman's faith in cause-and-effect thinking, the way in which he responds to his "peculiar sensitivity to what is revealed in the sky" is also far too individualistic to the latter's liking (*GR* 26). Instead of putting it into the service of the White Visitation, Tyrone allows it to make him suspicious of "Them," The Firm, who, as he finds out, want to use him only to further their own ends; who, as he also begins to suspect, have used him all his life. Tyrone rebels and flees to the Zone, not only in order to escape

---

2. James Fenimore Cooper, *The Pioneers* (1823; rpt. New York: Holt, Rinehart and Winston, 1966), 307. Future references to this edition will be cited parenthetically within the text (*PI*).

"Their" control, but also in order to find the Rocket to which he is related in such a mysterious way. It thus becomes his "Grail" which he must find if he is to know his self. No wonder that the thought of Tyrone "lost in the world of men, after the war," "historically, a monster" if his secret remains unsolved, fills Pointsman with "a deep dread" (*GR* 144).

If in the area of personal relationships the System's chief aim entails the denial of individual autonomy, in its dealing with the external world it will ultimately result in the annihilation of the organic world, as it is being transformed into a dead world. To understand this it must be realized that in both Pynchon's and Cooper's view the world is "a closed system, cyclical, resonant, eternally-returning," a "thing" that should not be tampered with but, on the contrary, left in good repair, an insight ignored by the System (*GR* 412).

What remains an intuitive understanding in *The Pioneers* — Natty condemning the wasteful ways of the settlers — acquires a scientific underpinning in *Gravity's Rainbow*. Many of the metaphors with which Pynchon seeks to explain the forces that structure the world, the physical as well as the human world, are drawn from the sciences. The metaphor that is relevant here is the one he derives from The Second Law of Thermodynamics which postulates that closed systems — and the earth is a closed system — decline into entropy, that is, into disorder, ending in (heat-)death if more heat (energy) is drawn from the system than it contains — a process that is irreversible. What the System — The Firm — in pursuing its aim does, is "to violate the cycle," leading, as the Second Law predicts, to a state of entropy, and the rest of the passage from which this and the preceding quotation have been taken is worth quoting in full, since it contains Pynchon's graphic description of the form this state of entropy is to assume in the human world:

> Taking and not giving back, demanding that "productivity" and "earnings" keep on increasing with time, the System removing from the rest of the World these vast quantities of energy to keep its own tiny desperate fraction showing a profit: and not only most of humanity — most of the World, animal, vegetable and mineral, is laid waste in the process. The System may or may not understand that it's only buying time. And that time is an artificial resource to begin with, of no value to anyone or anything but the System, which sooner of later must crash to its death, when its addiction to energy has become more than the rest of the World can supply, dragging with it innocent souls all

> along the chain of life. Living inside the System is like riding across the country in a bus driven by a maniac bent on suicide .... (*GR* 412)

No bus is to be discerned in *The Pioneers* yet, though with the compulsively energetic Richard Jones in mind it is not difficult to imagine who might have been the first "maniac" to drive it across the country; but what *is* discernible are the first signs of the removal "from the rest of the World" of "these vast quantities of energy to keep [the System's] own tiny desperate fraction showing a profit." In the townspeople of Templeton we already recognize the early representatives of the System, initiating on a local scale what on a global scale in Pynchon's novel is continued and completed by The Firm, the big corporations and cartels which in the world of today control the buying and selling, and consequently "productivity" and "earnings."

As for the "innocent souls" that are being dragged with it, "all along the chain of life," in both Pynchon's and Cooper's work they are not only present but also strikingly alike. In *Gravity's Rainbow* they are the people for whom the System has no use, the people who live amongst "the trivia and the waste" that it produces, the "passed over," the abandoned, the rejected, "The Preterite" as Pynchon, more of a Calvinist than Cooper, calls them.

Included in this category are in the first place the black Hereros, corrupted like Cooper's Indians by the white Europeans. These blacks are the survivors of Von Trotha's 1904 massacre in South West Africa, brought to Germany by another important character in *Gravity's Rainbow*, Blicero — Whiteman! — in Von Trotha's days a young officer, and now the driving force behind the production of the Rocket.

It is Blicero who has turned them into Schwarzkommandos, the black Rocket Corps, to serve the Third Reich, in which capacity they have become the first people to derive their identity from the Rocket (to Enzian, their leader, Blicero was a Jesus Christ, a "Deliverer"). But Blicero, once a young man "in love with empire, poetry" (*GR* 660), and still essentially a romantic, has changed into a corrupt Christ, a depraved Nazi, perverted like Kurtz by the Heart of Darkness. Since love among the whites "had to do with masculine technologies" (*GR* 324), he has taught the Hereros to be priests of the Rocket, the most advanced product of man's technology, but in actuality "an entire system *won*, away from the feminine darkness held against the entropies of lovable but scatterbrained Mother Nature" (*GR* 324).

In achieving this Blicero has not only alienated them from their own culture which informed them to believe in "Earth's gift for genesis" (*GR* 316) — their tribal totem is the Erdschwein, "earthpig" — but he has also infected them with his death-wish, his romantic sense of Gotterdämmerung, following the defeat of the Nazis. The Hereros can therefore be said to have been doubly victimized by what Pynchon in distinction with the Preterite and in accordance with Calvinist duality calls the Elect, the powerful, those who are in a position to control and manipulate the others.

But Blicero may still be regarded as an exceptional member of the Elect, a man regrettably destined to change from "prince to fabulous monster" (*GR* 660), a man yearning to achieve transcendence through a love-death. More representative is that other character who made the invention of the Rocket possible, Laszlo Jamf, like Pointsman a behaviorist, but turned chemist. It is also this man who is responsible for Tyrone's affinity with the Rocket: in the 1920s he conducted an experiment at Harvard for I.G. Farben which was carried out on the infant Tyrone, conditioning him to respond sexually to "a mystery stimulus." This stimulus, actually a chemical component, was later to be used as a vital part in the guiding system of the Rocket. Since Jamf was unable to extinguish entirely Tyrone's response to this chemical, it may furnish a "rational" explanation of the latter's affinity with the Rocket.

The symbolic significance of this fantastic experiment with regard to Tyrone is obvious. He too is in a double sense a victim of the Elect: not only has he been alienated from his human identity by the ruthless application of technology, he also continues to be deprived of his freedom by being kept under The Firm's close surveillance, and, after he has managed to escape from "Their" control in the Zone, by being relentlessly hounded. For suppose he might decide to trade his "secret" to either the Russians, or the Hereros, who, like The Firm, are also embarked on a frantic search for the German V-2s. This of course could never be allowed.

Tyrone, however, has no interest in "trading," for which, like his ancestors, he has never shown a great talent — one of the reasons why the Slothrops, although nominally belonging to the Elect, had actually always belonged to the Preterite. Tyrone's main interest is the redemption of his soul, an interest threatened by what The Firm considers the "real business" of the world, which of course *is* "trading," an activity even more rewarding in war-time than in peacetime since war, according to Pynchon, is basically "a celebration of markets" (*GR* 105).

Origin and character, then, destine Tyrone to take up his place among the Preterite, just like the Hereros, but unlike them he does not end up as another priest of technology, nor as a participator in the death-wish of those of the Elect who have experienced defeat. Tyrone's end, as we shall see, is different, resembling that of the Leatherstocking figure, although here too interesting differences begin to emerge.

In Cooper's work the "innocent souls" are also those for whom the System has no use. They are in the first place the Indians, reduced in *The Pioneers* to an inglorious existence of drunken depravity, the indirect result of the System's overriding concern with the profit-motive. True, Cooper makes them choose a fiery death on the mountain which he rather presciently calls The Vision, but the tribute he thus pays them, reiterated in the later Leatherstocking Tales by his revivifying Indian John as the brave warrior Chingachgook, noble Chief of the Delawares, issues from a personal dream rather than from historical reality. The historical reality was that the Indians, like Pynchon's Preterite, already belonged to the "passed over," the rejected, a category of men, however, which, as we shall see, also includes Natty Bumppo, the Leatherstocking figure.

Although one cannot say that in *The Pioneers* Natty submits to the Elect, represented by Judge Temple and his associates, without offering resistance, the fight he puts up to defend and guard his individual autonomy proves futile — what with his misplaced trust in the fairness of man-made law, and his own lack of duplicity with which he could have met his judges on their own ground. Rather than stay after the ignominy of being put in prison and in the stocks, he therefore turns his back on white civilization, and in the rest of the Leatherstocking Tales we only meet him on the frontier, the region where just as in Pynchon's Zone the System cannot yield power yet, and where Natty's particular "gifts" enable him to be in complete control of his own life.

But like his obsolete flint rifle to which he stubbornly sticks in preference to the more advanced models that have replaced it, Natty himself, worn out and miserable at the end of *The Prairie*, has become obsolete. His frontier skills of hunter and scout, once the pride of his manhood, are no longer needed and respected, are, in fact, rapidly becoming redundant, as the "sportsmen" hunters begin to slaughter the buffalo by the thousands, firing at them from open trainwindows.

Leatherstocking may die supported on the one side by Middleton, a white man, and on the other by Hard-Heart, an Indian, but the symbolic significance of this scene is illusionary too. The blessing he gives Hard-Heart is to some one who in the most literal sense already belongs to "the passed over," the abandoned, and Middleton, despite the friendship he feels for the young Pawnee, continues to look upon the Indians as "savages," whom he, a firm believer in the white man's "civilizing" mission, cannot but regard as inferior. Natty may stand between them, but he is no mediator since what he could mediate goes unrecognized: the Indians remain strangers to his Christian "gifts," while the whites find his Indian "gifts" embarrassing, since they stand in the way of "progress."

The Pawnees may honor Leatherstocking as "the just Chief of the Palefaces," but Natty, belonging to the Preterite himself, is in no position to save them from their impending fate. And even if he had been, it is doubtful whether he would have done so. To him, as to Middleton, the Indians are also basically "savages," "varmint," the only exceptions being the Delawares and the Pawnees, but even among these his heart only goes out to a few individuals — Chingachgook, Uncas, Tamenund, and Hard-Heart. Natty's indifference to the Indians in general is shown nowhere more clearly than in that passage from *The Prairie* in which he tells Bush that he too had fought under General Wayne, "Mad Anthony," the Indian-fighter. The reason why, is revealing:

> "I was passing from the states on the seashore into these far regions when I crossed the trail of his army, and I fell in on his rear, just as a looker-on; but when they got to blows, the crack of my rifle was heard among the rest, though to my shame it may be said, I never knew the right of the quarrel as well as a man of threescore and ten should know the reason of his acts afore he takes mortal life, which is a gift he never can return!"[3]

Not only is he ignorant of "the right of the quarrel" with the Indians, the right of the quarrel with the French, or with the English for that matter, escapes him as well. Thus in *The Pathfinder* he remarks that "there is no great difference atween an Englishman and a Frenchman, a'ter all,"[4] and the reason why he fights on the side of the English, and

3. James Fenimore Cooper, *The Prairie: A Tale* (1827; rpt. New York: Signet, 1964), 66.

4. James Fenimore Cooper, *The Pathfinder; or The Inland Sea* (1840; rpt. New York: Signet, 1961), 393.

in the War of Independence on the side of the revolutionists, is to all appearances the same as the one that made him fight the Indians under "Mad Anthony": he happens to be there, and being the man he is, cannot resist the call for action.

Natty's allegiance, then, is neither really to the Indians, nor to the whites, which incidentally can also be said of his bloodbrother, Chingachgook. They are in fact the first and the last of their kinds, and although Cooper dramatizes through their individual fates the one major historical event of nineteenth-century America, he has not attempted to make them representative of a solution that might have been an alternative to the one that was being enacted under his very eyes: the annihilation of one culture by another.

An explanation is not far to seek. Cooper, the man, never really doubted the prevailing nineteenth-century view that the true meaning of American history lay in transforming the state of the American wilderness into a state of civilization. And true civilization was white civilization, also to Cooper, no matter how severely he criticized the direction this transformation was taking, no matter how great his sympathy for the Indians (admittedly *his* Indians rather than *the* Indians) may have been.

Numbers and superior technology destined the latter to belong to history's "passed over," and Cooper was keenly aware of what this meant in terms of individual tragedy, as his Leatherstocking Tales impressively show. But he never squarely faced the moral problem inherent in the dispossession of the Indians of their lands and their culture. The character of Natty Bumppo was created to serve as an alternative to the type of backwoodsman that confirmed Cooper's worst suspicions about the course America's Manifest Destiny took, and hardly bears on the Indian problem. But he also must have realized that the Billy Kirbys were inevitable if the nation's westward movement was to succeed. It made his Leatherstocking stand outside history, and become a symbol. Which brings us back to Tyrone Slothrop, our modern Leatherstocking. Or is he?

The reason for Tyrone's escape to the Zone may be the same as the one that drove Natty to the frontier, but what complicates Tyrone's flight is that he, unlike the Leatherstocking figure, is never sure of his identity. Is he an American Army lieutenant sent on a secret mission to the Zone, about the purpose of which he is kept in the dark but which he nevertheless carries out? Or is he the man who has come to suspect that he is being used as a pawn in The Firm's world-wide game, the purpose of which is "to do business," with friend and foe alike? Tyrone must find out and in order to find out he must find the Rocket, The Firm's latest and costliest commodity in feeding the System's love of death, the secret of Tyrone's conditioning.

Under various mythic guises, the latest being a Wagnerian costume which makes him look like Rocketman, he sets out on his quest. It gets him involved in a series of pursuit-captivity-and-escape-adventures as exciting and fantastic as those Cooper regales us with, in which he matches in bravery and resourcefulness Cooper's hero, albeit on a note of hilarious zaniness entirely alien to the latter's writings. But the Rocket keeps eluding him, and so the secret of his identity.

However, what Tyrone does learn on his wanderings North in search of the Rocket is that the total freedom of the Zone appears to be a condition which "not many of us can bear for long" (*GR* 434). Instead of facilitating his search, it causes in the end his undoing. What the Zone lacks is a meaningful pattern, dooming those inside to go on "kicking endlessly among the plastic trivia ... and trying ... to make sense out of, to find the meanest sliver of truth in so much replication, so much waste" (*GR* 590). Conditioned to function within the System, primarily on the cause-and-effect principle, Tyrone lacks the means to make sense of his existence in the Zone, the world where there are no meaningful patterns yet, where everything is fluid. He consequently finds himself in a vacuum, and since he lacks a solid sense of self he is soon convinced that both outside and inside the separateness of the self there is nothing, a void. Like Natty, Tyrone cannot live in The Firm's rigidly patterned and deterministic world, but unlike the Leatherstocking figure, whom the nineteenth-century Cooper has furnished with an unshakeable sense of self, he cannot live in the as yet unstructured world of the Zone either. Chaos starts engulfing him, and instead of being present "at his own assembly," he witnesses his "disassembling."

Tyrone, the Rocketman, also becomes a symbol, a "charismatic" figure like Leatherstocking, but unlike the latter not one, as Joseph Slade believes, "without a following, never to be rationalized, never to redirect a death-loving System."[5] Pynchon's view of Tyrone — a character who can neither live inside nor outside the System — may seem to betray an even gloomier determinism than Cooper displays in the creation of Leatherstocking, but this proves to be deceptive. Pynchon is not really a nineteenth-century adherent of the principle of excluded middles, as Cooper was, who could only conceive dualities:

---

5. Joseph W. Slade, *Thomas Pynchon* (New York: Warner, 1974), 210.

civilization and wilderness, red and white (never to mingle), total control and absolute freedom, love and hate, good and evil, redemption and bondage, life and death, an approach largely responsible for his stereotyped characterization and the rigidity of his novels' ideological content.

That Tyrone was sent to the Zone to be present at his assembly, that is, to find and assert his recovered self, but "was being broken down instead, and scattered" (*GR* 738), is only one story about his end. There are also those who believe that "fragments of Slothrop have grown into consistent personae of their own," and if that is what happened, "there's no telling which of the Zone's present-day population are offshoots of his original shattering" (*GR* 742).

Considering the people towards whom the sympathies in *Gravity's Rainbow* are directed, there is little doubt that, if this is the true story of Tyrone's end, these "offshoots" should belong to the Preterite. Not only does this refute Slade's conclusion that Tyrone is outside history, which would put him on a par with the Leatherstocking figure, it also highlights another important difference in the symbolic significance of these two characters. To Pynchon it is only the Preterite who have retained "a few small chances for mercy" (*GR* 610), and the novel furnishes a number of instances to substantiate this view. If through Tyrone, Pynchon seems to demonstrate what may happen if conditioning by the System cannot be extinguished, Roger Mexico, the statistician for the White Visitation, is there to prove that the System's control need not be absolute. Roger, an anti-Pointsman, knows of the latest developments in the sciences, and he too has embraced the belief in the principles of indeterminacy, the theory that recognizes chance and hence the possibility of free will. He even looks forward to the day when scientists will "have the courage to junk cause-and-effect entirely, and strike off at some other angle" (*GR* 89), thus providing a scientific justification for the call to abolish a view of the world, determinism, which inevitably issues in "a culture of death" (*GR* 176).

Since the Preterite's stake in the affairs of The Firm is still negligible, it is among them that any organized form of opposition could arise, and when Roger sees that such an opposition, called the Counterforce, is actually taking shape — the Zone being increasingly controlled by The Firm again — he joins it. It is also Roger who still believes in the traditional idea of love as an antidote to "the culture of death," and it is he who does all he can to save Tyrone from Pointsman's evil machinations, causing in fact the undoing of Major

Harvey, one of Tyrone's most persistent pursuers, a lunatic version of Cooper's Hiram Doolittle in *The Pioneers*.

Tyrone can count on more loyal friends among the Preterite, one of the novel's few saving graces considering its all-persuasive apocalyptic mood: Geli Tripping, the witch, Bodine, the seaman, Otto and Felix, even Von Göll, the one-time filmmaker turned blackmarketeer, who eventually leads Tyrone to the Rocketbase at Peenemünde, "The Holy Center," although by then Tyrone has lost interest in the Rocket. Unable to find it, he has already started to "scatter."

There is no denying that Roger Mexico has secret doubts about whether the Counterforce will ever be forged into an organization sufficiently strong to challenge the System, the Preterite being notoriously unconcerned with ideas and therefore hard to unite for consorted action. But when at the end of the novel the Rocket — falling a mile per second — reaches the last delta-t, the book's hope that it remains "an unmeasurable gap" instead of becoming "the infinitesimal fraction of a second" before "this old theatre" will be destroyed, is pinned on the Preterite, not on The Firm. It is a slight hope, but as Pynchon's fascination with probability and indeterminacy theories may tell us, there is no longer a specific scientific reason to reject it out of hand. Chance seems to play its role in the universe — significantly, Ludwig's love for his lemming saves it from drowning, and Byron, the bulb, escapes destruction — , and determinism may not be the be-all and end-all of existence.

One of the numerous ideas underlying *Gravity's Rainbow* is that it was America's pursuit of Manifest Destiny that caused the world to miss "the fork in the road" (*GR* 556) that could have led it away from "the culture of death." This idea is also present in Cooper's work, and like Pynchon, he was inclined to put the blame on the Elect, the Haves. But unlike Pynchon, he did not expect anything from the Preterite, the People, as he called them, for reversing the invidious direction the world had taken.

Cooper believed in the right to property, holding that "most of the ordinances of civilized society, that are connected with this interest, are founded in reason, and ought to be rigidly maintained."[6] It firmly made him belong to the Elect, although he insisted on making an important distinction. There was on the one hand the financial élite, the bankers

6. James Fenimore Cooper, *The American Democrat, or Hints on the Social and Civic Relations of the United States of America* (1838; rpt. Harmondsworth: Penguin, 1969), 188.

and the emerging industrialists, whom he held responsible for much that had gone wrong in his country; on the other hand there was the landed gentry, a natural aristocracy, upholders of trusted moral values and virtues, of true civilization. In this class Cooper put his faith.

But it was a class that as a social and political force was already in the process of being rapidly replaced by the class of financiers and entrepreneurs. And in so far as Judge Temple is still a member of the landed gentry, he is a nostalgically remembered image of an idealized past; in so far as he too is becoming an entrepreneur considering his "bias to look far into futurity, in his speculation on the improvements" (*PI* 329), he reflects the shift that was taking place in the nation from an agrarian to an entrepreneurial stage, a shift Cooper deplored as a landowner, but which as an artist he merely registered. Yet, even his disappointment about the direction Jacksonian democracy had taken on his return from Europe in 1833 could not make him change his mind about the People, the Preterite among his compatriots, since, as he thought, their only interest was also money.

What informs the conception of both Natty Bumppo and Tyrone Slothrop, then, is a premise that does not seem to have changed over the past one hundred and fifty years: the premise that it is a man's right to exist as a man, as a uniquely defined individual, and to realize his humanity as fully as possible.

The forces that work against exercising this right are also basically the same for both characters. They are primarily technologies, co-opted by The Firm in pursuing its chief aim, which is "to do business," an activity that curtails individual freedom and that may eventually lead to a state of entropy if it is allowed to go unchecked.

The opposition against these forces assumes a similar form for both characters: they rebel, but in trying to escape from The Firm's control, they withdraw from civilization, Natty by retreating to the frontier, Tyrone by disappearing into the Zone, actions that are not inspired by any political or ideological motives. Natty's allegiance is neither to the Indians nor to the whites, while Tyrone is indifferent to the Allied cause in which he serves as an American officer. Their only commitment is to themselves, and is a strictly personal one: how to preserve individual autonomy.

The only way to achieve this leads to a return to nature, away from the labyrinthine complexity of civilization: Natty, a nineteenth-century creation, in the full understanding and acceptance of his mystic bondage to the wilderness, as exemplified by the last word he utters before he dies, an emphatic "Here!"; Tyrone, a twentieth-century creation, without any understanding, nature representing to him not much else than a source of undirected sexual energy, as exemplified by the image portending his dissolution in the Zone: "a stout rainbow cock driven down out of public clouds into Earth, green wet valleyed Earth, and his chest fills and he stands crying, not a thing in his head, just feeling natural ..." (*GR* 626). It makes both characters stand outside history. In Natty's case because Cooper has made him too much a man of one piece, a man who knows of no compromise between absolute freedom and total control, and who is therefore unfit to play a social role; in Tyrone's case because Pynchon has made him too little a man of one piece, and therefore equally unfit to break out of what has conditioned him.

Natty's position is particularly ironic. The qualities Cooper has invested in him are precisely those that would enable people to live in harmony with nature, the one way of recognizing true civilization, as Kay S. House puts it.[7] That Cooper did not envisage a way of making the Leatherstocking figure play a social role in furthering the creation of such a civilization must, as I have argued, also be ascribed to his own position as a member of the Elect. Through Natty he was able to vent his criticism of the deplorable direction American civilization seemed to be taking, while at the same time expressing his own nostalgia for an idyllic past without social and personal restraints. But his allegiance was to the Elect, not to the Preterite, the People, and it is from this stance that Cooper's efforts to distinguish the penniless and illiterate Natty Bumppo from the People derive their significance. He not only provided him with a set of aristocratic qualities (contempt for the merely mercenary, an absolute sense of honor and privacy), but he also took great pains in pointing out that his frontiersman moves on a foot of equality with officers and gentlemen, something that is especially noticeable in *The Pathfinder*, the novel where we meet Natty in the prime of life.

Tyrone's position in *Gravity's Rainbow* is equally ironic, and in much the same way as Natty's. His affinity with the Rocket seems to destine him to play a role in the state that "begins to take form in the stateless German night, a State that spans oceans and surface politics, sovereign as the International or the Church of Rome, and the Rocket is its soul" (*GR* 566). People like Tyrone who had been suspicious of the

7. Kay S. House, "James Fenimore Cooper: Cultural Prophet and Literary Pathfinder," in *American Literature to 1900*, ed. Marcus Cunliffe (London: Sphere, 1973), 123.

old state, could be expected to be useful in the construction of a new state. But Tyrone, though generous and brave, is too occupied with his own private affairs, too uncommitted, too much a product of "the mindless pleasures" fed to him by the mass media, the popular arts, to be able to understand the significance of the Rocket beyond the fact that in some mysterious way he is related to it.

With the invention of the Rocket — revolutionary technology — mankind has arrived for the second time at "the fork in the road" which, if it were missed again, would mean a continuation of "this cycle of infection and death" (*GR* 724), so characteristic of human history. But this time man might refuse to take the wrong fork. A rocket is not merely doomed to come down, symbolic of ceaseless destruction, it can also overcome earth's gravity, symbolic of transcendence. What is likely to happen is that the pull of earth's gravity proves the greater force. This apocalyptic view no doubt informs the conception of both Tyrone and Natty. When Tyrone dissolves at the end of *Gravity's Rainbow*, he hears the explosion of the atom bomb dropped on Hiroshima ringing in his uncomprehending ears; when Natty dies at the end of *The Prairie*, he dejectedly hears the shouts of Manifest Destiny ringing in his.

But the rigidity of Cooper's approach to both character and vision is lacking in Pynchon's. What Pynchon shows us is a healthy suspicion of any rigidity in the conceptualizing process, finding no doubt support in the discovery of the principle of indeterminacy. It may explain why he does not look upon the individual and society, the wilderness and civilization, as separate and opposite entities, but as fluid and interacting categories, infinitely variable as the spirit takes man. Chance, and therefore choice, is possible, enabling man to oppose the Systems which after all are as much the products of human ingenuity as the technologies he so cannily co-opts but which nonetheless remain the greatest threat to his humanity. It is this threat that gave rise to a concern which has not perceptibly changed over a span of one and a half centuries, as the work of both Cooper and Pynchon bears witness to.

ON THE TRAIL OF A CRAFTSMAN: THE ART OF *THE PATHFINDER*

RICHARD D. RUST

While the notion still persists that James Fenimore Cooper was more social-historian than artist, repeated readings of *The Pathfinder* reveal how carefully crafted that work is. The traditional view, accepted by Stephen Railton, is that Cooper wrote quickly, impulsively, and rather carelessly because he had a "nonchalant attitude toward the creative process."[1] John McWilliams in his review of Railton's book is correct, though, in suggesting that a bit more attention to the findings of recent Cooper editors might have revealed that Cooper was more of a conscious craftsman than has been believed.[2] This has certainly been my experience. I came to admire Cooper's artistry in the process of editing *The Pathfinder* for the SUNY Press edition of *The Writings of James Fenimore Cooper*. Reading the work over and over again helped me fully to anticipate the end from the beginning and to see how purposefully Cooper was shaping his materials. Further, I discovered in the manuscript of *The Pathfinder* many clues to Cooper's intentions with the work.

Cooper's art in *The Pathfinder*, as Balzac recognized, is certainly in its scenic portrayals and its rich characterization of Pathfinder: Cooper "owes the high place he holds in modern literature to two faculties: that of painting the sea and seamen; that of idealizing the magnificent landscapes of America," and the original creation of Leatherstocking "will live as long as literatures last."[3] For the Russian critic V. G. Belinsky, "*The Pathfinder* is Shakespearian drama in the form of a

1. Stephen Railton, *Fenimore Cooper: A Study of His Life and Imagination* (Princeton: Princeton University Press, 1978), 6.

2. John P. McWilliams, Jr., rev. of Stephen Railton, *Fenimore Cooper: A Study of His Life and Imagination*, *Nineteenth-Century Fiction* 34 (1979), 86.

3. Honoré de Balzac, *The Personal Opinions of Honoré de Balzac*, trans. Katharine Prescott Wormeley (Boston: Little, Brown, and Co., 1899), 114, 115.

novel — the only creation in this genre, entirely without equal, a triumph of modern art in the sphere of epic poetry."[4] Some of the elements in the creation of this art in *The Pathfinder* are Cooper's choice of names, the multivaried and intricate relations of characters, the elements of the plot, and the book's poetry. All of these are carefully, even subtly and intricately, interwoven, creating what George Dekker has called the "most unified of the Leatherstocking tales."[5]

As an example of manuscript clues to his intentions, Cooper first called his heroine Eve (as well as Agnes) rather than Mabel, and Jasper Western was first called Harry Harbor. (Incidentally, Arrowhead was also called Arrowflint, Killdeer was Doublesight, and Charles Cap was John Cap.) Although Cooper dropped the name "Eve," it is suggestive of the symbolic weight he had in mind regarding Sergeant Dunham's daughter. While too obvious, the name "Harry Harbor" also shows how Cooper envisioned this character as representing the man of the inland sea.

The name Pathfinder seems simple and appropriate at first in its reference to the Leatherstocking's role as a guide with the British forces during the French and Indian wars. He, however, is also a path-*maker*, saying, "I rather pride myself in finding my way, where there is no path, than in finding it where there is."[6] The name takes on further meanings when Cooper has Pathfinder speak of taking "the fare that Providence bestows, while we follow the *trail of life*" (19; italics added). After falling in love with Mabel Dunham, he acknowledges that this has been a false trail (272). He becomes a path finder for the dying Sergeant Dunham, helping him on his "longest journey" and contrasting it with that of the traitorous Arrowhead whose "path cannot be the path of the just" (439). Jasper is a pathfinder in locating Station Island among the Thousand Islands, and Mabel is a pathfinder to her father on his deathbed, helping put him in an eternal path.

4. V.G. Belinsky, "The Division of Poetry into Kinds and Genres," *Notes of the Fatherland* 15 (1841), trans. M.A. Nicholson; cited in George Dekker and John P. McWilliams, *Fenimore Cooper: The Critical Heritage* (London: Routledge & Kegan Paul, 1973), 195.

5. George Dekker, *James Fenimore Cooper: The American Scott* (New York: Barnes and Noble, 1967), 169.

6. *The Pathfinder, or The Inland Sea* (1840), ed. Richard D. Rust (Albany: State University of New York Press, 1981), 18. Future references to this edition will be cited parenthetically within the text.

Jasper Western is a subtler name than Harry Harbor, with the jasper being a precious stone most frequently green in color — suggesting Jasper's association with the color of the waters of the Great Lakes — while Western points to his being a frontiersman.

While the dun in *Dun*ham is a dull grayish-brown, the name Mabel is associated in the novel with the maple tree, known for its brilliant coloration. This connection is confirmed by Pathfinder's dream that he "had a cabin in a grove of sugar maples, and at the root of every tree was a Mabel Dunham, while the birds that were among the branches, sung ballads, instead of the notes that natur' gave" (275). Mabel shows her color often by flushing when her emotions are stirred. She and her father are also subtly associated with the trees described in the opening scene, starting with "the elm, with its graceful and weeping top," followed by "the rich varieties of the maple" (9). Near the end of the novel, Sergeant Dunham is buried "beneath the shade of a huge elm" (449). And the last tree described in the opening section foretells the characterization of Pathfinder: "the tall, straight trunk of the pine, pierced the vast field, rising high above it, like some grand monument reared by art on the plain of leaves" (9). Pathfinder is subsequently described several times as tall and straight; he rises above others, and he is a monument: "When last in view," we are told, "the sinewy frame of this extraordinary man was as motionless, as if it were a statue set up in that solitary place, to commemorate the scenes of which it had so lately been the site and the witness" (461).

Muir, as in "demure" (which means *affectedly* modest or shy), comes from a word meaning ripe or mature — which is certainly relevant to the older would-be lover. More directly applicable is his association with rebelliousness in the reference in the novel to the defeat of the rebel Scotch at Colloden Muir (337). As for crusty seaman Charles Cap, twice in the novel Cooper calls him "captious" — pointing to his quibbling and faultfinding. A typical example of his criticism is his disdaining "the bit of a pond, that you call the Great Lake" (12). The Big Serpent, otherwise known as Chingachgook, is named so not because he is treacherous but because "he is wise" (20). For his part, when allied with the Big Serpent, Pathfinder is said to have "acted with the wisdom of the serpent" (398).

Further analysis shows how Cooper pairs and contrasts his characters. Throughout the book he develops the implications of Pathfinder and Jasper having the domains of the woods and water; he also works out contrasts between Muir and Pathfinder; and in intricate ways he sets up various characters as foils. These foils include Lundie and Muir, the laird's son and the parson's son, who grew up together and now are close in age but are far apart in honor and capability in leadership. Arrowhead and Muir both want Mabel as an additional wife and both are subtle traitors. Mabel with Dew-of-June parallels to a degree the White-Indian relationship between the Pathfinder and Chingachgook. Arrowhead and the Big Serpent are Indian guides, one secretly serving the French and the other openly, according to his "natur'," helping the English; the first is deceitful, the second completely trustworthy. Jasper, the lakeman, is compared and contrasted with Cap, the seaman. Again, Cap regularly contrasts the seafarer with the soldier, such as his brother-in-law Sergeant Dunham. Pathfinder is like Sergeant Dunham in being a kind of father to Mabel, and he has respect for the French warrior Captain Sanglier, just as Sanglier has respect for the notable provincial hero.

While Pathfinder is honest and just, his putative rival Muir is described as being devious, resentful, and proud. Muir's sophistry is contrasted with Pathfinder's "upright, disinterested and ingenuous nature" (302). Cooper exposes Muir gradually, revealing his childhood-based rebellion against his father and against the laird, with the King being the premier authority figure whose name Muir invokes but whom he dishonors. In speaking about treachery, Pathfinder defines the difference between Muir and himself: "Now, when I find a man all fair words, I look close to his deeds; for when the heart is right and raally intends to do good, it is generally satisfied to let the conduct speak, instead of the tongue" (378). The narrator subsequently affirms that Muir's manner "denotes artifice" and his tongue "is out of measure smooth" (414). In pursuing his greed and envy, Muir is willing to deprive Pathfinder and sacrifice Jasper.

In the most dominant paired relationship of the novel, Pathfinder and Jasper are both friends and rivals. If Pathfinder is "a sort of type of what Adam might have been supposed to be before the fall" (134), and Mabel is an Eve, Jasper is a younger Adam, modeled after Pathfinder. (At one point, Cooper says Jasper and Mabel resembled "Milton's picture of our first parents" [457].) Pathfinder and Jasper reflect the major physical dualities of the book, land and water, which are reconciled in the title *The Pathfinder, or The Inland Sea* and in the closing chapters of the book.

At first, the plot sets up a dichotomy of land *or* water. Mabel is given the choice of going into the woods with Pathfinder or staying on the water with Jasper. She chooses to stay in the canoe rather than striking out through the woods, anticipating her later choice of Jasper over Pathfinder as a marriage partner. She even changes canoes to be with Jasper Western. At the garrison, she looks first at the "dense, interminable forest" then turns to view the "field of rolling waters" (108). While viewing the scene, she is joined by Pathfinder who explicitly says, "'Here you have both our domains, ... Jasper's and mine. The lake is for him, and the woods are for me'" (110). For the time, she is satisfied with both; later, she chooses a place reached readily from the water and finally goes to a settlement on the water's edge.

The overall plot puts emphasis first on the land and then on the sea. The first half of *The Pathfinder* contains a rescue under Pathfinder's direction, safe arrival at the garrison, and the rivalry of the shooting match, and ends with distress at sea in the *Scud* with Cap at the helm. The second half of the book, corresponding to volume two in the 1840 edition, begins with a rescue at sea under Jasper's direction, then has a safe arrival at Station Island, rivalry over control of the blockhouse versus surrender, distress under attack (with lives lost), and rescue by both Pathfinder and Jasper.

Resolution of the land-sea dichotomy is anticipated by Cooper's beginning description of the "ocean of leaves" and is reconciled in the end by the joined forces of Jasper and Pathfinder at an island — a small piece of land surrounded by water. While Cap makes sharp distinctions (he says, "ours is all water, yours [speaking to Pathfinder] is all land" [23]), Pathfinder is in between: "We border men," he says, "handle the paddle and the spear, almost as much as the rifle and the hunting knife" (23). And to the young sailor he says, I "find nothing very contrary, in our gifts, though yourn belong to the lakes and mine to the woods" (33). Yet at the very end, Pathfinder returns wholly to the forest, leaving Jasper and Mabel in their cottage at the edge of the woods. The conclusion is poignant in showing the distressed Pathfinder at parting to be "lost in the depths of the forest" (468).

In addition to those already mentioned, Cooper subtly presents many situations which anticipate later events. Early on, Pathfinder tells Jasper Western to speak his feelings (54); this is echoed in a later chapter. Also, several times Jasper is reluctant to relate his own exploits. At the beginning of the novel in their cover by the riverside, Jasper and Mabel converse together for an hour, unaware of how "the time flew by swiftly" (55); then near the end when they confess their love to each other, the two spend an hour without realizing how much time has passed.

Jasper's skill in going over Oswego Falls — despite Cap's disbelief, is repeated in running the *Scud* up near the shore to catch the undertow. Cooper emphasizes this connection by having Cap say, "the lad has a handy way with him in a gale, it must be owned," with Pathfinder responding, "And in coming over water-falls!" (405).

In wanting to win the shooting match and thus be able to present the calash to Mabel, Jasper is, according to Pathfinder, "Never satisfied with his own gifts, but forever craving that which Providence denies!" (166). Yet later in desiring marriage with Mabel, Pathfinder realizes that he himself is "craving that which Providence denies."

Other intricacies of plot are pointed out by William Owen, William Kelly, and Geoffrey Rans. In his essay "In War as in Love: The Significance of Analogous Plots in Cooper's *The Pathfinder*," Owen shows how the military and romantic plots have analogous narrative structures and themes — "the following of a false trail, the misuse of authority, and the need for experience."[7] Kelly develops the negative consequences of dependence in the novel as well as Cooper's "strenuous attack on unbridled originality,"[8] with the resolution of the novel showing the limitations and maturity of Mabel, Jasper, and Natty. Rans shows how "the process of choice lies at the thematic, generic, narrative, and structural heart of *The Pathfinder*."[9]

Just as Mabel and Jasper "become acquainted through their feelings rather than their expressed thoughts" (22), so Cooper's initial epigraph resonates throughout the novel. This epigraph is from the poet Cowper, " — Here the heart / May give a useful lesson to the head, / And Learning wiser grow without his books." The villain Muir is all head, and he accuses Sergeant Dunham of taking "counsel of his heart, instead of his head" (320). Both Cap and Muir are limited by their philosophizing, with the crusty seaman being led astray by his reason — especially in his discounting "seeing or feeling" in favor of "proving" Jasper's guilt by logic. (This illustrates Donald Ringe's point that

---

7. William Owen, "In War as in Love: The Significance of Analogous Plots in Cooper's *The Pathfinder*," *English Studies in Canada* 10 (1984), 290.

8. William P. Kelly, *Plotting America's Past: Fenimore Cooper and the Leatherstocking Tales* (Carbondale: Southern Illinois University Press, 1983), 138.

9. Geoffrey Rans, *Cooper's Leather-Stocking Novels: A Secular Reading* (Chapel Hill: University of North Carolina Press, 1991), 200.

Cooper had a fundamental distrust of unaided human reason.[10]) Jasper, on the other hand, is praised by Pathfinder for his true tongue and heart (170), and Pathfinder in countering Muir's perfidies affirms his favoring the heart, "Talk to me of no ensigns, and signals, when I know the heart — " (421).

Finally, Cooper's art in *The Pathfinder* is evident in his poetic prose. The epigraphs are all pieces of poetry, most of them inscribed at the time and some added later. There is a resonance between these epigraphs and the poetic qualities found in each chapter, with the narrator's and Pathfinder's voices being most poetic in their natural use of figurative language. Cooper's poetry is found in his rich scenic descriptions, exemplified by his description of "an ocean of leaves" in the western forest which formed "one broad and seemingly interminable carpet of foliage, that stretched away towards the setting sun, until it bounded the horizon, by blending with the clouds, as the waves and sky meet at the base of the vault of Heaven" (8, 9). An early example of Pathfinder's poetry is found in his response to Mabel: "And this poor flower, that first blossomed in the clearin's; shall it wither in this forest?" Cooper first followed this with "objected his friend." But he then changed the period to a comma and added, "with a poetry that he had unconsciously imbibed by his long association with the Delawares" (58) — thus emphasizing Pathfinder's poetic mode of speech. A natural poet, Pathfinder hears and describes the voice of God "in the creaking of a dead branch, or in the song of a bird" (93); he metaphorically calls Mabel "a ray of the sun" that had come "across the gloom of a cheerless day" (459); and he anticipates Whitman in his expansiveness: "With the heavens over my head, to keep me in mind of the last great hunt, and the dried leaves beneath my feet, I tramp over the ground as freely as if I was its lord and owner, and what more need heart desire?" (431-32).

Robert Spiller said that while Washington Irving and William Cullen Bryant "had helped to create an art for America, ... Cooper took the first strong step toward an American art."[11] *The Pathfinder* bears out the validity of Spiller's observation. With his characteristic stylistic expansiveness, Cooper in *The Pathfinder* has developed strong themes

10. Donald A. Ringe, *James Fenimore Cooper*, rev. edn (1962; rpt. Boston: Twayne Publishers, 1988), 124.

11. Robert E. Spiller, *The Cycle of American Literature: An Essay in Historical Criticism* (New York: MacMillan, 1955), 45.

such as identity, love, and death through thoughtful attention to names, character relationships, intricacies of plot and poetic discourse to give us a carefully crafted, fully realized work of art.

DIS-PLACING *SATANSTOE*

THEO D'HAEN

It is a commonplace in Cooper criticism that the Littlepage trilogy — of which *Satanstoe* (1845) is the first part, followed by *The Chainbearer* (1845), and *The Redskins* (1846) — is about how the original owners of large New York estates were "dis-placed" from their properties by the refusal of the descendants of their original leaseholders to continue to pay rent on land they considered their own through custom and usage. In his preface to *Satanstoe* Cooper himself stated that "'Satanstoe' and the 'Chainbearer,' relate directly to the great New York question of the day, ANTI-RENTISM, which question will be found to be pretty fully laid bare in the third and last book of the series."[1] In his view, New York at the time of anti-rentism was "much the most disgraced state in the Union, ... and her disgrace arises from the fact that her laws are trampled underfoot, without any efforts, at all commensurate with the object, being made to enforce them" (4). Later in the novel he will put it even stronger, when in his guise as editor he inserts a footnote complaining that a number of the oldest estates in New York "in our day, and principally through the culpable apathy, or miserable demagogueism, of those who have been entrusted with the care of the public weal, have been the pretext for violating some of the plainest laws of morality that God has communicated to man" (33).

In his discussion of Cooper's Littlepage and Wallingford novels in his *Political Justice in a Republic: James Fenimore Cooper's America*, John P. McWilliams, Jr. has demonstrated rather convincingly how Cooper — even though most critics since have taken him to task for his "conservatism" — had things correct not just from a divine, but also from a plain legal point of view, even if the settlers' claim may be

---

1. *Satanstoe, or The Littlepage Manuscripts. A Tale of the Colony* (1845), eds & introd. Kay Seymour House and Constance Ayers Denne (Albany: State University of New York Press, 1990), 3. All future references to this edition will be cited parenthetically within the text.

allowed to have had some moral ground to it.[2] And even though Cooper felt involved in anti-rentism for personal reasons — so that Eric Sundquist, as one of the more recent in a long line of critics, feels compelled to discuss the earlier *Home as Found* (1838), in which Cooper addresses the same issue, in terms of the degree to which it, and particularly the central incident in it concerning the ownership of Three-Mile Point, is autobiographical[3] — it is clear from the preface to *Satanstoe* that he also felt that there were a number of real principles at stake in the issue: "[a]greeably to our view of the matter, the existence of true liberty among us, the perpetuity of the institutions, and the safety of public morals, are all dependent on putting down, wholly, absolutely, and unqualifiedly, the false and dishonest theories and statements that have been boldly advanced in connection with this subject" (4). These principles — all of them closely linked to those issues of "genealogy" and "authority" Sundquist, in his readings not just of Cooper but also of Thoreau, Hawtorne, and Melville, defined as central to nineteenth-century America — Cooper saw as guaranteeing the stability and legitimacy of the American nation, and it is these principles he felt as being threatened, corrupted, and perverted, or which he, in short, felt as being in one way or another *dis-placed* in mid nineteenth-century America. In *Satanstoe*, then, as in most of his other work, and particularly his best known series of novels, the Leatherstocking tales, Cooper's concern is not limited to one individual, one family, one property; he is concerned with the destiny of the nation as a whole. In the novel under discussion he addressed these issues, as he saw them, and both on the level of the individual and of the nation, via his handling of two elements that are present in all of his fiction, and in most romance: the marriage plot and the problem of names and naming.

* * *

The issue of territorial displacement is central to the plot of *Satanstoe*. To begin with, part of the novel deals with Abercrombie's ill-starred

---

2. John P. McWilliams, Jr., *Political Justice in a Republic: James Fenimore Cooper's America* (Berkeley: University of California Press, 1972), 298-339.

3. Eric I. Sundquist, *Home as Found: Authority and Genealogy in Nineteenth-Century American Literature* (Baltimore: Johns Hopkins University Press, 1979), 3-8.

1758 expedition against the invading French, and hence implies the real possibility of foreign rule. However, even in the novel itself this possibility is never seriously advanced, and mainly serves to justify the raid upon the protagonists' wilderness settlements by the Indian allies of the French. The Indian issue has repeatedly been taken up by Cooper criticism, and I will not go into it here. More important, there is the struggle for supremacy between the English and the American colonials, and among the latter between those of English and those of Dutch descent. Last, there is the issue of individual ownership, and of anti-rentism. To both these latter points Cooper provides a solution via marriage, both on the level of his protagonists' genealogy and of the plot leading up to their own marriage. George Dekker, in his *James Fenimore Cooper: The Novelist*, argues that

> Like Scott's, Cooper's characters are usually representatives of a class — national, regional, racial, or social — and therefore their relations with each other are both individual and representative. Such is the case in, for instance, *The Pioneers*, or, more obviously, the first half of *The Spy*. An even better example is *Satanstoe*, a late novel dealing with pre-revolutionary America in which a colonial belle of mixed Dutch and English extraction is courted by a colonial of the same background and by a British officer from 'Home', i.e. England; she eventually chooses to make *her* home with the American. It does not require much cleverness to perceive that Cooper is here exploring the colonial schizophrenia which had to be healed before a national consciousness, and a nation, could come into being. Cooper almost invariably uses courtship and marriage in this way in his fiction: he doubtless saw his own marriage to Susan De Lancey as representative of the fruitful reconciliation of parties in the new nation. At its best, as in *Satanstoe*, it is a very effective device.[4]

It requires not much cleverness either to see that in *Satanstoe* it is not only Corny Littlepage and his "colonial belle" Anneke (in an editorial footnote Cooper tells us the name should be pronounced "On-na-*kay*" [35]) Mordaunt that fit the paradigm, but that they do so likewise in both their ancestry. Specifically, the marriages of both the Littlepage and the Mordaunt families legitimize on the individual and the

4. George Dekker, *James Fenimore Cooper: The Novelist* (London: Routledge & Kegan Paul, 1967), 67-68.

genealogical level the brute facts of politics: the transfer of the land from the original Dutch (the issue of the *real* original owners of the land, the Indians, never enters into the discussion in *Satanstoe*) to the new owners, the English. Both Corny's and Anneke's grandfathers are English, both marry Dutch heiresses; both their sons — Corny's and Anneke's fathers — likewise marry relatively well-off women of Dutch descent. Here again, then, we are faced with a literal dis-placement of one set of owners by another. However, the difference between this dis-placement and that as advocated and practiced by anti-rentism lies in the legitimacy of the former as compared to the illegitimacy of the latter, in the former being sanctioned by custom and law — notably marriage law — , and the latter's breach of custom and law. That is why Corny Littlepage, at the time of writing the owner of the New York estate "Satanstoe," and the autobiographical narrator of the novel, carefully details how his father, Major Evans Littlepage, inherited the property from his father and Corny's grandfather, Captain Hugh Littlepage: "it might, even at the time of my birth, be considered old family property, it having indeed been acquired by my grandfather, through his wife, about thirty years after the final cession of the colony to the English, by its original Dutch owners. Here we had lived, then, near half a century, when I was born, in the direct line, and considerably longer if we included maternal ancestors" (9).

That it is the "marriage" of the two, the Dutch and the English, that counts, is corroborated if we compare the other possible romantic connections in the novel. A marriage between Anneke and either Major Bulstrode or Dirck "Follock" — in the symbolic context of the novel it is not irrelevant that both are "cousins" to her, as is Corny, though the latter, "not too close"! — is undesirable, as it would imply backsliding into either the British or the Dutch orbit. A marriage between Anneke's friend Mary Wallace — colonial, though of one hundred percent British stock — and Guert ten Eyck — colonial, but of one hundred percent Dutch stock — is impossible. The restricted colonial milieu in which both have grown up has reinforced their respective "national characters" to excess. Clearly, the only solution is a marriage between those two characters that, through their mixed descent, are already "cross-sections" of the new nation to come. As Guert ten Eyck dies, and Mary Wallace, Major Bulstrode, and Dirck Follock remain single, the "future" of the new nation is clearly a matter for Anneke and Corny, and for what they stand for. With the union of Anneke Mordaunt and Corny Littlepage, then, American society, in the eyes of Cooper, reaches an almost ideal level of continuity and stability.

* * *

In an astute reading of *Home as Found* Eric Sundquist has demonstrated that "the problem of naming, and the right to a name, is always a central one for Cooper."[5] We can gauge the problem if we consider that the index to Richard Slotkin's *Regeneration through Violence: The Mythology of the American Frontier, 1600-1860* lists, as a subheading under the entry "Cooper, James Fenimore," "Leatherstocking tales," then subdivides "Bumppo, Nathaniel (Natty) in," and further particularizes "as Deerslayer," "as Hawkeye," "as Leatherstocking,"[6] and if we realize that even then there is one more "alias" missing from this list: "La Longue Carabine." This onomastic plurality of Cooper's in the Leatherstocking tales has often been remarked upon before, and through the writings of his imitators, not just American but also European, such as Karl May, it has become part and parcel of the western tale's generic stock-in-trade. However, this particularity of Cooper's is not limited to the hero of the Leatherstocking tales. It spreads to other characters in these tales, and via these characters to other works by Cooper. As instances in point we can refer to the various members, operating in various guises and under various aliases, of the Effingham family, which Cooper introduces in *The Pioneers* (1823), and which occupies center stage in the so-called "Silk-Stocking" tales,[7] *Homeward Bound* (1838) and *Home as Found*. In *Satanstoe* onomastic plurality assumes the threat of what I will call onomastic dis-placement doubling the territorial displacement that is the more overt subject of the novel, and that is countered by the marriage plot.

The most obvious instance of onomastic dis-placement in *Satanstoe* occurs in the very beginning of the novel, when Corny Littlepage explicitates the name "Satanstoe" to us:

> Before I enter into a more minute description of Satanstoe, it may be well perhaps to say a word concerning its somewhat peculiar name. The Neck [a local term for peninsula] lies in the

5. Sundquist, 12.

6. Richard Slotkin, *Regeneration through Violence: The Mythology of the American Frontier, 1600-1860* (Middletown, CT: Wesleyan University Press, 1973).

7. The phrase, as Sundquist notes, was coined by Arvid Schulenberg, *Cooper's Theory of Fiction: His Prefaces and Their Relation to His Novels* (Lawrence, KS: University of Kansas Press, 1955).

vicinity of a well-known pass that is to be found in the narrow arm of the sea that separates the island of Manhattan from its neighbour, Long Island; and which is called Hell Gate. Now, there is a tradition, that I confess is somewhat confined to the blacks of the neighborhood, but which says that the Father of Lies, on a particular occasion, when he was violently expelled from certain roystering taverns in the New Netherlands, made his exit by this well-known dangerous pass, and drawing his foot somewhat hastily from among the lobster pots that abound in those waters, leaving behind him as a print of his passage by that route, the Hog's Back, the Pot, and all the whirlpools and rocks that render navigation so difficult in that celebrated strait, he placed it hurriedly upon the spot where there now spreads a large bay to the southward and eastward of the Neck, just touching the latter with the ball of his great toe, as he passed Down East; from which part of the country some of our people used to maintain he originally came. Some fancied resemblance to an inverted toe (the devil being supposed to turn every thing with which he meddles, upside-down) has been imagined to exist in the shape and swells of our paternal acres, a fact that has probably had its influence in perpetuating the name.

Satanstoe has the place been called, therefore, from time immemorial, as time is immemorial in a country in which civilized time commenced not a century and a half ago, and Satanstoe it is called to-day. I confess I am not fond of unnecessary changes, and I sincerely hope this neck of land will continue to go by its old appellation, as long as the House of Hanover shall sit on the throne of these realms, or as long as water shall run and grass shall grow. There has been an attempt made to persuade the neighborhood, quite lately, that the name is irreligious and unworthy of an enlightened people, like this of West-Chester, but it has met with no great success. It has come from a Connecticut man, whose father they say is a clergyman of the "*standing* order," so called I believe because they stand up at prayers, and who came among us himself in the character of a schoolmaster. This young man, I understand, has endeavoured to persuade the neighborhood that Satanstoe is a corruption, introduced by the Dutch, from Devil's Town, which, in its turn, was a corruption from Dibbleston, the family from which my grandfather's father-in-law purchased having been, as he says, of the name of Dibblee. He has got half-a-dozen of the more sentimental part of our society to call the Neck, Dibbleton, but the attempt is not likely to succeed in the long run, as we are not a people much given to altering the language, any more than the customs of our ancestors. Besides, my Dutch ancestors did

> not purchase from any Dibblee, no such family ever owning the place, that being a bold assumption of the Yankee, to make out his case the more readily. (9-10)

From *The American Democrat*, Cooper's social and political primer, published in the same year as *Home as Found*, we know that to him giving in to public opinion equaled giving in to mob rule, a fear he saw come true in anti-rentism, where the — in all senses of the word — "popular" will was translated by demagogues into political majorities, and hence into political acts directed *against* custom and law.[8] In the context of Cooper's more general opinions on American democracy, then, it is important to note that the contest between "Dibbleton" and "Satanstoe" is the contest between the *opinion* of the neighbors, fired by hearsay and expedience, and the individual narrator's *knowledge* of tradition. With regard to the value he attached to the former we can cite *Satanstoe* itself, where Corny remarks:

> The neighbours! — what a contemptible being a man becomes, who lives in constant dread of the comments and judgments of these social supervisors! and what a wretch the habit of deferring to no principle better than their decision, has made many a being, who has had originally the materials of something better in him, than has been developed by the *surveillance* of ignorance, envy, vulgarity, gossiping and lying! In those cases where education, social position, opportunities, and experience have made any material difference between the parties, the man who yields to such a government, exhibits the picture of a giant held in bondage by a pigmy. I have always remarked too, that they who are best qualified to sit in this neighborhood-tribunal, generally keep most aloof from it, as repugnant to their tastes and habits, thus leaving its decisions to the portion of the community least qualified to make such as are either just, or enlightened. (40)

However, the contest between "Satanstoe" and "Dibbleton" is also a contest between Corny Littlepage and Jason Newcome, the Yankee — and as such one of Cooper's *bêtes noires*, together with those other manipulators of public opinion, newspaper editors and lawyers. Jason threatens the continuity and stability that Corny values so highly, and

---

8. *The American Democrat, or Hints on the Social and Civic Relations of the United States of America* (Cooperstown, NY: H. & E. Phinney, 1838).

that Cooper sought to shield and safeguard in the marriage of Corny and Anneke. In *Satanstoe* the threat is limited to the level of language, but in the later novels of the trilogy that threat will also pertain to the land of the Littlepages.

* * *

As will have been clear from my references to existing scholarship on Cooper, the importance of the marriage plot in *Satanstoe*, and of the particular passage I quoted earlier with regard to names and naming, has often been recognized. What has perhaps been less often recognized is that also the names of the characters in *Satanstoe* contribute to the various forms of displacement operative in the novel.

First, there is Jason himself, whose name is said to be

> Newcome, or, as he pronounced the latter appellation himself, Noocome. As he affected a pedantic way of pronouncing the last syllable long, or as it was spelt, he rather called himself Noo-comb — instead of Newcum, as is the English mode, whence he soon got the nick-name of Jason Old Comb, among the boys; the lank, orderly arrangement of his jet-black, and somewhat greasy-looking locks, contributing their share toward procuring for him the *sobriquet*, as I believe the French call it. (39)

In one paragraph we are here presented with five different appellations, most remarkable being the opposition between how Jason calls himself — "Noo-comb" — and how the community, here represented by the boys, calls him — "Old Comb". Of these two the latter is closest to that of "Leatherstocking," in that it corresponds to a physical attribute of the man it is applied to. Yet, whereas with "Leatherstocking" the *sobriquet* fits both the appearance and the spirit of the man, with Jason there decidedly is a split between the two. If anything, he is a "new comb," in his repeated clashes, fired by mistaken notions, with custom and tradition. In fact, as his own mistaken pronunciation of his name indicates, he has lost all touch with the continuity of custom and tradition. He adheres — literally — to the letter and not to the spirit of things; as with his advocacy of "Dibbleton," his own name is an instant genealogy, generated by the alphabet, and the authority he is after is that of his fellow ignoramuses.

Of course, through long acquaintance we have got used to the name of the hero of the Leatherstocking tales, but if we stop to think of it,

Natty Bumppo is such an incongruous, even ridiculous, name that it really only can function as a blank to be filled in by names won, honorifics earned for valorous deeds done, for superior qualities demonstrated. Not so in *Satanstoe*: it is Jason's original name — both in its orthodox pronunciation and in Jason's own peculiar sounds — that is the most appropriate measure, or handle, to the man, and this holds for all other characters in the novel. The later names given to the characters — Follock or Vollock for Van Valkenburgh, Yaap for Jaap — are mere corruptions of the originals, signs of a fallen age. Therefore the narrator takes great care to detail the place and circumstance in which he himself uses these corrupted names, and where appropriate he insists on the original names. In the case of his black servant, whom he has started out calling — or spelling — "Jacob, or Jaap, but who was commonly called Yaap," (28) and whom he then variously calls by one of these names, but mostly "Yaap" for the next few hundred pages, he resolves the matter with "Yaap, or Jaap, as I shall call him in future," (306) in favor of the original Dutch spelling. And as far as his friend "Follock" is concerned, he admits to using that appellation himself, but he does so in a passage in which the name is immediately linked to that of "Satanstoe" itself, and the reason he adduces for using the one name also holds for the other:

> I love old names, such as my father knew the same places by, and I like to mispronounce a word, when custom and association render the practice familiar. I would not call my friend Dirck Follock, any thing else but Follock, unless it might be in a formal way, or when asking him to drink a glass of wine with me, for a great deal. So it is with Satanstoe; the name is homely, I am willing to allow, but it is strong, and conveys an idea. It relates, also, to the notions and usages of the country, and names ought always to be preserved, except in those few instances in which there are good reasons for altering them. (434-35)

While the Leatherstocking tales, at least in origin, deal with unnamed country, in *Satanstoe* no Adamic naming of places and people remains possible. Hence, any "new" names can only be corruptions. It is worth making the point, once again, that the "original" names here are the Dutch, the corrupted the English.

The names Corny holds dear, then, are, like the various names of Natty Bumppo, earned ones. Throughout his work Cooper insists on this earned character of names, whether it be in his own guise as third-person narrator, as in *The Pioneers*, where the "leatherstocking" is visually presented to us, or in the guise of his first-person narrator in *Satanstoe* who insists that "Corny Littlepage is not a bad name, in itself, and I trust they who do me the favour to read this manuscript, will lay it down with the feeling that the name is none the worse for the use I have made of it" (12). Just as Corny is very much intent on establishing his own genealogy, and thereby the legitimacy of his ancestral right to Satanstoe, he is intent on establishing the legitimacy of the name of "Satanstoe," and the arguments by which he does so run exactly parallel to those he used in the other spheres. In a conversation with Major Bulstrode Corny explains: "Satanstoe; I do not wonder you smile, for it has an odd sound, but it is the name my grandfather has given the family place in West- Chester. Given I have said, though translated would be better; as I understand the present appellation is pretty literally rendered into English from the Dutch," (87) and earlier on he had stated that his grandfather "had married, and established himself at Satan's Toe; or as he spelt it, and as we all have spelt it, now, this many a day, Satanstoe" (22). Just as the English lineages from which Corny and Anneke issue literally as well as legitimately "begot" the present upon the original Dutch, just as the English bestow their English name New York upon the New Netherlands after the cession, just so, through another "happy marriage," then, the English language has "begotten" "Satanstoe" upon the original Dutch name of the property in a way parallel to the change of patronym of its owners. It is worth insisting that it is only the patronym that changes, because both with "Anneke" and with "Corny" from "Cornelius" the Dutch "base" to the dynasty remains firm.

The contest between "Satanstoe" and "Dibbleton," then, or between Corny and Jason, is also a contest between two views of America, two interpretations of its past and two blueprints for its future. Throughout *Satanstoe* Corny Littlepage is at great pains to establish the "material difference" in "education, social position, opportunities, and experience" between himself and Jason. The difference comes out clearly when we compare Corny's mixed English-Dutch "gentleman" descent, his schooling in the Classics by the English clergyman the Rev. Worden, his early travels in the colonies, and his college-education at Nassau Hall — later Princeton — , with the following description of Jason:

> Jason was the son of an ordinary Connecticut farmer, of the usual associations, and with no other pretension to education than such as was obtained in a common school, or any reading

> which did not include the scriptures, some half-dozen volumes of sermons, and polemical works, all the latter of which were vigorously as well as narrowly one-sided, and a few books that had been expressly written to praise New England, and to undervalue all the rest of the earth. As the family knew nothing of the world, beyond the limits of its own township, and an occasional visit to Hartford on what is called "election-day," Jason's early life was necessarily of the most contracted experience. His English, as a matter of course, was just that of his neighbourhood and class of life, which was far from being either very elegant, or very Doric. But, on this rustic, provincial, or rather hamlet foundation, Jason had reared a superstructure of New Haven finish and proportions. As he kept school before he went to college, while he was in college, and after he left college, the whole energies of his nature became strangely directed to just such reforms of language, as would be apt to strike the imagination of a pedagogue of his calibre. In the first place, he had brought from home with him a great number of sounds that were decidedly vulgar and vicious, and with these in full existence in himself, he had commenced his system of reform on other people. As is common with all tyros, he fancied a very little knowledge sufficient authority for very great theories. His first step was to improve the language, by adapting sound in spelling .... (41-42)

Apparently, Jason's attempts to improve upon the name of Satanstoe form only part of a much wider ambition to reform the English spoken in the colonies after his own idea of it, with all the faults pertaining thereto. What Cooper thought of such efforts, we can learn, again, from *The American Democrat*, where in the chapter "On Language" we find him saying that "[t]he common faults of American language are an ambition to effect, a want of simplicity, and a turgid abuse of terms. To these may be added ambiguity of expression. Many perversions of significations also exist, and a formality of speech, which, while it renders conversation ungraceful, and destroys its playfulness, seriously weakens the power of the language, by applying to ordinary ideas, words that are suited only to themes of gravity and dignity."[9]

With regard to the name "Satanstoe," then, we might echo Cooper when he says, in the same chapter "On Language" from *The American Democrat*, that "[n]othing is ... gained, while something is lost in simplicity and clearness by the substitution of new and imperfect terms,

9. *The American Democrat*, 117-18.

for the long established words of language. In all cases in which the people of America have retained the *things* of their ancestors, they should not be ashamed to keep the *names*."[10] As Satanstoe certainly is a "thing retained," the Littlepages should not let themselves be shamed into changing its name for the reasons offered by Jason, viz. that the name "'is irreligious and profane,'" as well as "'ungenteel and vulgar, and only fit to be used in low company. Moreover, it is opposed to history and revelation, the Evil One having a huff, if you will, but no toes. Such a name couldn't stand a fortnight before public opinion in New England" (46). In fact, doing so, especially under the pressure of "public opinion," would amount to succumbing to yet another fault Cooper, in *The American Democrat*, found with his country men, viz. a lack of candor: "It would be a singular and false effect of freedom, to destroy a nation's character for candor; but we are not to be deceived by names, it being quite possible that a tyranny of opinion should produce such results, even in a democracy."[11] As Sundquist argues, "the problem of giving names, of keeping and repeating them, and of making them respectable, is for Cooper intimately bound up with the backsliding of American values, the country's rampaging commercialism, and the decay of the English language."[12] For Cooper, then, eponymously naming his novel after a place so heavily invested with symbolic value amounted to exorcizing the various ghosts he saw threatening his most cherished beliefs.

* * *

If onomastic pluralism seems the rule with Cooper, at least in *Satanstoe*, it is worth pointing out the exceptions. Guert ten Eyck, Mary Wallace, and Major Bulstrode are never named any other way, and I think the immutability of these characters' names reflects their standing for historically already superseded and discarded possibilities for the American nation. A special case, however, is the name of Herman Mordaunt, in many ways the most shadowy character in *Satanstoe*. The first time his name is mentioned it is as

10. *The American Democrat*, 122.

11. *The American Democrat*, 116.

12. Sundquist, 19.

> Herman, or, as it is pronounced, Harman Mordaunt. He was a man of considerable note in the colony, having been the son of a Major Mordaunt, of the British army, who had married the heiress of a wealthy Dutch merchant, whence the name of Herman; which had descended to the son along with the money. The Dutch were so fond of their own blood, that they never failed to give this Mr. Mordaunt his Christian name, and he was usually known in the colony as Herman Mordaunt. (56)

Later, the narrator feels compelled to state that

> I can scarcely give a reason why this gentleman was usually called, when he was spoken of, and sometimes when he was spoken to, *Herman* Mordaunt; unless, indeed, it were, that being in part of Dutch extraction, the name which denoted the circumstance (Hermanus — pronounced by the Hollanders, Her*maa*nus) was used by a portion of the population in token of the fact, and adopted by others in pure compliance. But *Herman* Mordaunt was he usually styled, and this, too, in the way of respect, and not as coarse-minded persons affect to speak of their superiors, or in a way to boast of their own familiarity. (81)

The least we can say is that Corny — or Cooper — here seems to be creating a problem where there does not seem to be one. With Herman Mordaunt the total absence of any kind of onomastic pluralism is actively insisted upon, and it is thus raised to the level of a problem for the reader. The respect being paid to Herman Mordaunt, to his descent, and to his status in the colony, and added to this his activities as the founder of a new settlement on a large tract of land he owns in the wilderness, make of Herman Mordaunt both counterpart and heir to that figure so ubiquitously present in Cooper's work, and to which Warren Motley has drawn our attention in his *The American Abraham: James Fenimore Cooper and the Frontier Patriarch.*[13] Yet, as a patriarch Herman Mordaunt remains curiously passive and in the background. This circumstance is also aided by the fact that a lot of what he does and says is reported by Corny Littlepage, but not actually registered, at variance with most of the other (main) characters in the book. In many ways he is an "absconded" patriarch, even before he effectively vacates

13. Warren Motley, *The American Abraham: James Fenimore Cooper and the Frontier Patriarch* (Cambridge: Cambridge University Press, 1987).

the scene at the end of the novel. The reasons for this are to be found, once more, both on the individual level and on that of the nation.

By leaving his own properties to Corny by the latter's marriage with Anneke, Herman Mordaunt is paving the way for a bright "future" of the individuals involved, and by going to live in town he is gracefully handing over his authority to Corny. This is also what Cooper would have liked the English, whose rule Mordaunt supports by his initially favoring a union of his daughter and Major Bulstrode, to have done, thus pre-emptying the need for the American Revolution. In other words, Herman Mordaunt represents the authority, both genealogically and personally, of the founders and continuators of the particular kind of society Cooper, at the time of writing *Satanstoe*, would also like to have seen preserved in his own times, and this precisely by those "gentlemen" Cooper saw as preserving the appropriate language, customs, and laws. The American Revolution, however, involved an overthrow of paternal authority; as has been pointed out by Eric Sundquist and Warren Motley, but also by Joseph J. Ellis in *After the Revolution: Profiles of Early American Culture*, and especially by Jay Fliegelman in *Prodigals & Pilgrims: The American Revolution against Patriarchal Authority 1750-1800*,[14] in the contemporary debate on the issue the conflict is repeatedly stated in terms of a father/son conflict, and therefore it imperilled precisely that very continuity and stability Cooper held so high in *Satanstoe*. By having Herman Mordaunt act the way he does with his properties, and by insisting on the Dutch character of his name — thus seeking allegiance with an authority even older than that of the English — and on its immutability, Cooper is projecting his own ideal solution to the problem — continuity in discontinuity — while skirting the issue of what really happened with the revolution, and with the various transfers of authority between nations and generations. By thus masking the question, though, he is at the same time also begging it: trying to lay the ghost of a possible threat to the name of Herman Mordaunt by insisting on, and wondering at, its onomastic immutability, he is implicitly admitting its exceptionality. In other words, with the name "Herman Mordaunt" we notice the same gap opening up as we noticed earlier between the marriage plot and the linguistic level of the novel: here, too, we find the covert text belying its overt counterpart.

---

14. Joseph J. Ellis, *After the Revolution: Profiles of Early American Culture* (New York/London: W.W. Norton & Co., 1979; and Jay Fliegelman, *Prodigals & Pilgrims: The American Revolution Against Patriarchal Authority 1750-1800* (Cambridge: Cambridge University Press, 1982).

* * *

Just as we found overt and covert text meeting in the early passage concerning the name of Satanstoe, we find them meeting in a passage toward the end of the book:

> That there is such a thing as improvement, I am willing enough to admit, as well as that it not only compels, but excuses changes; but, I am yet to learn it is a matter of just reproach, that a man follows in the footsteps of those who have gone before him. The apothegms of David, and the wisdom of Solomon, are just as much apothegms and wisdom, in our own time, as they were the day they were written, and for precisely the same reason — their truth. When there is so much stability in morals, there must be permanent principles, and something surely is worthy to be saved from the wreck of the past. I doubt if all this craving for change has not more of selfishness in it, than either of expediency, or of philosophy; and I could wish, at least, that Satanstoe should never be frittered away into so sneaking a substitute as Dibbleton. (435-36)

This paragraph, with its appeal to Biblical patriarchal authority, to the "improvements" that time — and revolutions! — can bring, can be read as applying both to Corny's own individual circumstances, and to those of the American nation in the nineteenth century. In this light, the narrator's wish that "at least, Satanstoe should never be frittered away into so sneaking a substitute as Dibbleton" seems very modest indeed. And when somewhat further on he repeats that "I *do* love that venerable name [Satanstoe], and hope that all the Yankees in Christendom, will not be able to alter it to Dibbleton" (436), he already seems to be resigned to fighting a rearguard battle. If in a sense this confirms Corny's very first utterance to the reader, when he says that "[i]t is easy to foresee that this country is destined to undergo great and rapid changes" (7), it is in a sense totally opposite to the change Corny meant! At exactly that point in the novel where the resolution to the marriage plot calls for the greatest possible continuity and stability, the linguistic and onomastic level whispers that "all is mutabilitie."

* * *

To assess how the clash between the marriage and linguistic ecologies presented in *Satanstoe*, and the various dis-placements threatening as a result thereof, reflect Cooper's own sense of dis-placement in his own times is beyond the scope of this paper. Most of the secondary works I have referred to in passing address this issue much better than I ever could. In his introduction to the 1962 University of Nebraska Press Bison Book edition of *Satanstoe* Robert L. Hough remarks that "unfortunately, the Leatherstocking series has so dominated Cooper's modern reputation that his accomplishments in other areas are virtually unknown to the general reader ... but Cooper's comments on democracy *are* important, and *Satanstoe*, as the best book in which he discusses American society, deservedly holds a high rank in the Cooper canon."[15] It has been my concern to show that *Satanstoe* should hold this high rank not just because of its importance as a social document, but because of the way it sets up a tension between the linguistic level — here particularly with regard to names and naming — and that of the plot — here particularly as far as marriage is concerned — such as we find in many later American authors. I think that in this respect at least, Cooper can truly be termed the "father" of American letters in that the continuity between his work and that of later authors is not only greater, but also extends to other areas, than has generally been admitted to be the case. Specifically, I think that, if the autobiographical form of *Satanstoe* makes the novel into a fictional manufacturing both of the individual and of the American self, and if Cooper's fiction from an "American Studies" point of view is often seen as standing at the cradle of that "American literature" that aims to define an American national identity, the gap between language and plot, between overt and covert text cannot but have implications for "the American self," and for "American literature." In short, I hope that, through "Dis-Placing *Satanstoe,*" I have been able to "dis-place" Cooper a little with regard to customary American literary history, thus not only moving him — in the footsteps of George Dekker in his *The American Historical Romance* — perhaps a little closer to the Melville of *Benito Cereno*,[16] but even to the Melville of *Bartleby the Scrivener*, and a little bit further away both from those usually seen as his immediate successors in the genre of the historical romance and from western tale epigones. But then — in the tracks of John Cawelti in *The Six-Gun Mystique* and *Adventure,*

15. Robert L. Hough, ed., Introduction, *Satanstoe* (1845; rpt. Lincoln: University of Nebraska Press, 1962), xv.

16. George Dekker, *The American Historical Romance* (Cambridge: Cambridge University Press, 1987).

Mystery, and Romance — perhaps we could profit from moving Karl May, Margaret Mitchell, and Zane Grey a bit too?[17]

17. John G. Cawelti, *The Six-Gun Mystique* (Bowling Green, OH: Bowling Green State University Popular Press, 1971); and *Adventure, Mystery, Romance: Formula Stories as Art and Popular Culture* (Chicago: University of Chicago Press, 1976).

UNIFORMITY AND PROGRESS: THE NATURAL HISTORY OF *THE CRATER*

CHARLES H. ADAMS

One of the earliest critical essays on *The Crater* is W.B. Gates's 1951 *American Literature* piece on Cooper's extensive borrowings from two of the most important accounts of life in the Pacific region, *The Voyages of Captain James Cook* (in an 1846 collection) and Lt Charles Wilkes's *Narrative of the United States Exploring Expedition* (1844).[1] As a source study, Gates's essay is quite persuasive; he matches passages and details from the novel with remarkably similar material from the two books of exploration, and is especially convincing on the subject of Cooper's debt to Wilkes. This debt is not surprising, since the two men were acquainted, and Cooper's letters contain several references to his friend and the five-volume account of the four-year expedition that eventually came to be called by its leader's name. Gates's essay ends with an admission that his study cannot address the cataclysmic conclusion of the novel, since "Cook and Wilkes were of no assistance to Cooper" in "matters" like earthquakes and the disappearance of islands beneath the sea.[2]

For this, Gates might have referred his readers to another early source study of the novel, an 1947 essay by Harold Scudder, also published in *American Literature*.[3] Of course, writing in an era in which it was easier to keep up with Cooper scholarship, Gates might have assumed that his readers would be familiar with Scudder's demonstration of Cooper's dependence on Sir Charles Lyell's *Principles of Geology* (1830-33) for numerous descriptions of geologic phenomena. If credibility in source studies is a function of the number of specific

1. W.B. Gates, "Cooper's *The Crater* and Two Explorers," *American Literature* 23 (1951), 243-45.

2. Gates, 245.

3. Harold Scudder, "Cooper's *The Crater*," *American Literature* 19 (1947), 109-26.

parallels revealed, Scudder's essay is even more persuasive than Gates's, since he presents more than twice as many passages from Lyell embedded in Cooper's narrative than Gates finds from either Cook or Wilkes. And Scudder answers the question that Gates leaves hanging: the natural catastrophe that concludes the novel is, it turns out, Cooper's rewriting of the story of Graham's Island, a reef the rise and fall of which occupies a good deal of Lyell's attention in the *Principles*.[4]

Their evident narrowness of method and scope has, of course, relegated exercises like Gates's and Scudder's to critical obscurity, but the effort to recollect them is not necessarily a pedantic one. They offer, for instance, reminders that Cooper's Pacific Ocean is not quite "a blank slate," as Warren Motley calls it, on which the author "inscribes his major preoccupations as an American artist."[5] Nor is it entirely "a world by itself," as Daniel Peck argues.[6] Of course Cooper's Pacific serves important metaphoric purposes, both those intended in his allegory of the rise and fall of America, and the more subtle ones described by Motley, Peck, Wayne Franklin, and others. But Gates and Scudder illuminate the very important fact for criticism that the Pacific entered Cooper's awareness in very specific contexts. What little he knew about vulcanism, earthquakes, South Sea islanders, reef culture, or tropical weather patterns came wrapped in the values, prejudices, ideologies, and personal "preoccupations" of those whose books he read. What his imagination *made* of the Pacific — its people, geology, and role in western history — is inextricable from the shape in which his imagination received it. The critical act of recovering that shape helps to historicize the experience of reading *The Crater* more thoroughly than recent interpretations of the novel have done.

As Brook Thomas has demonstrated in connection with ante-bellum American law, the result of such historicizing, applied to Cooper or other writers, is frequently to reveal contradictions embedded in the conflicting discourses on which an author draws, and out of which she

4. Scudder, 114-16.

5. Warren Motley, *The American Abraham: James Fenimore Cooper and the Frontier Patriarch* (New York: Cambridge University Press, 1987), 152.

6. H. Daniel Peck, *A World by Itself: The Pastoral Moment in Cooper's Fiction* (New Haven: Yale University Press, 1977).

or he attempts to fashion a coherent novelistic whole.[7] Such is the case, for instance, in the source materials identified by Scudder and Gates. Even a casual reading of Wilkes's and Lyell's texts reveals that they embody opposing conceptions of history, whether human or geologic. Wilkes's expedition was a product of American expansionism, and an expression of the nation's growing sense of its importance in the world as a commercial, military, and scientific power. Navy Lieutenant Wilkes was authorized by Congress to sail around the Pacific rim for the same purposes that prompted Jefferson to send Army Captains Lewis and Clark to the coast of the same ocean thirty years earlier: to open trading routes, show the flag among the natives and secure their cooperation in American designs, and learn about lands that must one day form part of the flourishing young republic. Wilkes's *Narrative* often reflects the author's sense of participating in what journalist John O'Sullivan would call, the year after the *Narrative*'s publication, America's manifest destiny.[8]

The sense of history informing Wilkes's *Narrative* is resolutely linear: it is a report from the future, dedicated to preserving by means of specimens, drawings, and narrative the ephemeral present of a Pacific culture destined to disappear as surely as Native American culture seemed to be disappearing in 1844. But Sir Charles Lyell's *Principles* is essentially an extended argument for a conception of history that is just as resolutely cyclical. Lyell's "uniformitarianism" — the faith expressed in the subtitle of the *Principles* that "former changes of the earth's surface" can be explained by "reference to causes now in operation" — is directly opposed to the more familiar evolutionary

7. Brook Thomas, *Cross-Examinations of Law and Literature: Cooper, Hawthorne, Stowe, and Melville* (New York: Cambridge University Press, 1987).

8. On the subject of California, for instance, Wilkes announced that it "will become united with Oregon, with which it will perhaps form a state that is destined to control the destinies of the Pacific" (*Narrative of the United States Exploring Expedition During the Years 1838, 1839, 1840, 1841, 1842*, 5 vols [Philadelphia: C. Sherman, 1844], IV, 171). Wilkes's views on California are among the topics covered in E. Jeffrey Stann's very interesting essay "Charles Wilkes as Diplomat" (*Magnificent Voyagers: The U.S. Exploring Expedition, 1838-1842* [Washington, DC: Smithsonian Institution Press, 1985], 189-205). Wilkes's jingoism is made especially conspicuous by the fact that he was, as Cooper put it, "most foully used" by the Navy Department on his return from the expedition: he was court-martialed for illegally punishing members of his crew during the journey (*The Letters and Journals of James Fenimore Cooper*, ed. James Franklin Beard, 6 vols [Cambridge, MA: Harvard University Press, 1960-68], IV, 430).

model of natural change.[9] Rather than conceiving geologic time as a series of discrete events, connected in a causal chain leading from past to present, Lyell posited a geologic "uniformity of state" in which all past events are explicable by a set of immutable natural laws whose operations are, of course, still observable in the present.[10] Stephen Jay Gould summarizes Lyell's position with the incredulity of a committed evolutionist:

> No old causes are extinct; no new ones have been introduced. Moreover, past causes have always operated — yes, always — at about the same rate and intensity as they do today. No secular increases or decreases through time. No ancient periods of pristine vigor or slow cranking up. The earth, in short, has always worked (and looked) just about as it does now.[11]

The geology of Lyell's *Principles* is thus profoundly ahistorical: change is continuous, but nothing really changes. All conditions are reiterations of previous states, and the history of the world is a perpetual restatement of the immanent order of things.

I will return to Lyell's vision of earth history a bit later, but this opposition of linear and cyclical history deserves some attention since it is, I believe, at the heart of *The Crater*. The assumption informing criticism of the book is that time in the story is linear; the novel takes us, as the title of one of the most perceptive essays on the book has it, "from creation to apocalypse" in the history of Mark Woolston's republic,[12] an allegorical journey that recapitulates the birth and collapse of American republicanism. In this sense, the novel is a parody of the image of American history offered by Wilkes's *Narrative*; "commerce," "knowledge," and "faith" constitute the lexicon of the

---

9. Sir Charles Lyell, *Principles of Geology, Being an Attempt to Explain the Former Changes of the Earth's Surface by Reference to Causes Now in Operation* (London: John Murray, 1830-33).

10. See Lyell, *Principles*, ch. 14. Also see Stephen Jay Gould, *Time's Arrow, Time's Cycle: Myth and Metaphor in the Discovery of Geological Time* (Cambridge, MA: Harvard University Press, 1987), 117-26; and Martin J.S. Rudwick, *The Meaning of Fossils: Episodes in the History of Palaeontology*, 2nd edn (1976; rpt. Chicago: University of Chicago Press, 1985), 164-91.

11. Gould, 105.

12. Motley, 152.

mediocrities — lawyers, editors, and clergymen (excepting, of course, the Episcopalian) — who bring the colony to ruin.

More metaphorically, this assumption informs the sense, shared by the best recent critics of the novel, that the narrative represents an imaginative space in which Cooper could achieve the sense of authority that had been, by 1847, denied him by press, publishers, and public alike. According to this argument — articulated in distinctive ways by Franklin, Peck, and Motley, among others[13] — the adventures of Mark Woolston offer Cooper a means to create a world from scratch, develop it according to fantasies of power, structure its social and moral order according to each of his cherished principles and whims, and abandon it to violent destruction when the logic of history overwhelms it. This reading, obviously, depends on our being able to take "discovery" and "apocalypse" as unique events in the imaginative structure of the book, and trace a chain of distinctive events — the "history" of the book's world — between them.

Such an argument is compelling. But in its assertion that Cooper's choice of setting is largely accidental — the Antarctica of *The Sea Lions* (1849), or indeed any uncharted space, would serve as well for a "blank slate" on which Cooper might "project" his "preoccupations" — it artificially isolates Cooper's imagination from any meaningful engagement with the rhetorical context from which the setting is derived. In fact, the origin of Mark Woolston's island in Lyell's *Principles* invokes a cyclical conception of time that resists and undermines the linear history of the colony. In the geologic history of the earth, as Lyell developed it, notions of "change," "creation," and "destruction" become meaningless, since all change is part of a persistent "uniformity of state." The reef changes — indeed, it changes more dramatically than any other natural setting in Cooper's canon — but this change is circular; the movement is from emptiness to absence. The image of eternity in the forests of Cooper's woodland tales may be compromised by the depredations of settlers, and his fictional seas may be tormented by storms, but the reef is his only natural setting that achieves changelessness by its involvement in cycles of change inherent in the very structure of the earth.

Several commentators have discussed the importance for understanding Cooper's sense of history in *The Crater* of his allusions to Thomas Cole's monumental series of canvases entitled "The Course

13. See Peck; Motley; and Wayne Franklin, *The New World of James Fenimore Cooper* (Chicago: University of Chicago Press, 1982).

of Empire." Cole's paintings, which trace an idealized empire from inception to collapse, is rightly seen as a key to Cooper's allegory of the linear history of America. But the deeper significance of the presence of "The Course of Empire" is that America, like all empires, must inevitably repeat this pattern found, as Lyell argues, in the natural order of things. In this novel, then, all creation is merely reiteration, and all apocalypse the condition for another cycle of history.

The two central events of the novel are, of course, Mark's discovery of the reef, and the destruction of the colony that he founds there. These are the terminal points of the linear history of the reef. But a close look at both of them reveals something more than the beginning or ending of a world in either case. Although, on the morning after the storm that carries off the captain and the crew of the *Rancocus*, Mark and his companion Bob Betts find themselves stranded within the intricate maze of shoals that surround the reef that comes to be called Mark's, the two men are hardly in desperate need of the necessities of life. The *Rancocus*, as they quickly discover, is packed with virtually everything that a settler could want. In the course of cultivating their island hermitage, Bob and Mark excavate from the seemingly bottomless hold of the ship an extraordinary catalogue of supplies: guns, bread, flour, tools, pigs, rugs, fruit seeds, chickens, earthenware, gunpowder, wheelbarrows, grass seed, barrels enough of salted meat to last "five to six years,"[14] vegetable seeds, ducks, and the materials from which to build not one boat but two. The explanation for this cornucopia is that the owner of the vessel, a Quaker consistently referred to as "Friend Abraham White," intended the fated voyage for two purposes: to make money in "the Chinese market" by trading in sandalwood (32), and, in order to ease the Quaker's conscience both for the materialism of the venture and for dealing in a commodity that the Chinese reputedly put to idolatrous ends, to carry a cargo of goods intended to bring the blessings of Christian civilization to the "Feejee" islanders (111).

If Mark's experience on the reef resonates with the rhetoric of a New World — if, as many readers assume, it enacts the freshness of discovery before the disillusionment of experience — the protracted unloading of the *Rancocus* must be read as either unintentionally comic or seriously ironic. The apparently endless stream of goods from the

14. *The Crater; or, Vulcan's Peak. A Tale of the Pacific* (1847; rpt. New York: W.A. Townsend & Co., 1859), 82. Future references to this edition will be cited parenthetically within the text.

ship far exceeds, in both quantity and kind, the supply that Cooper needed to give his hero for survival, or to keep the plot going. Mark's bounty makes the entire section of the novel describing the development of the reef virtually a parody of the idea of "the new." There is nothing new here; indeed, the fact that the material in the hold is intended to spread American civilization suggests instead that history is being reiterated — beginning all over again — and not denied or revised. The language of discovery is invoked again after the earthquake that raises the reef ten or fifteen feet further above the ocean, and thrusts the volcanic island that becomes the Vulcan's Peak of the novel's subtitle high into the air. "His limits," Cooper says of his hero, "were so much enlarged as to offer something like a new world to his enterprise and curiosity" (175). When Mark visits the Peak for the first time, we learn that, "like Columbus, he knelt on the sands, and returned his thanks to God" (196). But a second Columbian moment occurring so quickly after the first, which is itself a parody of discovery, points to the possibility that the concept of beginning is itself an ironic one in this novel.

Warren Motley has noted the important relationship between the first and second parts of *The Crater* — the sections before and after the great upheaval of the earthquake. Events in the first part are echoed, sometimes virtually repeated, in the second part, so that the two sections develop parallel narratives of the growth of Mark Woolston's world.[15] Motley's argument focuses mainly on the distinctions between these sections, but his observation that the second section is in a sense a rewriting of the first is a valuable one. The scale is enlarged in the second part, but the activities repeated there retain their identity with those described in the first: Bob Betts's solitary trips to Loam Rock to collect compost for the Crater's garden are reflected in the major loam recovery effort mounted to establish the colony's agriculture; the castaways' meticulous efforts to fashion rude shelters against the brutal tropical sun are restated in the construction of complex fortifications against the depredations of the ruthless Waally and his band; Mark's assembly of the boats from the parts found in the *Rancocus* reappears as the construction of the colony's navy; and so on.

Reiteration is thus integral to the form of the novel. Repetition and restatement act as structuring devices; beginnings and endings become contingent and equivocal. Indeed, *The Crater* begins at the end of its story, and in several senses. The narrative opens with a short

15. Motley, 162.

description of Mark Woolston's career after the destruction of his colony, including the news that he has "recently ... died at a good old age" (viii), after enduring the "ignorance, envy, love of detraction, [and] jealousy" of "neighbors" who seem very much like the colonists from whom he fled just before the final catatrophe. Apparently Mark Woolston's drama in the long second part of the novel, between the two earthquakes, plays itself out again after his return to Pennsylvania at the end of the novel. The hero's finally antagonistic relationship with his social world — which, as everyone who writes about the book points out, is his creator's — lends the conclusion of his life as a Craterino an air of inevitability, as the two endings mirror each other across the intervening years of the character's life. In addition, the petty bickering between Doctors Woolston and Yardley with which the narrative begins resembles, as Wayne Franklin has indicated, the "inherent littleness of mind" that finally undoes Mark's Pacific paradise.[16] "Ignorance, envy, and ... jealousy" thus create the conditions that characterize both the initiation and consummation of the narrative.

Considering this relentless evocation of cycles and repetitions, *The Crater* might be described as an extended argument against the possibility of linear history, insofar as that phrase implies significant change in any given direction. Cooper's attack throughout the novel (and indeed throughout the second half of his career) on the cherished American notion of "progress" finds here a resonant intellectual context; not only are his countrymen's ideas of progress trivial and misguided, but an essential sameness in human experience renders such an idea meaningless. Nature, human and nonhuman, is defined by a "uniformity of state" that cuts across time and place to make renewal an empty gesture, and closure an echo of countless similar endings. William P. Kelly has detected a comparable circularity in another novel of Cooper's final decade, *The Deerslayer* (1842). Noting that the last of the Leatherstocking tales ends where it begins, with a description of the unspoiled New York landscape, Kelly argues that Cooper here "abandons" the sorts of dialectical resolutions of conflict offered in the Tales of the 1820s as "naive": "American history, [Cooper] concludes, is a contradiction in terms. There is only human history, and insofar as history implies progress toward an ideal, it is itself a fiction."[17] The

---

16. Franklin, 193.

17. William P. Kelly, *Plotting America's Past: Fenimore Cooper and the Leatherstocking Tales* (Carbondale: Southern Illinois University Press, 1983), 182.

American dream of "originality" and "transcendence" collapses with the recognition that, as Tom Hutter puts it, "the consciences in the settlements [are] pretty much the same as they are ... in the woods.[18]

History is indeed Cooper's greatest adversary in his late novels. The approach to the present is invariably littered with shattered idols and broken promises, so that, as many commentators have recognized, these novels are marked by numerous strategies for subverting time's progress and/or delaying the arrival of the unbearable now. The corruption of Mark's colony in *The Crater* occurs quite late in the action, and with remarkable rapidity, as though the author wished to prolong the expansion of the Woolston empire as long as possible, and describe its inevitable moral collapse with the greatest dispatch. The Littlepage novels, completed just before *The Crater*, describe a linear descent out of idyllic Dutch New York into a modern nightmare; throughout, Cooper poses such supposedly timeless principles as the common law and the Littlepage family character against the irresistible flow of history. But if he had already tried to deny the authority of history by invoking a cyclical view of time in *The Deerslayer*, the circularity of *The Crater* is rooted less in the sort of "eternal return" described in our century by Eliade than in the science of Cooper's day.[19]

Cooper derived from Lyell's *Principles* more than a justification for making his island rise and fall. The cyclical view of geologic time that Gould, like all modern geologists, finds so astonishing is fully comprehensible only in the context of the great debate in the Euro-American geologic world of Cooper's age between the Uniformitarians, for whom Lyell was the chief spokesman, and the Catastrophists, represented most famously by Louis Agassiz and Georges Cuvier, the latter an acquaintance of Cooper's from his Parisian days. This controversy has been described and analyzed by numerous historians of science,[20] but the essence of the debate, and its relevance to *The*

---

18. Kelly, 183-84.

19. Cf. Mircea Eliade, *The Myth of the Eternal Return* (Princeton: Princeton University Press, 1954).

20. The best discussion of the subject is undoubtedly Gould's, in chapter 4 of *Time's Arrow, Time's Cycle*, although other studies are available, especially Reijer Hooykaas, *Natural Law and Divine Miracle: The Principle of Uniformity in Geology, Biology, and Theology* (Leiden: Brill, 1963); Richard Morris, *Time's Arrows: Scientific Attitudes Toward Time* (New York: Simon and Schuster, 1984);

Crater, can be related fairly simply. Lyell's "uniformity of state" is posed in the *Principles* against the Catastrophist belief in what we now recognize as a relatively modern historical view of geologic time. For the Catastrophists, the earth's history was defined by an intermittent series of cataclysmic geologic events, each of which transformed the face of the globe and initiated a distinct period in geologic time. The long periods between these convulsions were marked by changes made by the inexorable operations of wind and water on the unique landscapes created by each catastrophe. So, rather than study the planet's past by reference to "causes now in operation," as Lyell's subtitle put it, the Catastrophists believed that the earth's present appearance bore very little relation to its past, since its past consisted of unique geologic events of unimaginable scale. At its least sophisticated, Catastrophism was a transparent effort to provide an ostensibly scientific explanation for Biblical events like the Flood. At their best, though, as Agassiz's work demonstrates, the Catastrophists' historical sensibility anticipated the sense of "deep time" imagined by Darwin and his successors in every field of natural history.

Cooper's argument in *The Crater* thus closely parallels Lyell's in his *Principles*. Both writers write in opposition to a conception of history that is linear; both resist the idea of progression in history in favor of a cyclical vision of time. Cooper found in Lyell's work a scientific articulation of the same sense of permanence underlying change that he sought to define in all of his works, but especially in his later novels. Lyell's Uniformitarianism offers a vision of nature that makes change part of a greater changelessness. The vagaries of Mark's reef — patterned after Lyell's rendering of Graham's Island — represent Cooper's effort to express in the language of science the same idea that he makes Leatherstocking speak a quarter-century earlier in *The Pioneers*, when the hunter tells Edwards that the double waterfall deep in the Catskills has been "playing" over its rocks in the same way "since He made the world."[21] Cooper knew from his reading of Lyell that such assertions of nature's stability were no longer tenable in 1847, but that His abiding presence could be traced nevertheless in nature's

---

Paolo Rossi, *The Dark Abyss of Time: The History of the Earth and the History of Nations from Hooke to Vico*, trans. Lydia G. Cochrane (Chicago: University of Chicago Press, 1984); and Rudwick.

21. *The Pioneers; or, The Sources of the Susquehanna. A Descriptive Tale* (1823), eds James Franklin Beard *et al.* (Albany: State University of New York Press, 1980), 293-94.

cycles. God's providential history moves ineluctably forward — "the only thing that can be termed stable," he says in *The Crater*, "is the slow but sure progress of prophecy" (153) — but by this point in his career Cooper can see no relation between God's "progress" and America's. On earth — and this novel is concerned in several senses with earthly matters — the last word is Ecclesiastical: "… the earth revolves; men are born, live their time and die; communities are formed and are dissolved …; good contends with evil, and evil still has its day" (478).

Lyell, of course, was not much concerned with God in his geology,[22] so the *Principles* does not suffer from the difficulty of reconciling a linear providential history with a cyclical earthly one. But, as Cooper virtually confesses, his interest in geology is less the science itself than the use to which he can put it. Just after the earthquake has created Mark's second "new world," Cooper paraphrases his scientific reading to explain the geological processes which could bring about such an event (176). He admits, though, that "such speculations" are very uncertain, and concludes that "so many unknown causes exist in so many unexpected forms, as to render precise estimates of their effects, in cases of physical phenomena, almost as uncertain as those which follow similar attempts at an analysis of human motives and human conduct" (176). The tendency — correct or not — in the latter arena is for "one man" to "judg[e] his fellow by himself," and thus create the other in one's own image. The logic of the analogy suggests an implicit recognition that the same tendency marks "speculation … in cases of physical phenomena" as well. Geology affords Cooper a lexicon by which to articulate his deepest convictions about the relationship between the individual life and the structures — natural and human — that condition it. Like the law elsewhere in his canon, science in *The Crater* becomes a means of imagining the world: a metaphoric structure describing the "uniformity of state" that Cooper sought to establish in his fiction, however he might despair of finding it in the world.

---

22. Cf. Rudwick, 188.

LIST OF CONTRIBUTORS

CHARLES H. ADAMS, Department of English, University of Arkansas. He is the author of *"The Guardian of the Law": Authority and Identity in James Fenimore Cooper* (1990), and has published articles on Cooper's *The Spy* and *The Red Rover*. He has also written on Hawthorne, the American canon, African-American literature, and William Bartram's *Travels*. He is currently at work on a book about American nature writing from Bartram to Dillard.

JAN BAKKER, recently retired from the Department of English, University of Groningen. His books include: *Fiction as Survival Strategy: A Comparative Study of the Major Works of Ernest Hemingway and Saul Bellow* (1983); *Ernest Hemingway in Holland, 1925-1981: A Comparative Analysis of the Contemporary Dutch and American Critical Reception of his Work* (1986); and *The Role of the Mythic West in Some Representative Examples of Classic and Modern American Literature: The Shaping Force of the American Frontier* (1991).

JOHN G. CAWELTI, Department of English, University of Kentucky. He is the author of *The Six-Gun Mystique* (1971), and *Adventure, Mystery, and Romance: Formula Stories as Art and Popular Culture* (1976).

GEORGE DEKKER, Department of English, Stanford University. He is the author of *James Fenimore Cooper: The Novelist* (1967) and *The American Historical Romance* (1987). He is also co-editer, with John P. McWilliams, Jr., of *Fenimore Cooper: The Critical Heritage* (1973).

THEO D'HAEN, Department of English, Leiden University. He has published extensively on modern European-language literatures, both in Europe and the United States. He is the author of *Text to Reader* (1983), and co-author of *Windows on English and American Literature* (1991). He has edited and co-edited several collections of essays, including *Convention and Innovation in Literature* (1989), *History and*

Post-War Writing (1990), and *Shades of Empire in Colonial and Post-Colonial Literatures* (1993).

ROBERT LAWSON-PEEBLES, American and Commonwealth Arts program, University of Exeter. He is the author of *Landscape and Written Expression in Revolutionary America* (1988), and co-editor of *Views of American Landscapes* (1989). He has published essays on transatlantic relations, on American Performance Arts, and on such figures as George Washington, Edgar Allan Poe, Henry George, and Williams Carlos Williams. He has contributed an essay to *New Essays on The Last of the Mohicans* (ed. H. Daniel Peck; 1992).

A. ROBERT LEE, American Studies program, University of Kent at Canterbury. His publications include *Black American Fiction since Richard Wright* (1983), eleven essay-collections in the Vision Critical Studies Series — among them *Herman Melville: Reassessments* (1984); *Edgar Allan Poe: The Design of Order* (1985); *Scott Fitzgerald: The Promises of Life* (1989), and *William Faulkner: The Yoknapatawpha Fiction* (1990) — and three Everyman editions of Melville, *Moby-Dick* (1973, 1993), *Typee* (1993), and *Billy Budd, Sailor and Other Stories* (1993).

JOHN P. McWILLIAMS, Jr., Middlebury College, Vermont. He is the author of *Political Justice in a Republic: Fenimore Cooper's America* (1972), *Hawthorne, Melville and the National Character* (1984), and *The American Epic: Transforming a Genre, 1770-1860* (1989). With George Dekker, he edited the Critical Heritage volume on Fenimore Cooper (1973). He has also contributed essays on Cooper to *Law and American Literature* (1983) and *James Fenimore Cooper: New Critical Essays* (1985), and has edited *The Last of the Mohicans* (1990) for the OUP World's Classics series. An expanded version of his article on *Lionel Lincoln* has recently been published in *American Literary History* 5 (Spring, 1993).

DONALD A. RINGE, Department of English, University of Kentucky. He is a member of the Editorial Board of the SUNY edition of *The Writings of James Fenimore Cooper* and the author of *James Fenimore Cooper* (1962; updated edition 1988). He has recently written an introduction and notes for the OUP World's Classics edition of *The Prairie*.

RICHARD D. RUST, Department of English, University of North Carolina, Chapel Hill. He has written extensively on nineteenth-century American literature, and is the editor of *Glory and Pathos: Responses of Nineteenth-Century American Authors to the Civil War* (1970). He has published an edition of Washington Irving's *Astoria, or Anecdotes of an Enterprize beyond the Rocky Mountains* (1976; reprinted 1982), and has edited the SUNY edition of Cooper's *The Pathfinder* (1981). Also he is the General Editor of *The Complete Works of Washington Irving* (1976-1989).

SUSAN SCHECKEL, Department of English, Memphis State University. She is currently working on a book-length study entitled "Shifting Boundaries: The Poetics and Politics of the American Frontier." She has recently published an essay entitled "Mary Jemison and the Domestication of the American Frontier" (1992).

W.M. VERHOEVEN, Department of English, University of Groningen. He is the author of *D.H. Lawrence's Duality Concept: Its Development in the Novels of the Early and Major Phase* (1987), and has published essays on William Godwin, Charles Brockden Brown, Fenimore Cooper, Melville, Anne Tyler, Michael Ondaatje, and others. He is also the editor of *Rewriting the Dream: Reflections on the Changing American Literary Canon* (1992).

THE POLITICS OF ART: ELI MANDEL'S POETRY AND CRITICISM

Edited by Ed Jewinski and Andrew Stubbs.

Amsterdam/Atlanta, GA 1992. xviii,156 pp. (Cross/Cultures 8)
ISBN: 90-5183-404-7 Hfl. 55,-/US-$ 32.-

The criticism and poetry of Eli Mandel, one of Canada's most important literary figures, have both defined and described the direction of modern Canadian writing. This critical conspectus by several hands explores his contribution to both fields more comprehensively and intimately than any other single work of scholarship. *The Politics of Art: Eli Mandel's Poetry and Criticism* surveys the main tendencies dominating discussion of the complex issue of Mandel's critical theories and poetic practices, and pulls together previously scattered materials into a cohesive whole. Thirteen engaging new essays some by those who have worked with Mandel, others by those who were directly taught by him comprise the main section. They are written from many points of view on a variety of topics, including: Mandel's use of "silence"; his view of Self; his poetic techniques; his concern with politics; his wrestling with tradition; and his role as literary critic and theorist. The book also features an extensive bibliography of publications by and on Mandel a section of particular interest to scholars, who should find this listing especially valuable. Contributors include: Douglas Barbour; William Butt; Ben Bryant; Dennis Cooley; David Cook; Susan Rudy Dorscht; Ed Dyck; Ed Jewinski; Smaro Kamboureli; Robert Kroetsch; Gloria Alvernaz Mulcahy; Ann Munton; Ian Sowton; and Andrew Stubbs.

USA/Canada: Editions Rodopi, 233 Peachtree Street, N.E., Suite 404, Atlanta, Ga. 30303-1504, Telephone (404) 523-1964, Call toll-free 1-800-225-3998 (U.S. only), Fax (404) 522-7116

And Others: Editions Rodopi B.V., Keizersgracht 302-304, 1016 EX Amsterdam, The Netherlands. Telephone (020) 622.75.07, Fax (020) 638.09.48

New books:

Who Climbs the Grammar-Tree

Edited by Rosemarie Tracy

1991. XII, 521 Seiten. Kart. ca. DM 226.–. ISBN 3-484-30281-x (Linguistische Arbeiten. Band 281)

The aim of this collection of articles is to give an overall picture of the central concerns in present-day linguistic research with reference to a number of specific issues. The following subjects are given particular prominence – history of linguistics, language change, selected structural phenomena (phonetics, phonology, orthography, syntax, semantics), first and second language acquisition, computer linguistics.

Leonhard Lipka

An Outline of English Lexicology

Lexical Structure, Word Semantics, and Word-Formation. Second Edition

1992. XI, 212 Seiten. Kart. DM 48.–. ISBN 3-484-41003-5 (Forschung & Studium Anglistik. Band 3)

This introduction for university courses gives a survey of approaches to all aspects of words and their functions, and offers a perspective on new directions in the field, viz. categorization, metaphor and metonymy, the relationship between words and world, and interdisciplinary connections (especially with psychology).
Chapter I discusses general problems of the vocabulary and dictionaries of English, while Chapter II introduces basic notions about words, viz. models of the sign, kinds of meaning, and the concepts morpheme, word, and lexeme. Chapters III and IV treat the internal structure of words (word-formation, semantic features, componential analysis) and the structure of the lexicon (paradigmatic and syntagmatic relations between words) respectively. The critical evaluation of research on morphological and semantic structure, the question of polysemy vs. homonymy, lexical rules, and sense-relations is combined with novel suggestions on a typology of semantic features, the advantages of Prototype Semantics, the notion of semantic processes, and the distinction between *lexemes* and *lexical units*. The concepts *collocation*, as a neutral syntagma, and *lexical sets* vs. *lexical fields* are stressed and words are considered also in context and in the mind. The consequences of lexical research for lexicography, language learning, and teaching are extracted and outlined in Chapter VI.

Matthias Heyn

Zur Wiederverwendung maschinenlesbarer Wörterbücher

Eine computergestützte metalexikographische Studie am Beispiel der elektronischen Edition des »Oxford Advanced Learner's Dictionary of Current English«

1992. X, 231 Seiten. Kart. ca. DM 98.–. ISBN 3-484-30945-8 (Lexicographica. Series Maior. Band 45)

This is a computer-aided meta-lexicographic study of a machine-readable dictionary with a view to utilizing the linguistic information in the dictionary on (unification-based) language processing systems. The author modifies the methods of analysis developed in dictionary research, using an analysis of structure and content to develop critical approaches to the prevalent hypotheses in computer lexicography on the utility of traditional dictionaries. The different views taken on this by the disciplines lexicography and information science are also discussed.

Max Niemeyer Verlag GmbH & Co. KG
Postfach 21 40 · D-7400 Tübingen

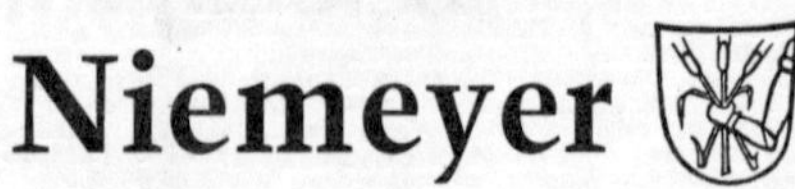